ISSUES IN ADVERTISING

A Conference Sponsored by the
American Enterprise Institute for Public Policy Research

ISSUES IN ADVERTISING

The Economics of Persuasion

Edited by David G. Tuerck

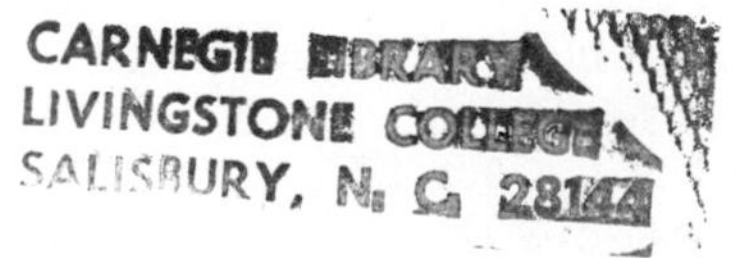

American Enterprise Institute for Public Policy Research
Washington, D.C.

Library of Congress Cataloging in Publication Data

Main entry under title:
Issues in advertising.

(AEI symposia ; 78D)
1. Advertising—Economic aspects—Congresses.
I. Tuerck, David G. II. American Enterprise Institute for Public Policy Research. III. Series: American Enterprise Institute for Public Policy Research. AEI symposia ; 78D.
HF5827.I83 338.4′3 78-6139
ISBN 0-8447-2127-1
ISBN 0-8447-2126-3 pbk.

Printed in the United States of America

MAJOR CONTRIBUTORS

D. A. L. Auld
Professor of Economics, University of Guelph

David M. Blank
Vice President and Chief Economist, CBS, Inc.

Robert H. Bork
Professor of Law, Yale University
and Adjunct Scholar, American Enterprise Institute
former Solicitor General of the United States

Gerard R. Butters
Assistant Professor of Economics, Princeton University

William S. Comanor
Professor of Economics, University of California, Santa Barbara

Harold Demsetz
Professor of Economics, University of California at Los Angeles

James M. Ferguson
Associate Professor of Business Economics
Graduate School of Management, University of Rochester

John A. Henning
Professor of Economics, Syracuse University

Yehuda Kotowitz
Professor of Economics, University of Toronto

Kelvin J. Lancaster
Professor of Economics, Columbia University

Wesley J. Liebeler
Professor of Law, University of California at Los Angeles
former Chief, Office of Policy Planning and Evaluation
Federal Trade Commission

Steven Lustgarten
Associate Professor of Economics
Baruch College, City University of New York

Michael P. Lynch
Assistant Director, Bureau of Economics for Industry Analysis
Federal Trade Commission

Roland N. McKean
Commonwealth Professor of Economics
University of Virginia

H. Michael Mann
Professor of Economics, Boston College
former Director, Bureau of Economics
Federal Trade Commission

Phillip Nelson
Professor of Economics
State University of New York at Binghamton

Stanley I. Ornstein
Assistant Research Economist
University of California, Los Angeles

Robert Pitofsky
Professor of Law, Georgetown University Law Center
former Director of the Bureau of Consumer Protection

Federal Trade Commission
Michael E. Porter
Associate Professor of Business Administration

Harvard University
Sherwin Rosen
Professor of Economics, University of Chicago

Richard Schmalensee
Associate Professor of Applied Economics
loan School of Management, Massachusetts Institute of Technology

Julian L. Simon
Professor of Economics and of Marketing
University of Illinois at Champaign-Urbana

Lester G. Telser
Professor of Economics, University of Chicago

David G. Tuerck
Director, Center for Research on Advertising
American Enterprise Institute

Donald F. Turner
Professor of Law, Harvard University
former Assistant Attorney General, Antitrust Division
U. S. Department of Justice

Thomas A. Wilson
Professor of Economics, University of Toronto

Ralph K. Winter, Jr.
Professor of Law, Yale University
and Adjunct Scholar, American Enterprise Institute

CONTENTS

PART THREE
Advertising as Information

PART FOUR
Advertising, Concentration, and Profits

INTRODUCTION

David G. Tuerck

Among business practices, advertising is unique for the amount and variety of attention it receives. As a field of study, it concerns psychologists, marketing analysts, economists, and lawyers. As a regulatory issue, it arises in connection with antitrust, consumer protection, and, lately, energy conservation and the preservation of free speech. Inherent in advertising, there seem to be certain intriguing, even mysterious, qualities that explain what Robert Bork describes below as "the immense volume of literature" that it has engendered.

Why then should we add, as we do here, to this volume of literature? The answer lies not only in the importance and urgency of the issues involved but also in the hope that some narrowing of the debate might be achieved. That the outcome is often the reverse comes as no surprise in view of the juxtaposition of opposing points of view in which the organization of this work has resulted.

Issues in Regulation

The issues to which the writings that follow are directly or indirectly addressed are laid out by Professor Winter in his opening paper: (1) whether advertising "is a prime source of consumer deception," (2) whether it distorts consumer tastes, and (3) whether it promotes monopoly power. All three issues might be reduced to the more general question of how alternative regulatory policies toward advertising affect the efficiency with which the industrial system delivers goods to the consumer. Should there be more government regulation of advertising or less? Should the Federal Trade Commission be empowered and directed to pursue a more activist policy of the kind urged upon it by, say, Robert Pitofsky, or should it assume instead the more noninterventionist stance taken by Ralph Winter and Robert Bork? Papers and comments bearing on these questions are organized here along both disciplinary and substantive lines. Part 1 is largely legal in approach and Parts 2 through 4, mainly economic. Part 4 has implications for antitrust policy, while Parts 1 through 3 bear on consumer protection as well.

The appearance of this volume coincides with an acceleration in recent years of regulatory activity directed toward advertising. Until recently, the Federal Trade Commission had to rely primarily on the "cease and desist order" as a remedy for business practices that it found to be "unfair or deceptive." Now, under the Federal Trade Commission Improvement Act of 1975, it can promulgate "trade regulation rules" that impose detailed and comprehensive restraints on certain broadly defined kinds of advertising. Accordingly, it has proposed trade regulation rules that would restrict the advertising of over-the-counter drugs to language approved by the Food and Drug Administration and that would ban certain comparative claims by food advertisers and require the "affirmative disclosure" in food advertising of selected facts bearing on nutrition.

In tandem with its acquisition of new rule-making powers, the commission has developed or proposed substantive remedies that portend a significant expansion in its enforcement powers. Important among these is the requirement, mentioned below in connection with the *Listerine* case, that manufacturers run advertisements correcting, in language specified by the commission, past deceptions of which they have been found guilty. As this volume goes to press, the commission staff still presses a 1972 complaint against three analgesics manufacturers from whom substantial outlays for corrective advertising are sought. In a complaint of similar vintage, the commission recommends another remedy—compulsory trademark licensing—for the "shared monopoly" and "barriers to entry" that the four largest cereal manufacturers have allegedly brought about through excessive advertising. An administrative law judge has ordered the same remedy in the FTC case against Borden, Inc. Under the judge's order, which has been appealed to the commission, Borden would be required, for a given period of time and in exchange for a nominal fee, to permit any maker of reconstituted lemon juice to use its ReaLemon brand name. Generously applied, compulsory trademark licensing could become an antitrust remedy of great consequence—good or bad—to consumer welfare.

These examples, however, merely represent the surface of public opinion, beneath which there may be found a collection of attitudes and ideas favoring a far more activist regulatory policy. A recent survey of consumer and consumerist attitudes toward business, conducted by the Marketing Sciences Institute of Harvard and by Louis Harris and Associates, revealed widespread discontent over advertising. Of the respondents who made up the "total public" survey sample, 44 percent identified "the failure of many companies to live up to claims made in their advertising" as a matter of "great" concern and 76 percent identified the same worry as a matter of at least "some" concern. Of the same respondents, 46 percent identified "most" or "all" TV advertising and 75 percent identified at least "some" TV advertising as "seriously misleading." For newspaper and magazine advertising, the percentages were 28 percent and 78 percent, respectively. Only 6 percent identified the advertising industry as one they regarded as doing a "good job," whereas 95 percent supported corrective advertising, and 78 percent agreed that companies found guilty of deceptive advertising should "be barred from advertising for a period of time."[1]

Proposals that would provide for more regulation of advertising emanate steadily from the academic community and from government. Donald Turner, who has served in both, once suggested, for example, that "it would be quite appropriate to impose, for a period of time, an absolute or percentage limitation on promotional expenditures by a firm or firms that have obtained undue market power through violations of the Sherman Act."[2] Representative Benjamin Rosenthal has suggested the formation of "a quasi-governmental testing laboratory" that would "certify the quality standards available to the consumer."[3] FTC Chairman Michael Pertschuk has warned that advertising may encourage "waste" and that advertisements aimed at children may be especially suitable targets for stricter regulatory standards.[4]

This volume does not attempt to consider the wide variety of regulatory targets and remedies that may be discussed in connection with advertising. It does provide some evidence bearing on the most prominent issues in consumer protection and antitrust, along with some refinements and extensions of existing economic and legal theory. One of the difficulties that arises in the regulation of advertising is, as Harold Demsetz points out below, the lack of an adequate theory of advertising expenditure. Several of the papers that follow are aimed explicitly at repairing this deficiency. The hope that the publication of this volume will contribute to the evolution of a more general and empirically supportable theory of advertising appears to be borne out by the convergence of the authors on certain points of view.

According to one of these points of view, the application of a particular remedy to a given act of unfairness or deception should

---

[1] *Consumerism at the Crossroads* (Cambridge: Marketing Sciences Institute, 1977), pp. 5, 12-13, 76.

[2] Donald F. Turner, "Advertising and Competition," *Federal Bar Journal*, vol. 26 (Spring 1966), p. 96.

[3] *Advertising and the Public Interest* (Washington, D.C.: American Enterprise Institute, 1976), p. 32.

[4] "Pertschuk Hits Ads that 'Encourage' Energy Waste," *Advertising Age*, June 6, 1977, p. 10.

hinge on a determination whether the expected social benefits will exceed the expected social costs of applying that remedy. All six of the contributors to Part 1 share the view that regulation gives rise to costs as well as benefits and that any rational approach to public policy formation requires a consideration of both. The differences of opinion, though strong, arise over the perceived *magnitudes* involved (that is, the size of the expected costs and benefits) and over the prospects for a regulatory standard that reflects an accurate perception of those costs and benefits. Thus, for example, Professor Winter's claim that "the burden of demonstrating the cost-benefit judgment ought to be placed on those calling for the regulation of advertising" causes him to express "grave doubts" about the corrective advertising remedy, with which Professor Pitofsky is able, on the other hand, to find considerable sympathy. (Both, however, would tolerate at least that amount of consumer deception for which the market itself provides adequate remedies.) Whereas Professors Bork and Liebeler reject unambiguously Pitofsky's defense of an activist FTC policy toward advertising, Professors Turner and McKean are able to provide some defenses of their own. Turner stresses the costs of alternative remedies for deception, in particular the costs of private actions. McKean, who nevertheless sides on balance with Winter, mentions the "fraud-deterrent atmosphere" to which an antifraud regulatory policy might contribute.

As Professor Winter observes below, "No commentator seriously contends that advertising should be regulated regardless of the cost imposed on the consumer." That the truth of his observation remains undiminished by the publication of this volume represents progress of a kind toward a more general theory of advertising regulation. Apparently, from Pitofsky's documentation of the FTC's one-time preoccupation with deceptive price advertising cases, Winter's observation would not have been true just a few years ago.

Advertising and the Firm

Any inquiry into the social costs and benefits of advertising leads ultimately to a consideration of the buyer-seller interface that is provided by the advertising media. In his examination of that interface, Lester Telser draws an analogy between the market for ordinary commodities and the market for advertising messages. The existence of such an analogy is germane, as Telser suggests, to questions about the viability of a *laissez-faire* policy toward advertising. Would a completely free, that is, unregulated market for advertising messages cause "too many" or "too few" such messages to be produced?

A free market in "ordinary" commodities causes them to be produced in amounts that are "just right," that is, in amounts that yield the maximum social net gain (excess of social benefits over social costs). Since, according to Telser, a free market in advertising can be expected to generate a system of implicit supply-and-demand determined prices, it can be expected to approximate the same result. One public policy implication concerns the regulation of television: an increase in the availability of pay TV would increase the diversity of TV entertainment without eliminating "popular" programs supported by advertising.

Questions about the likely effects of regulation or its absence on the quantity and character of advertising lead ultimately to questions about the individual firm's marketing strategy. Any attempt to assess the public policy implications of observed advertising patterns within industries that may be targeted for regulation requires consideration of the origin of those patterns in intra-industry variations in sales and product lines. In his examination of the canned and frozen food industry, Michael Porter tests a theory of the role of advertising in the firm's marketing strategy. He finds evidence that the level of a firm's advertising and the distribution of its advertising across different media will vary predictably with the breadth of its product line, the number of different brands that it advertises, and the rate at which it expands the size of its product lines. These findings suggest, as Porter points out, that any consideration of the relationship between advertising intensity and industrial concentration cannot ignore the marketing element in the firm's overall competitive strategy and that public policy toward advertising must take into account the differences between industries in the marketing strategies of individual firms.

In their comments on the papers by Telser and Porter, David Blank and Julian Simon stress the changeability and diverse character of the advertising media. Changes in the market for entertainment and variations between media in the price (positive and negative) of advertising messages make the accumulated experience with any one medium a poor basis for prediction or policy. What we know about commercial broadcasting today is not sufficient to allow any confident predictions about its future viability or about the future regulation of advertising in general.

In his comments, Gerard Butters reiterates some of the arguments made in Part 1 about the dangers of bias and of distorted consumer tastes ascribable to advertising. The public-good nature of advertising argues for governmental subsidization of alternative sources of information and for governmentally provided corrective advertising.

Thomas Wilson argues, contrary to Telser, that distortions between consumers' and producers' evaluations of advertising messages cause too many such messages to be produced. Tracing these distortions to (among other factors) elements of monopoly power in product and media markets, he suggests deregulation of pay TV as a partial remedy. The greater the competition between the media for the advertiser's dollar and for the viewer's time, the more closely the advertising messages produced will be matched with consumer demands for those messages.

Advertising as Information

There is increasing interest nowadays not only in the quantity of advertising messages produced but also in the qualitative differences between advertising messages. In their papers, Ralph Winter and Robert Pitofsky try to identify product categories for which advertisers are and are not likely to make truthful claims. More generally, the goal is to distinguish between those business practices that do and do not yield accurate information about the real alternatives facing consumers. The lack of market information and of competition that would prevail in the absence of advertising would be costly to consumers: as some sellers offering bargains failed to attract buyers, others would find it possible to exploit a degree of monopoly power. Hence, the choice again is not whether advertising is perfect but whether the benefits of advertising outweigh the costs, so that the social welfare is greater. Does advertising or do certain identifiable kinds of advertising serve to keep consumers reasonably well informed about the best available bargains and about the true social costs of the products actually or potentially available to them? If so, is the additional information provided by the advertising worth less or more than the alternatives forgone as a result of its provision?

In his paper, "Advertising as Information Once More," Phillip Nelson offers theoretical and empirical support for the argument that, although the advertising of so-called experience goods is literally not believable, it nevertheless provides valuable information, namely, the information that the goods *are* advertised. (Experience goods like tea and tuna fish have to be consumed before the consumer knows whether or not he likes them; search goods like carpets and clothes do not.) This information is valuable because consumers know what Nelson himself sets out to prove—that the more heavily advertised experience goods are likely to be the better buys. Taking what he calls the utility-adjusted price of a good as an inverse measure of the bargain it offers to the consumer, Nelson provides a detailed analysis of the likely relationship between that price and the amount of money spent advertising the good. He finds (1) that the relationship is probably negative in the absense of advertising economies of scale and (2) that such economies of scale are rare. Evidence on the relationships between five "market characteristics" (each of which provides a proxy for the intensity with which a particular good exhibits experience characteristics) supports Nelson's hypothesis that experience goods are more heavily advertised than other goods.

In his paper, Sherwin Rosen explores a theory of monopolistic competition in which consumers are viewed as seeking products not as ends in themselves but as means of obtaining certain product "attributes" that are the ultimate ends of consumption. He examines the role of competition in the introduction and pricing of new products. This approach, unlike an older approach to monopolistic competition theory,[5] permits different advertising messages to be considered for their welfare effects, not only according to the cost of disseminating them but also according to what they say. In Rosen's model, the firm positions its product's price and design by making comparisons with the prices and real or perceived design attributes of competitors' products. Through advertising, firms might attempt to bring about perceived but not real changes in the amounts offered of given attributes and, in the process, provoke a self-defeating struggle to position their products at the most preferred location along the price-attribute spectrum. On the other hand, the consumer's ability to verify cheaply at least some advertising messages and the firm's incentive to establish and protect a reputation for credibility limit the scope for deception. The information provided by advertising tends to be more valuable the greater the consumer's search costs, the greater the dispersion of consumer preferences, the greater the dispersion of prices and of product attributes associated with given product varieties, and the larger the expected size of the market.

In comments directed mainly at Nelson's paper, Yehuda Kotowitz argues that producers derive significant temporary gains from false advertising owing to the slowness with which consumers evaluate product characteristics. This slowness, which is traceable to product complexity, infrequency of product use, and the lack of consumer knowledge, combines with advertising economies of scale to reduce the amount of accurate information that advertising might be expected to transmit.

James Ferguson, who finds himself in general agreement with both Nelson and Rosen, uses Rosen's analysis to criticize the argument that

[5] See, for example, Edward H. Chamberlin, *The Theory of Monopolistic Competition*, 7th ed. (Cambridge: Harvard University Press, 1969), and Joan Robinson, *The Economics of Imperfect Competition* (London: Macmillan & Co., 1933).

advertising wastes resources by merely shifting consumers among different brands. The advertising of product attributes increases welfare by reducing search costs and by enabling consumers to select brands with characteristics that closely match their tastes. Contrary to the argument that advertising wastes resources, it expands sales by attracting additional consumers and producers into the market. Even if it did not expand sales, advertising would make a positive contribution to consumer welfare by bringing about a better matching of brands and tastes.

In a comment that mainly complements Rosen's paper, Kelvin Lancaster draws a distinction between "vertical" and "horizontal" product differentiation—the former being the kind in which quality and price vary from product to product, the latter being the kind in which quality and price are constant but other characteristics vary. Finding Rosen's paper to be concerned primarily with product differentiation of the vertical kind, Lancaster examines producers' incentives to reveal the true location of horizontally differentiated products along given characteristics spectra. His conclusion that those incentives may be weak leads him to support "compulsory labeling or other forms of information provision that minimize the total cost of providing that information."

D. A. L. Auld, who raises some technical questions about both papers, nevertheless finds them a valuable contribution to the public policy debate. Contrary to Lancaster, Auld finds little in the product attributes approach to support the argument for regulation. Limits or controls on the advertising of experience characteristics would be "futile."

Advertising, Concentration, and Profits

The question whether advertising causes monopoly has motivated a great deal—probably most—of the research to date on the economics of advertising. This research has, in turn, been mainly empirical and mainly directed at the relationship between advertising, on the one hand, and certain measures of monopoly power, particularly of industrial concentration and profitability, on the other. Despite what Professors Ornstein and Lustgarten reveal as elements of confusion in the underlying economic theory, industrial organization economists have struggled at length over the question whether there exists a statistical association between advertising and concentration, between advertising and profitability, or both.[6]

[6] For a review of the literature bearing on the advertising-concentration issue, see Stanley I. Ornstein, *Advertising Intensity and Industrial Concentration* (Washington, D.C.: American Enterprise Institute, 1977).

Whether this question has any bearing on public policy is itself questionable in view of the foregoing remarks and the papers to follow. It seems necessary to probe beyond mere dollar estimates of "advertising" or "advertising intensity" and into the markets for advertising messages and for product attributes in order to identify the competitive and anticompetitive effects involved. We may or may not be able to conclude from a properly identified theory of the firm that a positive correlation between advertising and concentration or profitability is evidence that advertising "causes" either.

In their paper, Stanley Ornstein and Steven Lustgarten offer several tests of the advertising-concentration relationship, using a large sample of four-digit SIC industries for which advertising data are reported by the U.S. input-output tables. From their estimates of the effect of concentration on advertising and of changes in advertising on changes in concentration, they find evidence of a significant, positive relationship between concentration and advertising and between changes in advertising and changes in concentration. However, they find this evidence too mixed and the advertising-concentration relationship too weak to support any inferences for theory or policy. The question whether advertising causes monopoly will, according to their interpretation of the evidence, remain unanswered until a better theory of the firm qua advertiser has evolved.

In their paper, John Henning and Michael Mann observe that, although there are "certain empirical regularities" suggesting a positive relationship between advertising and concentration and between advertising and profitability, there remains the question of causation. Does a change in one or two of the variables cause a change in one or both of the remaining variables? From a "statistical experiment" on fourteen industries, they conclude that advertising and profitability are "causally prior" to concentration but that it is not clear whether advertising is causally prior to profitability, or the other way around. The explanation, they suggest, may lie in the determining role of brand proliferation in firm behavior: the introduction of new brands triggers a round of advertising through which innovating firms try to expand their market shares at the expense of their rivals, who in turn try to protect their market shares against invasion. Concentration increases as the proliferation of competing brands reduces the number of firms that the market is able to accommodate. Public policies aimed at reducing concentration might therefore reflect a concern with the rate at which firms introduce new products.

Both papers evoke criticism of the authors' interpretations of the data. In his comments, Harold Demsetz attacks the Henning-Mann method of determining causality. Any legitimate interpretation of the observed advertising-concentration-profitability relationship requires more knowledge than we currently have about the firm and why it advertises.

William Comanor comments primarily on the weakness that Ornstein and Lustgarten attach to their own results. According to Comanor, it is not the strength of the advertising-concentration relationship that should, in the light of their results, be questioned, but rather the relevance of that relationship to the question whether advertising causes monopoly power. Concentration is not, in his view, "a very good measure of either entry barriers or of the degree of monopoly power in an industry."

In his remarks, Michael Lynch finds fault not with the way in which Ornstein and Lustgarten interpret their results but with the fact that their results are consistent with many interpretations. For example, the finding that increases in advertising are related to increases in concentration may or may not support the hypothesis that advertising creates barriers to entry. Likewise, Lynch questions the Henning-Mann allegation of one-way causality running from profitability to concentration and from innovation to advertising. He nevertheless views with considerable interest the brand proliferation model that Henning and Mann offer in defense of their findings. He recommends further attention to advertising at the firm and at the brand level.

Finally, Richard Schmalensee, like Demsetz, finds deficiencies in the Henning-Mann method of determining causality. Discussing the hypotheses that are implicit in their results, Schmalensee argues that the authors may have produced an oversimplified model of the firm's advertising behavior and that the destabilizing effects of brand introduction may be inconsistent with the observed positive relationship between advertising and profitability. Commenting on Ornstein and Lustgarten, Schmalensee expresses a doubt, also expressed by Comanor, that the observed positive association between advertising and concentration in the authors' producer goods sample invalidates their finding of a similar association for consumer goods. He further questions their interpretation of the evidence bearing on the effects of changes in advertising on changes in concentration.

On the Economics of Persuasion

As mentioned, one purpose of this volume is to see whether, in assembling it, some narrowing of the regulatory debate could be achieved. Whether, in fact, it has served that purpose can be judged only by the reader and only after he has read beyond the summary comments above. What can be said, perhaps, is that, despite the contributors' differences of opinion, there are certain ideas on which most appear to agree. One is the need for a cost-benefit evaluation of any proposed regulatory standard. Another is the idea that this evaluation requires a consideration of the media through which advertising is disseminated and of the firm's overall marketing strategy. Statistical associations between advertising, on the one hand, and concentration or profitability, on the other, may be meaningful, but only insofar as they reveal the effects of advertising on consumer welfare.

Advertising is, by design at least, persuasion. Yet, as we know, it is also information. Whether and how market incentives operate to make advertising a socially cost-effective way of disseminating information is a question around which the writings that follow are directly or indirectly united.

Acknowledgments

The publication of this volume has been made possible by the patience and cooperation of several people, in particular, the authors and commentators, who responded generously to repeated demands on their time. Richard W. Barrett, William Breit, and Kenneth Elzinga served as session chairmen for the conference at which the papers and comments were originally presented. I am especially grateful to my research assistant, Elizabeth Griffith, and my secretary, Lynn Martin, for their assistance in preparing the volume for publication.

PART ONE

ISSUES IN REGULATION

ADVERTISING AND LEGAL THEORY

Ralph K. Winter, Jr.

Advertising and Its Critics

Integral to many critiques of the private sector and particularly of American business are allegations that advertising inflicts injuries on consumers and that its overall role is harmful. Such charges are generally of three kinds.

The first allegation plays on what an American Bar Association study of the Federal Trade Commission called "a general conviction that marketing frauds against consumers are widespread in this country and constitute a problem of major national concern."[1] Central to this charge is the view that advertising is by nature peculiarly useful if not essential to carrying out frauds, and is thus a prime source of consumer deception.

A second allegation is that advertising is a device by which "artificial" tastes are created. Consumers, it is argued, would be better off employing their income according to their own preferences, and would enjoy more leisure once released from the pressure of having to earn and buy more than they need. Professor John Kenneth Galbraith has stated that "advertising and salesmanship" are simply "the management of consumer demand" and are "vital for planning in the industrial system."[2] His point is that, without advertising, persons would find a terminal satisfactory income and not continue on the treadmill of earning more and more income in order to purchase more and more presumably superfluous goods. He thus argues that the link between production and consumer desires is almost the opposite of that described in classical economics. Instead of production following consumer wants, the producer must create the want to justify the production. Galbraith argues:

1 Report of the American Bar Association Committee to Study the Federal Trade Commission, 1969, p. 36.

2 John K. Galbraith, *The New Industrial State* (New York: Signet, 1967), p. 281.

> Modern advertising and salesmanship . . . cannot be reconciled with . . . independently determined desire. . . . A new consumer product must be introduced with a suitable advertising campaign to arouse an interest in it. The path for an expansion of output must be paved by a suitable expansion in the advertising budget. Outlays for the manufacturing of a product are not more important . . . than outlays for the manufacturing of demand for the product.[3]

A final allegation is that advertising is anticompetitive; that is, large advertising expenditures create a "barrier to entry" that reduces competition. Those who hold this conviction have even suggested that legal measures be taken to restrict advertising expenditures.

The Limits of Advertising

Advertising's critics attribute to it a power that even the most immodest dweller of Madison Avenue would hesitate to claim. Widespread deception and fraud, the endless creation of artificial tastes, and the erection of barriers to competitor entry would be possible only if the advertising industry were able to manipulate consumers virtually at will and to evoke the desired response with Pavlovian regularity.

I make no claim to exhaustive research of the literature of psychology and social psychology relevant to these matters. I do have some familiarity with it, however, and students of mine have from time to time undertaken studies of various aspects of it. The conclusion invariably reached is that the alleged manipulative powers of advertising are simply not established in the literature and that even subliminal advertising is a very limited tool. To be sure, all agree that advertising is a useful and often indispensable tool to sellers. But all also agree that it can never guarantee undivided public attention, much less commercial success, and that deceptive advertisers cannot freely engage in extensive fraud by reducing the hapless buyer to an endlessly willing victim.

These conclusions are merely consistent with common observation. Advertising is one of numerous elements (level of education, views of peers, views of family, previous experience with the product, individual judgment, and so on) that influence a consumer's spending decisions. Because advertising is available to all who would sell a product or service, no single message can possibly dominate our attention. This applies as much to decisions between kinds of products as to different brands of a particular product. The advertisement for a Caribbean vacation

[3] John K. Galbraith, *The Affluent Society* (New York: Mentor, 1969), p. 141.

competes not only with other vacation ads, but also with reminders from a bank or investment broker about providing for one's future. If common observation reveals anything, it is that the market share of a particular brand is remarkably unstable, as is the relative market share of particular products. Studies indicate that most consumers experiment with a variety of brands and are in no sense wedded by advertising to any given product.[4] The history of political repression strongly suggests that the ability to silence competitors' advertising is a far more effective manipulative device than issuing one's own advertising.

Advertisers face an exceedingly complex task in seeking to persuade, much less manipulate, the public. Individual perceptions vary widely, and the impact of an ad on one person is generally different from its impact on another. In addition, consumers are aware of the self-interest of the commercial advertiser and are naturally skeptical of his advertised claims. Much of mass advertising is, as a consequence, little more than an attention-getting device seeking to increase brand name recognition. Nor is there any evidence that advertising can, in any but exceptional cases, offset a previous bad experience with a product. There is a strong temptation for advertisers to exaggerate the benefits of their products but much less of a temptation to employ outright lies, which tend to be self-defeating. The goal of most advertisers is to entice the consumer to purchase the product and then to satisfy him through experience.

One may well question, therefore, whether allegations of widespread fraud are in fact accurate. Not only would the seller have to construct an effective deception to begin with, but he would also have to be, somehow, immune to consumer retaliation and loss of patronage in the market afterwards. To be sure, plenty of examples of fraud exist, but they constitute a tiny fraction of commercial transactions. The Federal Trade Commission prosecutes only a couple of hundred deceptive practices cases a year, of which almost half are in the protectionist textile and fur mislabeling areas. One suspects similar agencies in the states have a comparably small caseload. Given the size of the American economy, the claims of widespread fraud seem more exaggerated than the advertising they deplore.

Mr. Galbraith's allegations about the creation of artificial consumer wants seem equally shaky and surely imply a very bleak view of democracy. As a genre, commercial advertising is anything but unique. The tools of persuasion employed by advertising are used by everyone who engages in mass persuasion. My colleague Arthur Leff once noted, for

[4] James M. Ferguson, "Advertising and Liquor," *Journal of Business*, vol. 40 (October 1967), pp. 414-434.

example, that the "Nader Reports" were a form of franchising similar in merchandising technique to Colonel Sanders' Kentucky Fried Chicken.

Every segment of society in fact employs such techniques. In the 1960s, for example, a major topic among the campus intelligentsia was "the urban crisis." It was not enough to study economics, sociology, history, political science, or law. If a course did not bear the brand label "urban," it was irrelevant; if it did, a sizable enrollment was guaranteed, no matter what the content. The lack of urban studies was regarded as a sure sign that a university was on the way to obscurity. A decade later "urban" studies still draw interest but on a very reduced scale, even though the "crisis" has assumed a more tangible form and its existence is less subject to doubt. As another example, political advertising employs techniques indistinguishable from those employed in commercial advertising. Name recognition is of critical importance, and sloganeering, hyperbole, and symbols are used pervasively.

The point is that virtually every aspect of our lives is affected by attempts at persuasion and that the techniques of advertising are common to every form of persuasion. Either we believe that citizens are capable of independent and balanced judgment or we do not. If in fact consumers are endlessly manipulated by advertising, then the same consumers are no better able to avoid manipulation in their political judgments. The case for fearing "artificial" desires for more and more government regulation is as good as the case for deploring "artificial" wants for more and more consumer goods. It is for this reason that I find Mr. Galbraith's view profoundly antidemocratic.

The Benefits of Advertising

A wholesale legal assault on advertising would entail great costs. It would predictably diminish the flow of goods, reduce the diversity of products and brands, decrease consumer satisfaction, and increase poverty because of the general decline in the level of commercial activity.

This is so because advertising performs the critical function of informing consumers about the availability of certain goods at certain places and at certain prices. Critics of advertising frequently slip over this point by arguing that in an academic model of "perfect competition," no advertising would exist because the flow of information would be perfect; therefore, according to this argument, the existence of advertising illustrates the lack of competition. In any case, the issue is not perfect or imperfect competition in an academic model but the maximization of consumer satisfaction in everyday life. Perfect competition is nothing but an abstraction useful for analytic or pedagogic purposes, and a departure from its assumptions in no sense implies a net injury to consumers. For example, when economies of scale invalidate the model's assumption of an atomistic market, industrial concentration may benefit consumers since the price effects of the reductions in cost may exceed the price effects of the restrictions in output. Similarly, because the collection and transmittal of product information consumes resources, the attainment of perfect information, even if possible, would be prohibitively expensive for consumers. Information is a commodity that itself should be allocated by a price system that reflects its costs. Advertising does just that, as the cost of providing information about a product becomes part of the price of the product.

Many dispute this view of advertising on the grounds that the information provided in mass advertising seems inadequate to inform consumers about much more than the existence of a product. But is this so? One would be hard put to find examples of advertising that did not also inform us what the product is for, the advantage of using it, where to get it, and so on. Advertising may well be the least costly method of introducing the basic features of the product to the consumer. Should more information be desired, interested consumers may thereafter seek out further details from dealers or from people who already own the product. This is far less costly than attempting to transmit every conceivable detail on a mass basis.

To be sure, ads of a general nature are sometimes accompanied by hyperbole that may overstate the merits of the product or simply fail to inform. Claims that a product is "unique" or the "best buy" do not give the consumer hard information, but what evidence is there that consumers take them seriously? If they did, they would either be paralyzed by indecision or go sleepless trying to purchase every advertised product. Compared to the rhetoric of others engaged in mass persuasion, like political candidates or some so-called consumer advocates, commercial advertising is a model of restraint. Hyperbole in commercial advertising is part and parcel of the advocacy necessary to attract attention to the name and kind of product. Without the advocacy, the incentive to advertise would be greatly reduced.

Similarly, many criticize advertising for creating product images that they believe are not consistent with the actual physical qualities of the product. To the extent that consumers disagree and find psychic pleasure in a product in addition to "practical" utility, this is not an illegitimate function. If advertising enables purchasers of certain beer to suppose themselves more rugged and manly, or purchasers of cosmetics to think that they are more beautiful as a result, that attribute of advertising itself seems a good worth paying for. The critics are merely substituting their judgment for the consumers'.

Advertising also provides a benefit in that it facilitates competitive behavior. A businessman who wishes to cut price, for example, will think twice if news of the price cut cannot be quickly transmitted to his competitors' customers. And it is surely the case that established firms wishing to bar entry by newcomers would find a prohibition on advertising a means well tailored to that end. Indeed, prohibitions on advertising almost always have the suppression of competition as their goal.

Many of the benefits gained through advertising are denied by the critics. They contend that in the absence of regulation, the octane content of gasoline usually would not be revealed to the consumer and the practice of unit pricing would not exist. My suspicion again is that this criticism is second guessing the consumer. In reading some of the literature in preparation for this conference, I learned for the first time about the disclosure of octane readings. Now I remain puzzled over what I am to do with them, particularly since my purchase of gasoline is for the most part governed by my desire for a reliable repairman. Similarly, I have never mastered the art of deciphering the hieroglyphics underneath products in supermarkets. One's personal view of whether the information produced by advertising is adequate is rarely relevant to the issue of whether consumers in general are receiving the optimal amount of product information, given the cost of producing it. Tastes for information are as varied as tastes for the performing arts, and it is not enough for the critics to argue that all the information that might be relevant in lawyers' terms is not disclosed by advertising.

Advertising and the Law

No commentator seriously contends that advertising should be regulated regardless of the cost imposed on consumers. Nor should anyone seriously contend that the regulation of advertising be undertaken for any reason except the protection of consumers.

The issue thus is whether or not the costs of a particular regulation are greater or less than the benefits to consumers gained thereby. Estimating costs and measuring them against the estimated benefits invariably lead to a substantial measure of disagreement, although much of that disagreement can be resolved by locating a burden of proof in the proper way. The burden of demonstrating the cost-benefit judgment ought to be placed on those calling for the regulation of advertising rather than on those who object to it. This is so for three reasons.

First, the benefits derived from advertising are more verifiable than the costs of deceptive or other harmful advertising practices. The latter are in many ways avoidable on the consumer's part and claims about the extent of damage from them are almost always impressionistic. What we do know is that the suppression of advertising impairs competition. It is difficult to see what could replace advertising as a means of informing the consumer if its role is diminished.

Second, because law schools and economics departments are so often fully engaged in their assigned task of discovering market failure, all too little has been done in the way of examining the costs of regulation and the incidence of regulation failure. Not only the bureaucratic budget and the overt costs incurred by those regulated, in the way of lawyers' fees and the like, are involved. Every mistake an agency makes in the regulation of advertising is as harmful to the consumer as fraud. The consumer who does not buy a product he would have enjoyed because advertising is suppressed or because the product is not produced because of the disincentives created by FTC rules is also injured. Injury to consumers is thus as easily accomplished by regulation failure as market failure.

Third, the premises of a democratic society compel us to view the consumer as having powers of discernment and the ability to maintain a level of resistance to advocacy. We cannot consistently call for the vigorous straining of all commercial information received by the public while trusting the very same public to separate the wheat from the chaff in a robust open political debate. Unless we are to decide for the consumer what is best for him—a far cry from democracy—we ought to be as reliant on the marketplace of ideas in the commercial world as in the world of politics.[5]

The Regulation of Deceptive Advertising. As a threshold proposition all would agree that government ought somehow to provide a suitable remedy for fraud. This remedy might well be administrative if suits by consumers are thought to be too unwieldy procedurally or if it is believed that intervention is necessary because false advertisers are getting a "free ride" on the reputation of those who advertise truthfully and thus are diminishing the overall incentive to advertise.

Fraud should be narrowly defined to mean a demonstrated false statement. Government agencies should not be responsible for deter-

---

[5] See Ronald Coase, "The Market for Goods and the Market for Ideas," *American Economic Review*, vol. 64, no. 2 (May 1974), p. 385; also Reprint no. 28 (Washington, D.C.: American Enterprise Institute, 1975). Recently, constitutional protection has been extended to certain kinds of commercial speech. See Virginia State Board of Pharmacy v. Virginia Citizens Council, U.S. 48 L. Ed. 2d 346 (1976) in which the Supreme Court struck down certain state restrictions on the advertising of prescription drug prices. See also below, pp. 24-26.

mining whether a statement is simply misleading or deceptive, rather than false, since perception of the meaning of an ad varies so widely from individual to individual. To ask an agency to act on *its* perception is to ask it to engage in intuitive and highly subjective behavior that can never be reliably proconsumer.

Fraud so defined cannot in any sense benefit the consumer, and there would be no reason to permit it to exist *if* it could be eliminated costlessly. The suppression of fraud is costly, however, both in an administrative sense and in the "chilling effect," that is, the disincentive to engage in any advertising, that some kinds of antifraud rules may have on truthful advertisers. A first step in reducing these costs is the identification of the kinds of fraud that are clearly damaging and unlikely to be corrected by market forces and thus may be targets for regulation. As Richard Posner has noted, fraud is more likely in circumstances in which the performance of the product, for example, patent medicine, is uncertain or where the seller can leave the business easily, for example, a "fly by night" operation. In either case, market forces may insufficiently deter fraud. Similarly, where all brands of a product suffer from a common undesirable characteristic, for example, the effect of cigarettes on health, there is no incentive on the part of any seller to expose that characteristic. In contrast, where the costs to the buyer in discovering fraud are low or where competitors have an incentive to expose the fraud, more reliance ought to be placed upon the market.

To reduce the costs of enforcement, this kind of analysis should be the basis of the antifraud strategy. Not only will the more serious cases of fraud be detected but the number of cases uncovered will give us an idea of the probable level of fraud in other kinds of markets. If, for example, a relatively small number of cases of fraud are detected in markets peculiarly susceptible to it, we may rest easier as to the workings of other markets.

A general rule requiring that advertisers substantiate claims made on behalf of their products goes much too far. By its very terms it may suppress truthful claims that the Federal Trade Commission (FTC) decides have not been properly substantiated—and this is as harmful to consumers as failing to suppress fraudulent claims. As an adjunct to the rule against fraud, this rule seems far too costly unless restricted to markets in which a likelihood of damage through fraud exists and the costs of substantiation are moderate. Such a rule, broadly applied, would necessarily reduce the advertiser's power to engage in advocacy and thus reduce his incentive to provide even undisputed information to consumers. Proving a claim may be very costly—the lawyers' fees alone could be staggering—and substantiation would surely decrease the volume of advertising and the volume of new products introduced because of the increased difficulties in advertising them. Such reasoning was the basis of the decision in *The New York Times* v. *Sullivan*, which forbade defamation judgments against the media in cases involving public officials unless knowing falsity was proven.[6] The Court there specifically relied upon the fact that closer scrutiny of news stories by the judiciary would reduce the volume of news because of the higher costs of reporting stories that might be difficult to substantiate fully.

A requirement that manufacturers disclose particular information about their products can also be justified only in carefully defined circumstances. Where the information is such that some manufacturers of the product would have an incentive to disclose if consumers were sufficiently interested, the cost-benefit judgment should be left to those manufacturers. Where, however, the information is such that none of the competitors has an interest in disclosure—health information about cigarettes—required disclosure makes more sense provided the information is of importance.

The FTC has undertaken a program of requiring corrective advertising in cases in which a history of deception has supposedly been found. Since we know so little about the actual impact of deceptive advertising, I have grave doubts as to the worthiness of this program. The FTC's remedial powers may be inadequate as deterrents, but adoption of a remedy that may further injure consumers does not seem appropriate.

It has often been noted that one impact of rigorous administrative scrutiny of advertising may be to instill an unwarranted confidence in consumers, who believe that every ad meets government approval. I cannot help but note that among the most misleading ads currently in use today are the Environmental Protection Agency (EPA) estimated mileage figures for new cars. As I understand it, these figures are wildly inaccurate as a practical matter but come with a governmental stamp of authenticity and are thus constantly used.

One wonders whether the reverse impact of FTC vigor may not be of considerable importance, particularly since the scope of actual policing of advertising is so small. It has been suggested that government forgo a compulsory substantiation rule and, instead, invite advertisers to submit their claims voluntarily for authentication. The consumer then would be exposed to both authenticated and unauthenticated advertising claims and could use his own judgment. This, along with proper antifraud rules, seems to me a far more intelligent approach to the problem of advertising regulation than either substantiation or a requirement of product information disclosure.

---

[6] The New York Times v. Sullivan, 376 U.S. 254, 266 (1964).

Advertising as a Barrier to Entry. Of all the claims about the harmful effect of advertising, the most baseless are the allegations about its anticompetitive effect. It may well be that those who see in advertising a barrier to entry are like Mr. Nader and his associates, who recently declared that managerial talent and production techniques that give a firm a cost advantage are barriers to entry about which antitrust ought to concern itself. To be sure, superior managerial talent or production techniques are "barriers to entry," but antitrust ought not concern itself about such barriers since they work to the consumers' advantage. The purpose of antitrust is not to protect the least efficient producer but to insure that producers compete so that efficiency is maximized.

It is not enough, therefore, to show that advertising by one firm hampers entry by another. It must be also shown that this is anticompetitive. The advertiser who creates goodwill for himself has in fact created and paid for a capital asset like any other capital asset owned by a firm, and there is no reason for antitrust to be concerned about the fact that others cannot enter effectively without acquiring similar capital assets. Those who reject this argument are again simply demonstrating their distrust of the consumer, since it is his loyalty developed through experience with the product that makes entry difficult.

Nor can product differentiation be viewed as anticonsumer. What firm in its right mind would incur the costs of differentiation unless some consumers preferred its variant of the product? Indeed, I would think that product differentiation on its face should be treated as presumptive evidence of rampant competition. Advertising and product differentiation may in fact help rather than hamper entry. For example, heavy advertising of ready-to-eat cereals and a proliferation of brands make it easier rather than harder for new brands to enter since consumers are accustomed to a variety of choice and it is the brand name rather than the manufacturer's name that the consumer knows. People may also be more inclined to eat ready-to-eat cereals than if there had been no advertising, since brand advertising is advocacy of a product type—cereal as against bacon and eggs—and is thus a help to competing brands.

Those who criticize advertising for its anticompetitive effect have the matter exactly backwards. Advertising is an important weapon of competition. Its suppression, as in the case of prescription drugs, will almost invariably restrict competition.

Advertising and the First Amendment. It might seem to follow from the above that my inclination would be to argue that the First Amendment protects commercial advertising and to applaud the recent decision of the Supreme Court in *Virginia State Board of Pharmacy* v. *Virginia*

Citizens Consumer Council, Inc.[7] Regretfully, I have the most serious doubts about the validity of this decision—doubts which stem not from my view of whether advertising ought to be free, but from my view of the role of the Supreme Court in elaborating the values protected by the Constitution. An extended discussion and defense of the latter view is hardly called for here, but it is my conviction that the values served by the Court in interpreting the Constitution ought to be rooted in that document itself rather than in the personal value systems of the justices, however wise they might be about social policy.

Virginia State Board involved a Virginia rule prohibiting the advertising of the price of prescription drugs. The thrust of the decision can be found in the following statement from Justice Blackmun's opinion:

> The State's protectiveness of its citizens rests in large measure on the advantages of their being kept in ignorance. The advertising ban does not directly affect professional standards one way or the other. It affects them only through the reactions it is assumed people will have to the free flow of drug price information. . . . The only effect the advertising ban has on [the pharmacist] is to insulate him from price competition and to open the way for him to make a substantial, and perhaps even excessive, profit in addition to providing an inferior service. . . .
>
> It appears to be feared that if the pharmacist who wishes to provide low cost, and assertedly low quality, services is permitted to advertise, he will be taken up on his offer by too many unwitting customers. . . .
>
> There is, of course, an alternative to this highly paternalistic approach. That alternative is to assume that this information is not in itself harmful, that people will perceive their own best interests if only they are well enough informed, and that the best means to that end is to open the channels of communication rather than to close them. If they are truly open, nothing prevents the "professional" pharmacist from marketing his own assertedly superior product, and contrasting it with that of the low-cost, high-volume prescription drug retailer. But the choice among these alternative approaches is not ours to make or the Virginia General Assembly's. It is precisely this kind of choice, between the dangers of suppressing information, and the dangers of its misuse if it is freely available, that the First Amendment makes for us. Virginia is free to require whatever professional standards it wishes of its pharmacists; it may subsidize them or protect

[7] Virginia State Board of Pharmacy v. Virginia Citizens Council, Inc., 425 U.S. 748 (1976).

> them from competition in other ways. . . . But it may not do so by keeping the public in ignorance of the entirely lawful terms that competing pharmacists are offering.[8]

With all due respect, I do not think that Justice Blackmun's analysis supports the decision. Consider for a moment the right of free political speech that the opinion concedes is at the heart of the First Amendment. In the case of the political process, speech is protected not because some individual right or gratification is involved, but because an open political process itself entails leaving people free to comment on or to oppose governmental action. The right of free political speech, therefore, is derived from the nature of a democratic political process and enforced principally to ensure that this process remains free.

In the case of the speech involved in *Virginia State Board*, however, no such argument can be made because the competitive process is, under the Constitution, subject to considerable state regulation. There is in short no "free" competitive process which is constitutionally protected. For example, under existing Supreme Court decisions the State of Virginia is free to fix the prices of prescription drugs and thereby eliminate price competition entirely. Indeed, it is probably permissible for the state to give a monopoly in prescription drugs. Yet, no reason is given by Mr. Justice Blackmun to justify eliminating Virginia's restriction on the advertising of drug prices other than our strong interest in protecting a free competitive market. The speech protected in short has no value to the advertiser or to the public other than facilitating conduct and processes which themselves have no constitutional protection. How then can the speech be protected? *Virginia State Board* seems, therefore, a throwback to an older and now rejected notion of "substantive due process" which protected competitors from government regulation but which was based on the personal views of the justices rather than the Constitution.

[8] Ibid., pp. 769-770.

ADVERTISING REGULATION AND THE CONSUMER MOVEMENT

Robert Pitofsky

Regulation of false and unfair advertising was authorized at the federal level in 1914 when Congress enacted the Federal Trade Commission Act, declaring unlawful "unfair methods of competition."[1] Before the 1960s, government regulation of national advertising was sporadic and weak, frequently instigated by competitive (as opposed to consumer) interests, and often based upon arbitrary and literalistic standards of accuracy.[2]

The last decade has witnessed sharply increased government efforts at regulating advertising and significant departures from earlier approaches—more cases, new theories of truth and relevance, and imposition of more drastic remedies against violators. Much of this augmented regulatory activity reflects pressures generated by the "consumer movement," with many of the new cases, rules, and programs designed to require or encourage dissemination to consumers of accurate and relevant product information they can use to make informed choices among competing brands.

I believe a solid case in economics and law can be made in favor of government regulation of truth-in-advertising. Of course, ill-conceived regulation will suppress or diminish useful information in the marketplace, and generate unjustifiable costs. New regulatory approaches, and specific programs and cases, will be justifiable only if linked securely to an appreciation of the legitimate role of advertising in the free market process. I believe most recent advertising regulation efforts meet this test; many earlier federal efforts at regulation were wrongheaded and counterproductive precisely because they did not.

In succeeding sections, I will discuss (1) justifications for government regulation of advertising, (2) arguments that there is no proper

---

[1] 15 U.S.C. §45 (a) (1). A narrowing court interpretation of this provision was overruled by statute in 1936 by adding that "unfair or deceptive acts or practices in commerce" were also unlawful.

[2] Richard Posner, "The Federal Trade Commission," *University of Chicago Law Review*, vol. 37 (Fall 1969), pp. 71-78, and section entitled "Deceptive Comparative Price Advertising," in this paper.

role for government intervention—principally the contention that occasional instances of deception should best be left to correction by free market processes, and (3) recent government regulatory programs (and decreases in certain kinds of earlier regulation), which will be evaluated in light of purported justification for the regulatory effort.

Justification for Advertising Regulation

It is common ground that accurate and relevant information supplied through advertising is socially useful because it substitutes for search costs that otherwise would have to be undertaken by consumers. The law authorizes sellers to accumulate relevant data and transmit it to consumers because sellers are in a position to do so more efficiently than consumers, who would have to undertake the task separately for each of the large number of different products they buy. Since sellers cannot always be relied upon to provide accurate and relevant product information, accuracy must be insured and disclosure of key product information encouraged through some outside influence. In the absence of adequate incentives generated by the market or otherwise and given the significance of accurate product information to consumer interests, it seems inevitable that the role will and should be undertaken by the government.

Beyond any duty to provide consumers with truthful product data, advertising should also be regulated with a sharp eye to its influence in the competitive process. Competitive markets function most efficiently when consumers are aware of the availability and characteristics of substitute products.[3] Advertising can also facilitate entry by new companies or expansion of smaller suppliers willing to challenge larger rivals. Finally, advertising frequently is the lever that supports product innovation or makes feasible aggressive price competition.[4] Once advertising successfully takes up a product theme (miles per gallon for automobiles, tar and nicotine content in cigarettes, nutritional content of particular foods), it not only maximizes the rewards of the product innovator, but exerts pressure on all rivals in the product line to equal or surpass the innovations. These procompetitive effects occur, how-

[3] George Stigler, "The Economics of Information," *Journal of Political Economy*, vol. 69 (June 1961), pp. 213-225; Yale Brozen, "Entry Barriers: Advertising and Product Differentiation," in *Industrial Concentration: The New Learning*, ed. Harvey J. Goldschmid et al. (Boston: Little, Brown & Co., 1974), pp. 120-123.

[4] For example, see Lee Benham, "The Effect of Advertising on the Price of Eyeglasses," *Journal of Law and Economics*, vol. 15 (October 1972), pp. 337-353, for a description of how advertising made discount marketing feasible, which in turn led to lower prices.

ever, only if the information accurately reflects product improvement or price. False advertising can result in misallocation of economic resources (for example, purchase of products that cannot achieve the claimed result), or distortion of the competitive process so that companies seek to develop better and better advertising messages (whether truthful or not) rather than better or less costly products.

Viewed in light of these principles—specifically the principle that government intrusion should be viewed as a supplement to the general incentives of the market system, designed to help the system work more effectively—advertising regulation should not attempt to police every inaccuracy in the marketplace nor to require disclosure of all information that some class of consumers might regard as relevant or interesting. For example, there would be no reason to police fraudulent claims associated with low price, repeat purchase items where the fraud will easily be disclosed with use, and no reason to require disclosure of product information if the market already provides an adequate incentive for disclosure. Rather, ad regulation should be a highly practical enterprise designed to insure the availability and accuracy of key product information essential to the functioning of an effective competitive system.

Alternatives to Government Regulation of Advertising

Market Incentives Generating Accurate and Relevant Product Information. It is argued by some that the government has no legitimate role to play in the regulation of false advertising—or a very modest role at best—since there are adequate market incentives for sellers to provide accurate and relevant information and, in those rare instances where sellers misconceive their own best interests, adequate market incentives for rivals to challenge false claims through their own access to advertising channels.[5]

I grant of course that there usually are powerful incentives on sellers to disseminate accurate product information, but there are also on occasion powerful incentives to lie. Certainly a good deal of false advertising is disseminated in the marketplace and competitors are adversely affected. Federal and state authorities bring hundreds of false advertising cases each year and generally win upwards of 90 percent of them. Yet I can think of no instance either before or after government cases were filed in which competitors attempted directly to expose deceptions. Indeed, even when comparative demonstrations have been

5 For example, see Posner, "Federal Trade Commission," pp. 61-63.

successfully challenged by government authorities, rivals directly slandered by the false claim rarely countered the slander publicly.[6]

I suggest this is an area where economists and lawyers might sensibly put aside their models and graphs and take a look at the world around us. Where is this competitive counteradvertising and debunking advertising that many anticipate? One reason for the absence of competitor-generated counteradvertising may be the availability of the government as a low-cost enforcer of competitive rights. Government vindication of private rights also avoids exposing the counteradvertiser to a disparagement suit if the counteradvertising itself proves to be erroneous. But given the infrequent and relatively weak quality of government enforcement in the advertising area through the years, surrogate government enforcement hardly seems an explanation for the almost total absence of competitive counteradvertising. Until recently, networks made explicit counteradvertising against designated rivals impossible on television through self-imposed rules preventing advertisers from naming competitive products. Since those rules were eliminated—largely as a result of government pressure[7]—there seem to be more explicit comparative claims, but few instances in which sellers have attempted to expose to the public deceptions broadcast by rivals.

The explanation for the absence of counteradvertising appears to be that sellers see their best interest in meeting or exceeding questionable or deceptive claims by rivals rather than exposing competitive frauds. The charges contained in the Federal Trade Commission's pending complaints against the analgesics manufacturers,[8] if eventually established, reflect an industry-wide view that it is more effective merchandising to publish the results of a questionable study supporting the seller's claims about its products than to demonstrate the flaws, inadequacies, and irrelevance of rival studies; more effective to create a catchy slogan than to undertake advertising campaigns keyed to explain to consumers that a rival's emphasis on the "special ingredient doctors recommend most" (as a way of distinguishing its product from plain old aspirin) is a reference to aspirin.

A similar gap between theory and reality appears with respect to presumed seller incentives to make available essential information consumers need to make informed choices between competing brands. It has been asserted that where a plurality of sellers offers different prod-

---

[6] For example, see *American Home Products Corp.*, 81 FTC 579 (1972), where an order was entered against deceptive comparative claims for four different household products which, according to the complaint, unfairly depicted a series of rivals described as "Brand X."

[7] See 5 CCH Trade Regulation Rep. ¶¶50, 196 and 50, 205.

[8] For example, see In re Bristol-Myers Co., docket no. 8917 (1972).

ucts with unequal characteristics, there is a natural incentive in most situations for those sellers with superior products to make key product information available.[9] Where information is not made available, it is sometimes assumed the reason is that sellers believe consumers do not want and will not willingly pay the expenses of accumulating and disseminating the data.[10]

In the majority of situations, market incentives of course are adequate to insure the availability to consumers of essential product information. But there are exceptions. Absence of data may reflect imperfections in market organization. A monopoly may concentrate on public image advertising, explaining how it treats its special market position as a public trust, thereby steering clear of such worldly matters as price and efficiency of service.

Oligopolists may avoid claims about key product attributes—for example, octane rating of gasoline, price of funeral services, efficiency of air conditioners—because of recognition of oligopoly interdependence. An obvious example is the failure of cigarette manufacturers until recently to emphasize tar and nicotine content for fear of triggering a "tar and nicotine derby."[11] In addition to usual considerations of avoiding expensive advertising wars in an oligopoly context, any emphasis on comparative safety aspects of particular cigarette brands was bound to affect adversely total industry demand and likely to affect sales volume of the high tar and nicotine brands offered by each of the major sellers.

Finally, product information that a large segment of consumers might seek (and be willing to pay for) may not be available through advertising because sellers believe accumulation of the data is unjustifiably expensive, because unilateral disclosure is useless if comparative data are not available in the marketplace, or because sellers believe most consumers would not understand or for other reasons would ignore the additional information.

Until the government intervened and required or induced disclosure, accurate information was not available in the market as to durability of light bulbs, octane ratings for gasoline, tar and nicotine content

9 Posner, "Federal Trade Commission," pp. 61-62; Stigler, "The Economics of Information," pp. 213-225.

10 William C. Whitford, "The Functions of Disclosure Regulation and Consumer Transactions," *Wisconsin Law Review* (1973), p. 400; *FTC Office of Policy Planning and Evaluation Mid-year Budget Review*, pp. 1-2, reprinted in Bureau of National Affairs, *Antitrust and Trade Regulation Reporter*, April 1976, pp. A-6 to A-12.

11 Product improvement and vigorous advertising of tar and nicotine content followed, and probably was caused at least to a modest extent by, government induced disclosure of comparative tar and nicotine levels.

of cigarettes, mileage per gallon for automobiles, or care labeling of wearing apparel. There continues to be little accurate information to determine comparative prices of life insurance policies, funeral services, eyeglasses, relative efficiency of air conditioners and other electrical appliances, performance characteristics of tires, nutritional content of foods, and so on. I do not suggest with respect to every one of those categories that competitive and consumer advantages will justify the costs of required disclosure. Rather the point is that, in many product categories, when disclosure is cost justified, standard market incentives are inadequate to stimulate competitors to make product information available, and that government intervention is necessary to supplement market incentives if consumers indeed are to have access to key product information.[12] Whether disclosure of particular categories of product information should be required will depend on cost-benefit considerations with respect to each product line—considerations that will be discussed at a later point in this paper.

Fraud Viewed as Harmless or Benign. In the last few years, a second set of arguments has been advanced challenging the wisdom of government intervention to eliminate deceptive advertising—arguments frequently associated with the work of Professor Phillip Nelson.[13] Professor Nelson posits two categories of product characteristics described in advertising: information with respect to "search qualities" (product characteristics that a consumer can determine by inspection before purchase), and "experience qualities" (qualities authenticated or found wanting in the course of use). Under this analysis, search characteristic data are reliable though not very important because consumers can check their accuracy beforehand. Sellers have strong incentives not to embarrass themselves by putting out transparently fraudulent claims. Information with respect to the experience qualities is usually unreli-

---

[12] It is worth remarking that other institutions potentially available for controlling advertising fraud are largely ineffective in this country. Industry self-regulation can have significant hortatory impact but if a trade association attempts to coerce unwilling members to abandon questionable advertising campaigns, or requires disclosure of product data, it will encounter serious antitrust problems, *cf.* Radiant Burners, Inc. v. Peoples' Gas, Light and Coke Co., 364 U.S. 656 (1961); private legal actions by consumers challenging advertising campaigns are virtually impossible because of their considerable expense, the characteristically low dollar amount of injury to any particular consumer, and the Supreme Court rule that consumers may not aggregate their separate claims in a consumer class action, see Snyder v. Harris, 394 U.S. 332 (1969).

[13] This description of Professor Nelson's views is based on two of his articles: "Advertising as Information," *Journal of Political Economy*, vol. 82 (July 1974), pp. 729-754, and "The Economic Value of Advertising," in Yale Brozen, *Advertising and Society* (New York: New York University Press, 1974), pp. 43-66.

able[14] because sellers may exaggerate product quality claims in order to complete a sale and consumers will have no opportunity before purchasing to check the data. Professor Nelson then argues that consumers show good sense by ignoring "experience" quality claims, and concentrating instead on indirect indications of quality. A reliable "indirect" indicator is the frequency of advertising—thus "the more advertisements of a brand the consumer encounters, the more likely he is to try the brand," and the more likely that the consumer is making a wise decision.

The heart of these arguments is the contention that brands that provide the highest utility to consumers are those that are likely to advertise most. Under this view, advertising's main role with respect to experience qualities is reiteration to induce consumers to remember the product's name. This effort will pay off only if the product is likely to generate a high level of consumer satisfaction and repeat purchases. Hence, one can reliably infer value and quality from heavy advertising. By the same line of reasoning, government efforts to eliminate false advertising are wasteful and perhaps counterproductive[15] because the content of the ad is irrelevant; the only thing that is important is the number of exposures.

I must confess some uncertainty as to the substance of these arguments. If Professor Nelson is arguing that consumers, according to some economic model, have reason not to believe "experience" product claims contained in advertising, and therefore usually do not believe such claims, that thesis is demonstrably false. Consumer behavior studies show that consumers frequently believe and are influenced in their purchases by the content of experience-quality advertising claims, true or false. For example, the Federal Trade Commission recently found that Warner-Lambert's false claim that Listerine was effective in preventing colds and ameliorating cold symptoms was believed by an average of 53.8 percent of users and nonusers exposed to that claim during the period 1963–1971.[16] Surely advertisers in this country are not totally misguided in spending billions each year to develop and substantiate product claims. They spend that money because they realize that they cannot achieve the same results at less cost merely by repeatedly an-

---

14 One form of experience quality advertising that is relatively reliable, according to this analysis, relates brand to function—for example, a particular product is a stomach remedy or relieves athlete's foot—but all other descriptions of the qualities of the product are unreliable.

15 They are counterproductive in that they generate in consumers the false notion that information about experience qualities may be accurate.

16 FTC v. Warner-Lambert Co., docket no. 8891 (1975).

nouncing the name of the product and the fact that it was available for sale—in advertising otherwise devoid of content.

Perhaps Professor Nelson is making a different argument—namely, that sellers tend to expend maximum revenues in advertising superior products since advertising inferior products in the long run would be wasteful. If the products do not live up to the advertising, either in terms of search or experience qualities, consumers will recognize that fact and repeat purchases will not occur. One problem with this analysis has to do with the premise that all or most advertising consists of search and experience qualities—product characteristics that can be measured against claims before purchase or during use. I agree that where advertising fraud will be exposed by consumers sampling low-cost, repeat purchase items, there is less reason for the government to intervene. To the extent that Professor Nelson's analysis tends to spotlight the futility of fraud cases where the accuracy of claims can easily be judged during use (for example, the recent action charging that the deodorant Dry-Ban was "dry" upon application and left no "residue"), it is a useful analytical tool.

But most government charges of deceptive advertising have to do with product claims that are extremely difficult or impossible to measure by observation or use. How can a consumer determine the accuracy of a claim that a product has "twice as much vitamin C" as a competing brand? How can a consumer reliably evaluate a claim that a particular disinfectant "helps prevent colds and flu"? Even price claims can be difficult to evaluate—when the claim is "10 percent off manufacturer's list" or "lowest price in town."[17] The more complicated the technology of the product—automobiles, television sets, over-the-counter drugs—the more unlikely that consumers will be in a position to measure the validity of product claims relating to that technology.[18] Thus, an effective and persuasive advertising campaign can and does generate repeat purchases even though the product claims are utterly fanciful. Government regulation is essential to prevent the market distortion that such claims would otherwise produce.

---

[17] I even question whether simple descriptions of function—which Nelson generally regards as reliable (see note 13 above)—always can be evaluated during use. For example, consider the claim by the sellers of Geritol that it was a cure for "tiredness," which was found to be deceptive when applied to the overwhelming majority of users, see J. B. Williams Co. v. FTC, 381 F.2d 884 (6th Cir. 1967).

[18] Darby and Karni refer to these impossible-to-evaluate characteristics as "credence qualities" and rightly point out that the line between experience and credence qualities will often be blurred, depending on cost to check claims, time lapse before truth of claims becomes obvious, and so forth; Darby and Karni, "Free Competition and the Optimal Amount of Fraud," *Journal of Law and Economics*, vol. 16 (April 1973), pp. 67, 69.

New Programs for Advertising Regulation

Assuming government has some role to play in advertising regulation, questions remain whether the sharp departures from prior approaches are consistent with and reflect valid concepts of the legitimate role of advertising. Discussed below are the following recent developments: (1) requirement of prior substantiation of advertising claims, (2) required disclosure of key product information, (3) virtual abandonment of efforts to regulate deceptive price claims, and (4) corrective advertising.

Ad Substantiation. In 1972, the Federal Trade Commission decided that it would be a violation of law to make an affirmative product claim without reasonable prior substantiation,[19] and backed this decision with a program requiring sellers to produce data for a public record, usually on an industry-wide basis, substantiating recently circulated ads.[20] Unsubstantiated claims detected as a result of the program have been challenged in traditional enforcement actions.

One consequence of the ad substantiation rule and its implementing program is to facilitate the detection of false claims, since instances in which advertisers cannot satisfy a demand for substantiation often involve deceptive advertising. The substantiation rule goes further, however, and declares that promulgation of claims violates the law—even if the claims are true—if the seller did not have substantiation at the time the advertisement was published or broadcast. Advertising "puffs," that is, claims not capable of objective verification ("Tastes great!"), are excluded. In announcing the rule, the commission justified the imposition of the substantiation burden on sellers by pointing out that it was impractical to expect individual consumers to run product tests on thousands of different products and that it was much more efficient for a seller to discharge this responsibility before publication of the ad. If prior substantiation is a sensible policy goal, it is surely true that it can be discharged efficiently only by sellers; the question remains, however, and was never addressed in the *Pfizer* opinion, whether the costs of substantiation ought to be incurred at all.

Depending on what standards are adopted to define "adequate substantiation," costs of prior substantiation for all ad claims would be considerable. If advertisers believe the program will be enforced, this also could have significant effects on the amount and content of information disseminated through the advertising process. True claims that

19 In re Pfizer, 81 FTC 23 (1972).

20 See *Staff Report of the Federal Trade Commission on Ad Substantiation* (1973).

are expensive or difficult to substantiate may never be disseminated and, as a result, product superiority features would not be clearly communicated to consumers.

The program could also have beneficial consequences. Claims based on uncertain substantiation will be either withheld or accurately qualified to be co-extensive with available substantiation. Where claims involve health and safety considerations, it is likely that any additional expenses for prior substantiation undertaken as a result of the rule will be justified when compared with potential injury to consumers. Where the unsubstantiated claim does nothing more than fabricate a bargain (for example, "10 percent off" describing a price that was inflated 10 percent prior to the sale), it is more doubtful that consumer harm from occasional false or questionable claims justifies substantiation costs of true claims.

Beyond these fairly conventional cost-benefit considerations, I suggest that if the substantiation rule is justifiable at all, it is for reasons not touched upon in commission opinions. A prior substantiation rule should trigger a *process* of advertising review—involving at an early point in the clearance process professional experts on whose research or knowledge the claim is made and lawyers who may be called upon eventually to defend against a false advertising suit—which should help to eliminate or curtail the quantity of inaccurate information in the marketplace. Enthusiastic marketing people would no longer be able to put off demands for substantiation with the response that the data will be made available when and if needed, but would have to accumulate substantiating evidence before making the claim. Although the encouragement of this clearance process may offer a plausible theoretical justification for a prior substantiation rule, proof of its effectiveness and value can be judged only after measurement of costs and evaluation of the extent to which the rule has contributed to more effective self-regulation by advertisers. To date, no follow-up programs have been undertaken and published and until they are, it is impossible to conclude whether the costs generated by the program are worthwhile.

Required Disclosure of Product Information. It was earlier argued that there are many instances in which the market for one reason or another fails to stimulate the dissemination of competitively important information about product characteristics. Deception by silence has been a traditional form of actionable fraud, although, in previous enforcement efforts in this area, the government has usually acted only upon a finding that, in the context of express claims that were made or the nature of a product, a failure to disclose pertinent information would be misleading.[21]

Recently the commission has become far more aggressive and innovative in its programs of required disclosure. In a series of cases, it has charged that vocational schools violated the law by advertising job opportunities but failing to disclose the percentage of enrollees who failed to complete courses or to obtain employment on graduation. Listed earlier were categories of information that will be required to be disclosed under the commission's rule-making authority: octane ratings on gasoline, tar and nicotine content in cigarettes, mileage per gallon for cars, care labeling instructions on wearing apparel, and average durability of light bulbs. Other projects pending propose disclosure of information on nutritional qualities of food and the electrical efficiency of certain appliances. Free market enthusiasts should particularly applaud commission efforts to preempt under federal law, and thereby nullify, state and local regulations that make the disclosure of comparative price data on eyeglasses illegal.[22]

Required disclosure of octane content is an illuminating example of the proconsumer and procompetitive potential of government intervention in this area. Before the international oil cartel led to virtual elimination of retail price competition, octane content was masked under vague and imprecise labels describing gasoline as "high test," "premium," "regular," "sub-regular," and so on. In fact, unadvertised, off-brand gasolines frequently sold at prices five to ten cents below advertised gasolines of equivalent octane rating. Adequate octane levels are necessary for a car to perform properly. Inadequate levels are obvious to the motorist because of engine "knocking" and afterburn. Excessive octane content in gasoline cannot be detected in the course of use, however, and therefore most consumers, unaware of comparative octane ratings, had no convenient way of discovering that they were using and wasting excessive octane, and that low-price substitutes offered gasoline with adequate octane content for their cars.

Since the off-brand marketers depended for their survival in the market on maintaining a differential between themselves and highly advertised brands roughly equivalent to the savings from not advertising, they were at some disadvantage in any effort to clarify octane con-

[21] See Alberty v. FTC, 182 F.2d (D.C. Cir.), certiorari denied, 340 U.S. 818 (1950). A broader interpretation of Alberty, which would have denied the commission authority to require disclosure of any data adverse to the interest of the advertiser, was repudiated in Feil v. FTC, 285 F.2d 879, 900-901 (9th Cir. 1960).

[22] See *Report of the Presiding Officer on Proposed Trade Regulation Rule Regarding Advertising of Ophthalmic Goods and Services*, 16 C.F.R., part 456 (December 1976).

tent through their own access to advertising channels. Moreover, in the absence of comparative data on octane content in rival brands—information the lower-price marketers were unlikely to possess—any effective advertising campaign would be seriously hampered.

It is not possible at this time to determine whether this form of mandated disclosure will indeed have significant competitive effects. After the oil boycott, gasoline advertising avoided any price or product quality claims; as a result, there has been no occasion to discuss in advertising the comparative qualities of gasolines. It appears now that competition is returning to retail gasoline marketing, including some price competition by cut-rate retailers. It is not clear at present whether marketers will undertake competitive campaigns turning on octane disclosure, or whether consumers in purchase decisions will react to octane information if those data are made available. One hopes they will and that the pattern we now see in cigarette sales with aggressive product innovation and marketing of low tar/low nicotine cigarettes—following and presumably influenced to some extent by required disclosure of tar and nicotine content—will emerge in octane/price competition in retail marketing of gasoline.

Obviously, no information disclosure program will be successful if it attempts to require disclosure of more information than consumers care to know, can understand and "process," or would be willing to pay for (that is, exceeds the cost of consumers gathering the data for themselves). Required disclosure also should be limited to salient characteristics that bear in an important and direct way on the worth of the product. Government intervention is unjustified where the market is producing or predictably will produce the necessary data or where the cost of policing federal disclosure rules is inordinate. Finally, expensive disclosure systems could raise barriers to entry or favor large firms over small so that any adverse competitive effect on industry structure will have to be taken into account. Subject to all these constraints, however, there does appear to be a legitimate government role in this area and some justification for the decision in recent years to shift some enforcement resources away from case-by-case policing of fraud, in the direction of disclosure requirements.

Deceptive Comparative Price Advertising. New fashions in advertising regulation not only involve the institution of new programs but also should include reconsideration of some forms of prior regulation. Fifteen or twenty years ago, up to 30 percent of commission cases involved efforts to extract orders from advertisers against various kinds of deceptive price claims. Enforcement efforts in this area in recent years have been negligible[23]—a development that seems to me to be consistent with an enforcement program geared more to concern for consumer welfare than surrogate enforcement of what are in effect cross-claims by competitors.

When a seller deceptively asserts that he is selling at "20 percent off list" or giving something away "free," competitive or consumer injuries can result. Purchasers may be diverted from the more efficient low-price seller, and purchases may be executed that might not otherwise occur. On the other hand, much alleged deceptive pricing is almost certainly innocuous—either because consumers are in a position to check the validity of exaggerated claims (for example, because comparison shopping is relatively simple) or because the claims are so unlikely ("lowest price ever") or so ambiguous ("10 percent off") that they will be ignored by almost all consumers. Savings claims that exaggerate the comparative price may deny consumers the benefits of a bargain they thought they were receiving, but the sale may still be at a price lower than could be obtained at most other sales outlets in the marketing area. Much deceptive pricing enforcement also entails considerable social and economic costs. A natural target for such enforcement has been discount houses. The usual complainants have been nondiscounters, who emphasize service and reliability rather than price. Aggressive enforcement against discounters that forces them to hew close to the line of accurate information may tend to dampen competitive activity. Cents off, free goods, couponing, and other discount promotions have other procompetitive aspects; such programs are often a device assisting entrants to penetrate new markets and may tend to unsettle rigid pricing patterns. Couponing and free goods may be the only legal way a seller can effectuate a price cut to consumers when intermediate distributors choose to pocket all or most of a list price reduction. While the same procompetitive effects can be achieved by accurate price claims, the cost of ascertaining whether particular discount claims are accurate may deter sellers from making any such claims at all. For example, if a seller must survey area prices to make the claim "no lower price in town" or any other area price claim, the claim is almost certain not to be made at all.

Another aspect of the problem worth noting has to do with the role of advertising in price disclosure as opposed to the role of advertising of other product characteristics. At least in theory, there seems to be some reason to believe that price disclosure is particularly procompeti-

23 Cases charging "truth-in-lending" violations which are numerous and of questionable utility—but which do not involve the kind of comparative price claims discussed here—are excluded.

tive because it tends to "integrate" product markets—that is, it tends to advise consumers with relative accuracy that a variety of similar products is more or less substitutable in terms of price. Advertising focusing on product characteristics can have the opposite effect. It may take up products that are essentially identical and emphasize certain characteristics in order to convince consumers that the products are different and therefore should be considered in different "markets." For example, claims may be made that different brands of breads are more nutritious, fresh, or especially desirable for dieting; or that certain beers are similar to champagne, attractive to heavy drinkers, or more appropriate for women. In effect, such advertising "disintegrates" markets by exaggerating (or fabricating) minor product differences.

There are several reasons why price advertising has special procompetitive effects. Unlike product characteristic claims, price information is perfectly quantifiable (with little subjective distortion), is unidimensional in the sense that lower price is almost always regarded by consumers as better than high price, and is easily comprehensible to consumers.

It is also probably true that most consumers know more about the range of price in product categories than the range of other product characteristics. For example, they would know more about the upper and lower range of prices on particular models of automobiles than the upper and lower range of durability, and more about the upper and lower range of prices for brands of cereals than a similar range of nutrition. As a result, consumers can more accurately evaluate price claims and relate this to value, and avoid products that are priced out of line with value. Without attempting to offer a full explanation for the phenomenon, I would nevertheless maintain that the effect of price information on consumers is particularly procompetitive, and therefore that price advertising should be entitled to special treatment in terms of facilitating and encouraging disclosure.

A Supreme Court case summarizes in an interesting way competing policy considerations in this area. In *FTC* v. *Mary Carter Paint Co.*,[24] the commission challenged the Mary Carter claim that with every purchase of a can of paint (price: $6.98), it would give a second can of paint away "free." Since Mary Carter never sold single cans of paint, it did not meet the specific requirements of the FTC Guide that the word "free" be used only if the sales price for both products was the advertiser's usual and customary retail price for one (Mary Carter had no single can price), or, if the advertiser had not previously sold the article, the price for two may be the usual and customary price for one

---

[24] 382 U.S. 46 (1965).

in the relevant trade area (Mary Carter had sold the article previously in the area). The commission, rejecting an offer of proof by Mary Carter that each can of its paint matched in quality those paints usually and customarily sold in the $6.98 price range, found a violation of its pricing guides; the Supreme Court affirmed.

As in so many deceptive price cases, the problem is to figure out what possible consumer or competitive injury occurred. Competitors could hardly complain about Mary Carter's two-for-one campaign in light of its offer to prove that its paint was equivalent in quality to that sold for $6.98 a gallon. If the offer of proof was valid, Mary Carter was indeed offering two cans of paint at the price of one can sold by competitors. Similarly, consumers were receiving the equivalent of a second can of paint free. One plausible deception is that consumers may have been mislead into thinking that Mary Carter had a single-can price, but it is hard to imagine how this misconception could have led to any injury. Another was that Mary Carter was implying that the offer was of limited duration and that consumers should buy in quantity promptly or lose a special opportunity. The evidence showed, however, that Mary Carter in its ads went to some lengths to be clear that the offer was a permanent sales policy.

Assuming Mary Carter was a more efficient producer of a quality product, arguably there were alternative marketing approaches, presenting no possibility of consumer deception, that would have presented its products to consumers in a favorable light. For example, it could have sold single cans of paint at $3.49 each—presumably a price that would attract many purchasers. But that alternative would have deprived it of the opportunity to make use of a distinctive and memorable ad campaign that allowed it to overcome sales resistance by some consumers who associated low price in paint with low quality. All in all, the case seems an unusually clear example of enforcement that generated little or no consumer benefit and considerable competitive loss.

While few decisions present the case against fictitious price enforcement as clearly, the fact remains that the government policy decisions to downplay enforcement against deceptive pricing, thereby permitting some exaggeration and ambiguity on price claims, is consistent with the principle of minimum enforcement where consumers (as opposed to competitors) are unlikely to be seriously injured and where rigid substantiation requirements might suppress a useful form of competition. Extreme examples of deceptive price claims might still be challenged.[25] My suggestion is not that the government allow a free-fire zone for all price claims, but rather that discounters be allowed a little extra elbow

[25] See Tashof v. FTC, 437 F.2d 707 (D.C. Cir. 1970).

room to state their claims because of the special proconsumer and procompetitive effects of aggressive price competition. In that context, the past effort of government to clear the market of ambiguous or exaggerated price claims, often operating more like a Commission for the Purity of Language than a consumer protection agency, seems well ended.

Corrective Advertising. The most controversial innovation in advertising regulation in recent years involves corrective advertising. This remedy, designed to eradicate the effects of the previous fraud, requires advertisers who are found to have advertised falsely to purchase advertising time or space and disclose to consumers true information about the product (usually through the same media in which the false claim was disseminated). In its simplest form, this action would require the advertiser to announce that previous specified claims had been found to be false and misleading and then to state the truth about the product with respect to that claim. The problem to which corrective advertising is addressed should be one that economists would particularly appreciate. Put simply: under traditional law, the rewards for advertising deception were so great and the penalties so modest (especially when discounted against the remote likelihood of detection and suit) that it was virtually perverse for advertisers not to engage in certain kinds of false claims.

Under traditional advertising law, successfully prosecuted violations resulted in a "cease-and-desist" order that directed the advertiser not to engage in similar future frauds. Violations of these orders could result in prosecutions (extremely rare in practice) leading to fines of $5,000 per day per violation.[26] Since most advertising campaign themes run for a year or less, and most commission advertising enforcement proceedings span periods of two to five years—with one horrible example running to sixteen years[27]—the effect of any order was usually to direct the advertiser to discontinue an advertising campaign that had long since disappeared. Thus the major risk that an advertiser ran in disseminating a false claim was that the litigation expenses necessary to delay enforcement might exceed the value to the advertiser of the business advantage generated by the deception.

---

[26] The fine was recently increased by statute to $10,000 per day per violation.

[27] This was the notorious Carter Products Inc. v. FTC, 268 F.2d 461 (9th Cir.), certiorari denied 361 U.S. 884 (1959), where it took the commission sixteen years before it successfully ordered the elimination of the word "Liver" from Carter's Little Liver Pills.

A measure of the success of the commission's efforts in that case was suggested by a James Reston column reporting the lack of interest in the early presidential primaries in 1976: out in the west, he reported, most people thought Carter was a "liver pill."

Beginning in 1970, the commission claimed the authority to impose corrective advertising and has since brought complaints against a score of advertisers and imposed corrective advertising as a result of several consent settlements.[28] In December 1975, it ordered the imposition of corrective advertising to correct allegedly false advertising concerning the mouthwash Listerine.[29]

The theory underlying corrective advertising is that the effects of a false advertising campaign endure in the marketplace long after the campaign has been discontinued, with consumers who recall the deception continuing to make purchases on the basis of misleading information. A simple cease-and-desist order obviously does nothing to eliminate the consumer misimpression, nor does it return to competitors any lost market share misappropriated as a result of the deception. Incidentally, the notion that advertising has residual marketplace effects that diminish slowly over time is consistent with the view of many economists that advertising should be treated as an investment rather than an expense.[30]

The corrective advertising concept could embrace somewhat more exotic theories of residual effect. For example, it could be argued in some circumstances that deceptions, though no longer recalled, were the cause of an original purchase and that thereafter brand loyalty and consumer satisfaction took over to generate repeat purchases, or that while there was no present recall (and therefore no identifiable residual effect) of false claims, similar future campaigns would predictably trigger recall and then influence market behavior. To date, the commission has not needed to deal with these more imaginative theories. A likely disposition would be to grant that such marketplace effects can occur and put it to the government to prove their existence in any particular case—a problem of proof so overwhelming as to make successful enforcement under these later theories virtually impossible.

In what sort of cases will corrective advertising be applied in the future? Most likely, the remedy will be reserved for use against major advertising themes. Purchase of advertising space is expensive and the remedy unusually embarrassing to companies against which it is directed. More important, a corrective message broadcast after all but a few consumers have forgotten the original fraud is likely to be confusing. Similarly, a corrective message for an insignificant fraud or for a false

28 For example, see *American Home Products Corp.*, 3 Trade Regulation Rep. ¶19,673 (FTC June 1971); *ITT Continental Baking Co.*, 3 Trade Regulation Rep. ¶19,539 (FTC March 1971).

29 In re Warner-Lambert Co., docket no. 8891 (December 1975).

30 See Brozen, "Entry Barriers," p. 124, where a ten-year depreciation period was proposed as realistic.

claim of marginal significance in most consumers' purchasing decisions would disserve the goal of emphasizing key market information on which consumer choices should be made. Corrective advertising will almost certainly be limited to those situations in which the government is able to prove clear recall of the fraud by a substantial segment of consumers at the time the complaint is filed. If the commission moves with reasonable dispatch—that is, if it brings cases fairly promptly after deception is detected—even twenty-six week ad campaigns, assuming they include a vivid and memorable fraudulent theme, should be reachable under this remedial approach.

Conclusion. To a considerable extent, the "consumer movement" of the 1960s and early 1970s has been fueled by the fact that characteristic consumer injuries are usually so small in dollar amount that it almost never makes sense for individuals to seek compensation or relief through the slow and expensive processes of the courts. Frustrated consumers, feeling they have been exploited and unable to vindicate what they believe are their rights, have turned to government agencies (or have demanded the establishment of new agencies) to represent their interests. Also, many consumer advocates have turned their attention to the reform of institutions that protect consumers from injury before the event. Advertising regulation was an obvious target for that kind of approach. It is worth noting that most of the major departures in regulation described in this paper, including the ad substantiation program, corrective advertising, and required disclosure of product information, such as octane rating and tar and nicotine content, were initiated by petitions from consumer groups.

It is not my intention to argue that all cases, rules, and programs undertaken under the influence of a more consumer-oriented program of ad regulation have been sound and sensible. My point is a much more limited one of suggesting that many of the major changes that have occurred reflect a more realistic appreciation of the true role of advertising in a free market process and as such should result in higher levels of consumer welfare.

COMMENTARIES

Robert H. Bork

The immense volume of literature about advertising and the proliferation of government efforts to regulate advertising are both impressive. I suppose what is impressive about them is that so much concern is lavished on a range of problems that seem to me, for the most part, monumentally trivial. We have become enormously sensitive about anything that might cause the slightest degree of inconvenience to consumers, and, indeed, the word "consumer" has become talismanic.

Increasingly, the task of the law and of government is seen as the elimination of all inconvenience from the sacred function of consuming efficiently. We measure an individual's efficiency in consuming, of course, by standards that we, rather than he, would agree are rational.

For some reason, we treat no other recipient of messages in our society with the solicitude with which we treat consumers. We do not ask that the persuasion employed by clergymen, in advancing religious causes, or politicians, in advancing political causes, or, most certainly, the messages delivered by professors, in advancing education, meet the standards of prior substantiation, disclosure of key information, and counteradvertising that we impose upon the sellers of products. A very good argument could be made, nonetheless, that the volume of false claims and misstatements of fact, in each of those fields, easily meets and probably surpasses the volume of false claims in commercial advertising. Can anyone be sure that imposing the kinds of standards we are discussing here today would not devastate much of religious proselytizing, political discourse, and the curricula of our major centers of learning? Applying these standards would certainly greatly alter the practice of law, though that is a point I shall not dwell on. It would also greatly change the accepted tactics of courtship.

There is a mystery here. Why is it that in commercial advertising alone we take the possibility of a misstatement so seriously that we suggest government intervention? We do not even take commercial misrepresentations seriously unless a private company makes them. An example of government advertising that is decidedly misleading, and to which there is little public outcry, is the false advertising that accompanies the sale of U.S. savings bonds. The government not only falsely represents the bonds as a good investment, when it knows that they are a perfectly dreadful investment, but it compounds the damage in a way that no private advertiser can, because after it has sold the bonds it pursues inflationary policies that make the bonds an even worse buy.

There seems to be a mystery also in our very different attitudes towards private, commercial advertising and all other forms of persuasion. I think the concerns that intellectuals and regulators have shown about advertising represent their own special view more than any deep public antagonism to business and its workings. The type of intellectual who exemplifies that antagonism perfectly is John Kenneth Galbraith, who is mentioned in several of the papers given today. The kind of antagonism displayed by Professor Galbraith is, in turn, I think a reflection of an antibourgeois sentiment that lies beneath so much public policy and that has been explained by Irving Kristol and others in terms of class warfare between the intellectuals and the bourgeoisie.

This line of reasoning casts the issue in a somewhat different light. If we live easily with factual misstatements and dubious claims in so much of our lives, with no sense of real grievance or deprivation, I wonder what would be wrong with accepting an imperfect world in which consumers make mistakes; in which the claim of the lowest price in town is not accurate; in which the marbles in the soup can make the photo show more vegetables at the top than, in fact, you will find throughout; in which people buy the light bulb that does not last the longest.

I know of one light bulb that is promoted as lasting longer and, indeed, does. The promotion of the light bulb may be viewed as deceptive because it ignores one flaw: the bulb lasts longer because it gives less light. What can regulation do about that problem? If we begin to require a description of all the seemingly relevant aspects of products we will wind up with product advertisements that resemble an SEC prospectus.

Errors made in the marketplace due to advertising, such as buying marble soup or buying Listerine under a misapprehension that it reduces the chance of catching a cold, are really not disastrous. In comparison with other mistakes in life caused by misleading messages—such as sacrificing to a false religion, electing the wrong President, accepting social science quackery as scholarship, or marrying the wrong person—they are trivial.

One might say that, as compared with these other matters, the dangers of government intervention are also quite slight. But that is not a completely satisfactory answer because it does not allow for the possibility that the costs of regulation are greatly disproportionate to the evil feared. We are accustomed, in discussing these matters, to look only at the evil to be cured and not at all at the evil inherent in the cure. We assume imperfect markets and perfect regulation. If that were an accurate picture, regulation would always be the better choice. Of course it is not.

There is mention in both papers of cost-benefit analysis. I would like to consider the costs of regulation because I believe them to be vastly underestimated.

Starting with the most obvious, there are the dollar costs of regulation itself and the costs incurred by producers and distributors in their efforts to comply with or resist regulation. That there could be an offsetting dollar gain to consumers in fewer mistaken purchases seems to me dubious. It must be remembered that the costs of monitoring compliance with regulation fall upon all firms, those that are performing satisfactorily as well as those whose behavior is thought to require correction. Costs are thus imposed far more widely than benefits are attained.

Professor Pitofsky has criticized the commission for not making follow-up studies. Perhaps his point is valid, although the commission may have looked at such an undertaking and decided that it was impossible. We have seen a spate of articles attempting now, eighty-six years after its inception, to ask whether the costs of antitrust policy exceed the benefits of antitrust policy. The answer is that we do not know. Such things often must be decided on the basis of uncertain inferences from economic theory and on the basis of common sense.

It is not at all clear that the dollar costs of regulating advertising would not exceed, perhaps greatly, the dollar benefits conferred. But on top of that, there is the cost to consumers of regulatory mistakes—and we can be certain that they will occur. They are common in every regulatory scheme we know of and there is no reason to suppose that the regulation of advertising will proceed with any less error, any less adverse impact upon consumers, than other regulatory efforts. That is a chilling thought.

An additional cost is the disincentive to produce useful advertising because of the danger of legal involvement, which has been mentioned by the speakers.

Finally, there is a cost that I find hard to describe. It certainly cannot be quantified, but it seems to me in some ways more important than all the other costs we have been discussing. Advertising is simply one example of thousands of activities for which controls are proposed or are in place. We have become a very anxious people, and we are trying to guarantee, by law and by adjudicative processes, every minor right people think they ought, ideally, to possess. The total amount of government intervention in formerly private and free processes—social, economic, educational, political—is at levels that were, until quite recently, inconceivable. And the amount of intervention is growing.

I would suggest that the cost of this for the legal system, for the vitality of private institutions, for the integrity of governmental institutions, and for our morale as a community, is very great indeed. It is apparent, if you are close to them, that the weight of the regulatory welfare programs we increasingly engage in is, in fact, deforming the function of our federal courts, of the Congress, and of the presidency. The regulation of advertising, of course, is an infinitesimal part of that. But then, the regulation of anything is an infinitesimal part of the total regulatory effort.

I think we have to come to the point—or rather, I think we are well past the point—where we must severely ration ourselves in the number of activities we try to regulate. We are at the point where regulation in any context ought to be shown to be necessary to avert a very serious harm before it is adopted. Insofar as I know, nobody has made a showing of that kind with respect to advertising.

It is for this reason and the other reasons cited that Professor Pitofsky's excellent paper ultimately fails to persuade me to his viewpoint.

We are really dealing, in a sense, with an empty topic because advertising displays almost none of the evils attributed to it. It has been suggested that advertising does not work well in oligopoly situations since oligopolists do not point out particular product features or defects in their rivals' products because of something called "oligopolistic interdependence." The theory of oligopolistic interdependence is one I am quite dubious about, but in any case the phenomenon cited has, in fact, very little to do with oligopoly. If we look at competitive industries, we find the same thing is true or, perhaps, even more true: the pizza houses in New Haven are a prime example of advertising in a highly competitive market, and they certainly do not provide a great deal of information about their particular product or about defects in their rivals' products.

Professor Winter has adequately dealt with the issue of barriers to entry, which turn out merely to mean that a person who has been advertising successfully has an advantage, just as a person who has a plant or a managerial staff or a sales force in place has an advantage. Those are functions of efficiency, rather than artificial barriers.

On the question of fraud, I want to make one suggestion about Professor Pitofsky's comment that advertising disintegrates markets by playing up product differences. Professor Winter has answered that in part by saying that if the differences are real, we ought to let the advertising alone because consumers are responding to product differences, and that is part of their satisfaction. I would also suggest that emphasizing a vague product difference may be essential to the provision of the real information in the advertisement.

One of the problems a provider of information faces is recapturing the costs of providing it. If you advertise and fail to persuade anybody to try your product, you cannot recapture the cost of the real information you do provide. Some degree of product differentiation, even if it is not scientifically capable of being established, seems essential to recapture the cost of the information in this market and, therefore, ought not to be tampered with.

We have heard a lot about fraud. I suppose there is some, but it seems to be trivial. The question of whether some people are misled about Listerine or Carter's Little Liver Pills seems not to be terribly troublesome. I suppose that, if one could be sure that only the case of clear fraud would be dealt with, then I would accept Professor Winter's rule for dealing with it.

The difficulty is that we know something about the dynamics of regulatory agencies and people who have missions. If we start with a rule that clear fraud will be banned, I am afraid that, as the regulatory agency tries new cases and redefines fraud—and we have seen this in a variety of public programs—we will soon have rules and controls for things that are not real fraud. The Mary Carter paint case, which has been described to us, is an example of the FTC's starting with a valid objective and arriving at invalid conclusions. If the commission were as reasonable as Professor Pitofsky has proved to be this morning and as reasonable as his model of regulation requires that it be, it would not have moved into the Mary Carter paint case. I am afraid we may in general expect that sort of behavior from regulatory agencies.

For these reasons, I think the damage ascribable to advertising is slight, and I suspect that, in attempting to repair it, we are likely to do far more harm in the aggregate than good.

Donald F. Turner

Although I am inclined to agree with the other contributors that advertising is by no means one of the most important issues around, it is an issue about which people feel strongly on both sides. The emotional heat that is worked up is far in excess of the real importance of the issue itself. This may well suggest one of the reasons why we have regulation of advertising, and will probably continue to have it and, I think, probably should.

More than one have asked the question: Why step in and endeavor to preserve truth in the commercial advertising area, when we do not in any other area, such as political debate, education, and the like? I think one of the reasons is that the potential adverse consequences of attempting to control political debate or educational processes are vastly greater than the potential adverse consequences of excessive or poorly directed regulation of advertising.

Probably another reason is on the consumer side. I sense that consumers react directly and deeply when they feel they have been gouged or misled in the purchase of a product. This has an immediate impact: the product they bought is no good or is not what it was represented to be. They have spent hard cash for it, and they are mad. I think the feeling of having been cheated is much more direct and more deeply felt than the feelings that are aroused when they have been misled by politicians or educators (although I must say from my experience in academic life that the volume of distress there is still pretty high).

In other words, I think the real reason we are regulating advertising is that it is a matter about which people, on the whole, feel pretty deeply. They do not like to get directly taken when their pocketbook is at stake.

Now, apart from that, I must say I would find it hard to disagree with the proposition that if a set of priorities were established for what the government should regulate, if it were going to regulate anything, advertising might be far down the list. But I would not be entirely comfortable with such a list. We do not know what the volume of misleading advertising and the cost of it would be in the absence of existing regulations. I suspect that if everything were open—if advertisers could say anything they wanted to with no penalties, governmental or private—we would have a substantially greater volume of serious fraud and deception and, hence, more damage to consumers than we now have. Obviously, we cannot look at the situation as it now is and say, well, advertising is 99 per cent pure and conclude that regulation is unwarranted. If it is that pure, it may well be so because there has been government regulation.

By and large, businessmen are honorable people, and advertisers are honorable people, in the sense that they wish to be law abiding and do not want to be categorized as lawbreakers. After all, the media give substantial publicity to FTC suits against companies for false or misleading advertising, and I do not think that companies like to receive publicity of this kind. So, concerning the proposition that regulation of advertising is an extremely low priority item, I rather suspect that it would be a problem of considerably more serious proportions if we did not regulate.

Now, in the few additional remarks I have to make, I will proceed on the assumption that the government has a proper regulatory role, though surely more circumscribed and more careful than it has been a lot of times in the past. Within government agencies there ought to be some presumptions against intervention. Agencies ought to try to allocate their resources to situations of general significance, but I am inclined to say that the continuation of government regulation in some form is appropriate.

It seems quite clear to me that, unlike political debate, the market does not adequately take care of misrepresentations in advertising. Moreover, if there is to be some control over advertising in the form of some kind of sanction or regulation, government regulation with all its weaknesses—and it certainly has them—is much more appropriate than private rights of action. That is, it misses the critical point to argue that we need no government regulation because if people are really hurt, they have, or ought to have, a private right of action.

I would suppose that if somebody proposed to make consumer class action suits for false advertising feasible, advertisers would view that as a terrifying alternative to FTC regulation, and properly so. The problem is not so much that money would be at stake, although that is certainly one thing. More fundamentally the problem is that government regulation is vastly superior in this kind of matter. It is more likely to be wise than the kind of law that would evolve from purely private rights of action, unless the substantive provisions of the law that gave the private right of action were tightly controlled and very severely circumscribed.

The problem is very similar to that in an area with which I am much more familiar, namely, antitrust law. It has been only within the last few years that people have begun to realize that private rights of action in the antitrust area, formerly thought to be a wonderful adjunct to government enforcement of antitrust, are in fact creating some very serious problems.

This is partially attributable to the fact that substantive antitrust law is rather vague, giving a lot of judges the power to make bad law, or scaring them so badly that they will not grant summary judgment against frivolous cases. They let the cases go to the jury, where the little guy is likely to win.

The serious problem is that antitrust can very well become, through poor interpretation or through the threat of lawsuits, a device for discouraging businessmen from engaging in perfectly legitimate competitive activity. If businessmen become subject to a treble damage action by engaging in any activity that might arguably hurt a competitor, they simply will not do it. I think in the antitrust area, unlike advertising, the social costs of this kind of a threat are likely to be very, very great. The short of it is that government regulation or government enforcement policy in the antitrust area, for all of its faults, is more likely to be reasonably sane than the kind of law that evolves out of private actions.

I have said that I did not think the social costs of overregulating advertising were all that great. I do not think they really are. Ralph Winter and Bob Bork suggest that regulation failure can cost consumers as much as the fraud they are seeking to stop. I am just a little puzzled by the argument. Surely government regulation of advertising does not keep products from getting to the market. That is not the danger. What would happen, if there were a rather serious threat of prosecution for false advertising, is that people would not conduct dubious advertising campaigns.

The threat is not that products will not be able to get to the market, or anything of that kind. The concern is more that, if too heavy a campaign is launched against specific product claims, and it becomes very costly to make those claims, advertising will simply be deflected into more noninformational, nonrational forms. So consumers will not lose the product; they will lose the kind of information that we would like to see them get. That is the risk of unwise regulation.

Wesley J. Liebeler

In reviewing the foregoing papers and comments, a couple of thoughts struck me that I want to express before moving to my main subject, which primarily concerns Professor Pitofsky's paper.

The point was made that consumers apparently suffer more anguish when they have been misled by commercial advertisements than when they have been misled by law professors, politicians, and other people engaged in some sort of persuasion. The theory offered in explanation was that, perhaps, their pocketbook was involved more directly when they were misled by commercial advertising. But surely their pocketbooks are involved, often in a big way, when they are misled by politicians and educators.

I think that if consumers do become more upset when they have been misled by commercial speech, that should be taken as testimony of the high esteem in which they hold businessmen. They apparently expect more from businessmen than they do from politicians and professors. Or to put it another way, they rarely get taken by business; when it does happen, they are understandably surprised and upset. Those of you who have felt that businessmen are held in low esteem should take heart from this.

It is heartening that Professor Pitofsky appears to recognize the importance of market forces and to argue that sensible advertising regulation should supplement and reinforce them. But I have the feeling that this recognition is more apparent than real, for two reasons. First, Pitofsky seems to think that the Federal Trade Commission has stopped doing silly things in the area of advertising regulation. I do not believe it. The second reason lies in the nature of the examples that Pitofsky puts forward to show that the commission is now doing sensible things. I do not believe that the current regulatory devices (advertising substantiation, corrective advertising, and affirmative disclosure) are well designed to supplement and reinforce market forces.

It is not surprising that Pitofsky does not defend the commission's historical record in the field of advertising regulation, for that record is dismal beyond ready belief. For example, recall the commission's proceeding against an advertisement that was taken to claim that certain waterwings were invisible, impalpable, and in effect nonexistent.[1] Other examples, that most observers would find fatuous, or worse, include the proceeding that argued that a soap called "palm and olive oil soap" would be taken by consumers to be 100 percent palm oil soap or 100 percent olive oil soap, whichever the case may be,[2] and the proceeding that concerned itself with the "claim" that one could shave sandpaper using a certain shaving cream.[3]

One gets the impression, listening to Professor Pitofsky, that while the commission may have done a lot of foolish things in the past, it is on the right track now. Pitofsky implies, for instance, that due recognition is being given by the commission to recent theoretical work such as that which divides product attributes into search qualities, experience qualities, and so-called credence qualities.[4] Since false advertising will be most difficult to detect—and therefore most likely to be profitable—in the case of credence qualities, we should expect the commission to redouble its efforts in this area and pay less attention to search and experience qualities. Let me review, by way of checking this prediction,

---

1 Matter of Kirchner, 63 FTC 1282, 1963, affirmed 337 F.2d 751 (9th Cir. 1964).

2 Wrisley Co. v. the FTC, 113 F.2d 437 (7th Cir. 1940).

3 FTC v. Colgate-Palmolive Co., 380 U.S. 374 (1965).

4 Phillip Nelson, "Advertising as Information," *Journal of Political Economy*, July/August 1974, pp. 729-754; Michael R. Darby and Edi Karni, "Free Competition and the Optimal Amount of Fraud," *Journal of Law and Economics*, vol. 16 (April 1973), pp. 67-88.

some current or recent activities in the commission's advertising regulation programs.

When I was director of policy planning and evaluation at the commission, I discovered that the Bureau of Consumer Protection had a program designed to deal with "advertising techniques." I did not know what an "advertising technique" was or just how it might be expected to injure consumers. I was told that, among other things, the program was designed to deal with the problem of dangling comparatives. But that was no help, since I did not know the meaning of a dangling comparative. To enlighten me the Bureau of Consumer Protection sent my office a number of print ads illustrating the "problem." A dangling comparative, I learned, was a claim that a product had more or that it was better. What it had more than or what it was bettter than, the ad did not say.

Before I looked at the ads I asked myself why business firms, which I do not take to be irrational all the time, would run ads that did not contain more explicit information. I indulged the apparently common assumption that consumers would tend to respond to more informative ads, and that, therefore, businessmen trying to boost sales would tend to provide more information rather than less.

The only plausible explanation I could think of was that the products involved must have qualities about which information could not be readily communicated in an ordinary print ad. I conjectured that most of the products involved would be those with experience-type qualities. The most cost-effective way for a consumer to get information about these qualities would be to buy the product and try it. I predicted that the products beset by dangling comparatives would be frequently purchased and that they would have a relatively low purchase price.

Of course, I would not be reporting these thoughts if they had not turned out to be correct. They were confirmed the next day when I talked to one of my staff who had reviewed the ads. In looking through the ads we found one that was particularly threatening. It was an advertisement for a certain brand of Scotch whiskey which, it was claimed, had better balance. The ad contained a picture of Zero Mostel with a glass perched on his head, presumably to indicate that the Scotch did indeed have better balance. But the question that concerned the Bureau of Consumer Protection was, "Better than what?"

Obviously this advertisement, like others using dangling comparatives, was trying to persuade consumers—perhaps by sparking their curiosity about what the Scotch was better balanced than—to try the product and decide for themselves whether it was good or not. It is beyond me how the qualities of a whiskey can be communicated directly in a print ad, at least in one not longer than the average SEC prospectus.

And I think that most of us would rather just buy a bottle and try it than read an ad like that. The point that sampling the product is the most efficient way to get information about experience-type qualities seems to have been completely lost on the commission and its staff, at least up to now.

The commission did not, of course, make a federal case out of the Scotch ad. But it did something just as silly when it investigated an advertisement that claimed that Dry Ban was dry.[5] I would have supposed that interested consumers could have tested this claim by the ready expedient of buying a can of Dry Ban, spraying it on some appropriate part of their body, and observing whether it was dry. Even if it was not totally dry, they could presumably use the rest of the can. Barring allergies or extreme dissatisfaction with the product, the purchase price would not be totally lost. The consumer loss from ads of this type cannot conceivably be large enough to justify the expensive attentions of a federal agency.

But even proceedings like this appear sensible when compared with other FTC actions, such as an investigation of a "money-making" machine. Apparently there is an advertisement that shows a device with two rollers mounted on a wooden frame with a sheet of fabric running between the rollers. If the operator rolls up a dollar bill on one roller, and then inserts a plain sheet of paper from the other side, it appears as if the machine is making money. The Magic Money Maker sells for less than two dollars. The commission has on file a complaint from a parent stating that his child believed that he could print the real thing and spend it.[6]

This is one of a series of similar ads that, according to the budget review, "if developed into a case . . . might establish the precedent that comic book publishers are responsible for advertising that is 'clearly deceptive on its face.' " Another ad in the series broadcasts the claim: "Drive a spike through metal with your hands."

The budget review, displaying a sense of humor and proportion apparently not shared by the regional office that spent 154 man-hours on this ridiculous proposal, remarks that cases such as these "might be justified as a long-term investment. If the expectations of young wayfarers are preserved now, the agency [the FTC] may have more business later." [7]

---

[5] Briston-Myers Co. (Dry Ban), 85 FTC, pp. 688-752.

[6] See discussion on Commission Program I-01 (Advertising Monitoring and Substantiation), Mid-Year Budget Review, FTC Office of Policy Planning and Evaluation, January 1976, p. 6.

[7] Commission Program I-01, p. 7.

That the commission's efforts at advertising regulation are not confined solely to the protection of fools is shown by another investigation in the same regional office involving an ad for a product that gets rid of unsightly and unwanted hair on the upper lips of females. The concern of the regional office is that it is false and misleading to suggest that hair on the upper lips of females is unattractive. But what if men in fact want their partners to be less hirsute than Professor Bork? The young lady promoting this investigation replies that this would be irrelevant; people *should not have* such feelings. The Federal Trade Commission is there to make sure that they do not.[8]

While matters like these do have a certain value as entertainment, they hardly support Pitofsky's view that advertising regulation at the Federal Trade Commission is on the right track. Nor are we convinced by his argument that the commission has reformed itself because it has stopped trying to suppress advertisements that inform consumers of reduced prices. This is a matter of changing styles, not substance. The commission has merely adopted an indirect approach.

Instead of directly attacking the advertising of lower prices, the commission now has a very substantial program aimed at the unavailability of advertised specials. A grocery store, for example, will advertise a certain number of special low prices on specified items. Since it is very hard to gauge in advance the demand for these bargain items, the advertised specials sometimes sell out before all customers can be satisfied. When this happens, most stores have a policy of either giving a raincheck so the special can be obtained when it is back in stock or giving the closest available substitute product at the reduced price. This, however, is not enough for the FTC. The commission has spared little expense making sure that retail stores have the advertised specials on hand for all the consumers who come in to get them.[9]

This seems like a laudable program until we realize that the operation of market forces will tend to create an optimum trade-off between the degree to which advertised specials are available and the cost to advertisers (and thereby to consumers) of making them available. Economic theory suggests that stores will expend additional amounts to increase the percentage of availability until those marginal expenditures equal the marginal revenue gained by the store from having such increased availability. Since there is no apparent reason to believe that such revenue is less than the marginal costs to consumers of lower

[8] See discussion of Commission Program P-01 (Regional Advertising), Mid-Year Budget Review, FTC Office of Policy Planning and Evaluation, January 1976, p. 4.

[9] See discussion of Commission Program J-01 (Point of Sale Practices), Mid-Year Budget Review, FTC Office of Policy Planning and Evaluation, January 1976.

availability, there is no reason to think that the market has failed or will fail to produce the optimal level of availability, from society's point of view, without the help of the Federal Trade Commission. It should be obvious that the optimal level of availability will not be 100 percent; the high costs of achieving that level would almost certainly exceed any conceivable benefit which consumers would realize from having it.

If the market does operate to produce the optimal level of availability, any attempt by the commission to increase the degree of availability from that level must operate to reduce consumer welfare. It will do that either by increasing the costs of having items available at a higher than optimal percentage of the time or by reducing the extent to which food stores advertise the availability of low-priced specials. If, as I suspect, it does the latter, the commission's advertised specials program must be seen as an indirect attack on the advertising of low prices. Even if such advertising does not cease entirely (and it probably will not), the increased costs of such advertising which result from the commission's program would tend to reduce the amount of such advertising.

The actual effect of the commission's program in this area is, of course, an empirical matter. The argument outlined above is based on theory. Even if an empirical examination of the effects of this program were conducted, however, and did not show that the principal effects of the program were to increase grocery prices or to reduce the amount of price advertising, it is hard to see how this program would reinforce or supplement market forces, as Pitofsky rightly argues sensible advertising regulation should.

The commission's overall performance in the field of advertising regulation cannot, of course, be judged on the few examples which I have discussed. But I am prepared to defend the general proposition that the commission's programs in that field are for the most part quite insensitive to market considerations and, as a result, quite unlikely to increase consumer welfare. The fact that Pitofsky seems to believe that the commission is improving and doing, if not terribly well, at least tolerably better, leads me to suspect, as I have said, that his recognition of the importance of market forces is more apparent than real.

That suspicion is reinforced when I turn to the three principal programs that Pitofsky offers as examples of sensible advertising regulation—advertising substantiation, affirmative disclosure, and corrective advertising. I will confine myself to some brief remarks about the first two.

The development of the advertising substantiation notion is rather odd. It came to first flower in the *Pfizer* case, which involved a product called "Unburn" that the maker claimed would stop sunburn pain faster than a girl could slip out of a bikini.

The commission's opinion in that case was written by its then chairman, Miles Kirkpatrick. The opinion stated in effect that consumers could not practically run laboratory tests to determine the truth of an ad claim. Since the manufacturer can do this more cheaply and efficiently, he should be required to do it beforehand.[10]

It seems to me that the *Pfizer* ad was peculiarly inappropriate as a vehicle for developing the advertising substantiation concept, even assuming that the concept makes sense in some cases. It certainly did not make sense in *Pfizer*. The effectiveness of a cure for sunburn pain is something that even the most foolish wayfarer among us can readily determine for himself. The product either eases the pain or it doesn't. Even if we are "manipulated" by intensive advertising into believing that the product is effective, the result is the same: We don't hurt anymore! The product is obviously laden with experience qualities. In this situation the likelihood of false advertising or fraud is almost nonexistent. And so, one would think, is the need for advertising substantiation.

Though constrained from developing the idea to its fullest, I am prepared to defend the general proposition that advertising substantiation is not appropriate for products that are characterized primarily by search or experience qualities. Goods heavily laden with credence qualities are a more difficult problem, but even here it is not at all clear that a *mandatory* substantiation program is the best approach.

If the commission feels that it must do something in this area, it might develop a system of property rights that would enable advertisers to claim different degrees of substantiation.[11] This system could entail a number of degrees of substantiation for any particular claim, which could be established by the commission. If an advertiser makes a claim and states that it is "substantiated to Level A, FTC Standard," a consumer could take the claim to be true insofar as it could be effectively tested. A claim substantiated to Level B would be entitled to less credence in the marketplace and so on. A claim that was stated to be "not substantiated" would be the equivalent of a caveat emptor warning.

If consumers regarded substantiation of the ad claim as important, they would patronize the firm that made the most appropriate claim to

---

10 Matter of Pfizer, Inc., 81 FTC 23, 1972.

11 I must give credit for this idea to Mark Grady, who advanced it, among other places, in a paper that he presented to my class in Law and Policy to Consumer Protection at the UCLA Law School.

the highest level of substantiation. If consumers did not regard substantiation as important enough to pay a premium for the product, they could buy products for which claims were not substantiated. No doubt individual consumers would derive different utility from different degrees of substantiation among various products. There is no reason to believe, given a system of well-defined and enforced property rights in degrees of substantiation, that the market would not produce an efficient mix of ad claims, product characteristics, and prices that would tend to maximize consumer welfare.

This is the kind of program that would reinforce and supplement market forces. The Federal Trade Commission does not have very many of them. None of the three programs mentioned above, on which Pitofsky relies for his claim of sense in advertising regulation, falls within this category.

The commission's pending action against suppliers of house plants illustrates the issue of affirmative disclosure. The action involves the claim that not everyone knows how to take care of house plants, with the result, it is alleged, that many of them die. In order to solve this problem the commission has authorized an investigation looking toward an order that would require the sellers of house plants to provide affirmative product information, in the form of a card or booklet attached to the plant or its container, on how to care for and feed the plant.[12] The justification offered for this action was that few such sellers, presumably as casually observed by some member of the commission staff, were now providing such information at the point of sale.

If one is to fit this case into a market theory of advertising regulation, some plausible explanation of how and why the market has failed to provide this information—if indeed it has—would seem necessary. Needless to say, no such explanation was attempted by the commission staff when they sought authorization to proceed.

The week after the commission authorized the investigation, over the Policy Planning Office's objection and against the vote of two commissioners, *Woman's Day* magazine, which costs less than a dollar, appeared in the check-out lines of the grocery stores of America, with about 115 pages devoted to how to care for plants. In addition to the extensive information it provided, the magazine listed other sources for more information, if desired. Indeed, there is an enormous and readily available literature on house plants. The commission is, however, proceeding with its investigation.

The question one must raise about an affirmative disclosure program, in the context of a market-oriented system of advertising regula-

[12] FTC, file no. 752 3100.

tion, is why do we think that the market has not already produced the optimum amount of information about various products? Information about particular products need not always be supplied by their makers; the information supplied by a competitor may be much more interesting and valuable. This leads to the issue of comparative advertising.

Many people, including Professor Pitofsky and myself, believe that there is not as much comparative advertising as there "should be." Pitofsky advises us to put aside our economic models and look at the real world. We will see that there is not a great deal of such advertising, even though a market model might predict that we would be likely to find some (or more) if we looked. But as we put aside our models, we are advised that "oligopolistic interdependency" probably explains the dearth. The proffered explanation is, of course, based on an economic model.

The model in question tells us that "oligopolistic interdependency" is merely a form of collusion, presumably tacit in nature, in its most rarefied form. But those of us who might doubt that collusion is so easy, even when there are only a few firms in a given industry, would be led by the model to look for more explicit types of collusion. And in this case, I believe, we would be rewarded.

For an example, I refer to the March 15, 1976, issue of *Advertising Age*, which reports that the National Advertising Division of the Council of Better Business Bureaus received thirteen challenges to national advertising in February. I will quote an excerpt of one report of such a challenge, regarding the claims of the Ford Motor Company for Pinto based on an earlier Volkswagen ad:

> "How come that $3,330 VW Rabbit costs most people $4,100? . . . They've got you by the extras." The ad includes a list of six items that come as standard equipment on the Pinto, but are extra on the Rabbit. Since there was no comparable list of standard equipment on the Rabbit that costs extra on the Pinto, NAD felt it placed the consumer at a disadvantage in comparing the two cars. Ford disagreed, but said it would discontinue the ads.[13]

This is only one example of many, many cases in which the self-regulatory agencies of the advertising industry, for the most part with the encouragement and support of the Bureau of Consumer Protection of the Federal Trade Commission, have acted to prevent comparative advertising claims from being made. It is a good one to make my point, however, because I understand that another automobile company took

[13] *Advertising Age*, March 15, 1976, p. 4.

the approach of asking the FTC to move against the VW ad, rather than trying to deal with the "problem" itself, as Ford did, by waging a comparative ad campaign.

Government policing of advertisements like the one for the VW Rabbit is intended to guarantee the availability of product information. But it cannot be said that such a system reinforces and supplements market forces. Government policing of the usual type operates more as a substitute for market forces, or as a device that changes and distorts those forces, producing nonoptimal levels of information.

Instead of requiring affirmative disclosure of certain specific information, which may interest commission staff members but be of limited use to consumers, the commission might better approach the goal of optimal amounts and types of consumer product information by striking at the institutional and legal arrangements that inhibit comparative advertising. To its credit the commission has moved in this direction by authorizing the Bureau of Competition to investigate the kind of "self-regulatory" (collusive) restrictions discussed above, which are imposed by the Council of Better Business Bureaus, through its National Advertising Division and the National Advertising Review Board (NARB).[14]

A study of various tort rules that may inhibit comparative advertising might also be appropriate. The commission could recommend restricting the scope of such laws to increase the incentives to engage in comparative advertising.

Programs like the commission's efforts to strike down state laws prohibiting or restricting the right to advertise the prices of prescription drugs or eyeglasses [15] truly do reinforce and supplement market forces. Unfortunately programs of this type remain a very small part of the commission's total advertising regulation program.

The commission has not reformed itself much, although it has been trying. Notwithstanding Professor Pitofsky's sanguine views to the contrary, things are not well at the Federal Trade Commission. If we are going to have sensible advertising regulation, the commission will have to get moving in the right direction—and that almost always means toward more, not less, market freedom.

---

[14] See memorandum of N. E. Beckwith to Mark Grady, acting director, Office of Policy Planning and Evaluation, set forth at the end of the specific program analysis in the Mid-Year Budget Review, FTC Office of Policy Planning and Evaluation, January 1976.

[15] "Report of the Presiding Officer on Proposed Trade Regulation Rule regarding Advertising of Ophthalmic Goods and Services," 16 CFR, part 456, December 1976.

Roland N. McKean

Like some of the other discussants, I tend to agree with the general conclusions of Professor Winter's paper. I do not quite agree that advertising rarely fools us. I know my family and I get hooked every so often, mainly because we do not follow some simple rules of thumb, such as to ignore flamboyant direct mail advertising from places like the Intercontinental Cheese Lovers' Club. But basically, I have to admit it is our fault. We know there is a middling probability of being hooked but go ahead and order anyway without acquiring more information. Consumers in general, in my opinion, can behave as though they are pretty gullible about advertising, education, politics, marriage, and so on. (I do not quite mean it, but I sometimes say that the consumer has made a fool of himself, so now it is the government's turn.) A major and often neglected reason for consumer mistakes, however—and I will say more about this later—is that it costs too much to ponder most alternatives in detail and to guard too closely against being taken.

What really gives me pause about regulation of advertising, though, is the fact that most of the interventions I can think of would probably make matters worse. I am not fond of advertising. I am even tired of a lot of the innovations that go along with advertising—including both new products, such as low-calorie dog food, and style changes, like the cyclical shifts in the width and lengths of neckties. Nonetheless, when the dust settles down, I feel that advertising is a good deal like life itself: pretty objectionable but better than the alternative.

Turning to Professor Pitofsky's paper, I do not quarrel with his individual arguments, but I do disagree with some of his emphasis and to some extent with what I believe are his general conclusions. For example, he gives some attention to the virtues of markets for information, yet I think he underestimates the ability of markets to gauge the usefulness of information, and I think he especially overestimates the incentives of government personnel to do this effectively. He says that "until the government intervened and required or induced disclosure, accurate information was not available in the market as to durability of light bulbs, octane ratings for gasoline, tar and nicotine content of cigarettes, mileage per gallon for automobiles, or care labeling of wearing apparel." Let me assume that this is correct. The absence of such information may still have been appropriate. I would still bet that, on these repeat-purchase items, the market would have elicited the

Thanks are due to the Center for the Study of American Business at Washington University, where the author was Visiting Scholar during the first half of 1976.

information that consumers were willing to pay for at about the time they became willing to pay for it. Until the energy crisis, I do not believe many people strongly desired to know more than they did about octane ratings, the durability of light bulbs, or mileage per gallon. Until the newer synthetic fabrics became numerous and *widely* used, there was probably little demand for labels indicating how to clean them. If people are paying attention to these pieces of information now, I would bet that altered demand conditions rather than required labels are bringing this about. Even now, however, I doubt that the newly required information about several of those items is very valuable to consumers. (I notice that big cars are selling well again.)

It may sound callous or cynical to say that people do not care much about mileage per gallon or cancer per cigarette, but introspection suggests that such indifference is often the case and is often surprisingly sensible. In choosing a product, the consumer does not benefit enormously from extra knowledge about *one* out of a dozen relevant features —unless that feature is of overriding importance to him. Thus, the *marginal* value of extra knowledge about tar content of cigarettes may not be great when one is also concerned about taste, price, convenience, prestige, stimulant effect, and so on,[1] particularly before the evidence piled up that tobacco was related to cancer.

With respect to health hazards in general, even after the hazards do become convincing, people will not attach much importance to more precise information if the risks are *comparatively* unimportant to them. Most people demonstrate time and again that they are willing to risk serious consequences in pursuit of activities they find pleasurable. Most of us eat too much, drink too much, and exercise too little, knowing full well it may injure our health. The risk of life becoming an empty exercise in marking time—of life's costs exceeding its benefits—probably looms large in most minds compared to the risk of termination. We are much like the farmer who said, "Why should I read these pamphlets? I already know how to farm twice as good as I do." If a person "cannot" or will not lose ten excess pounds, is it worth much to him to compare cholesterol and nicotine numbers?

Most important of all, decision-making costs cause the sensible consumer to grope for some halfway useful index of quality—or of features he desires—rather than attempt to weigh numerous combinations of technical characteristics against each other. He is likely to adopt economical if crude rules of thumb—for example, to use brand

[1] In his paper, particularly in one footnote, Professor Pitofsky implicitly recognizes this point, but I feel that it deserves much more attention. In fact, throughout my comments, I mention arguments that he may agree with; we may differ only in our judgments about the significance of these considerations.

names, or "regular" gasoline, or dealer reputation, in making purchase decisions. In a recent government survey, only 13 percent of the purchasers of nonprescription drugs studied the labels. This may seem sad, yet it may be intelligent to look at a blurred picture of the forest rather than to try to study the individual trees. In selecting automobile tires, for example, I think I would be better off to pick a dealer who had a good reputation, ask him a few questions, and look at the warranty, than I would be by trying to decode information molded into the tires or compare technical characteristics, and risk neglecting other features not reflected in the quantitative proxies. Economizing on decision-making costs may be particularly appropriate in an affluent society, though I doubt that even the poor (who may be relatively unproductive at evaluating technical characteristics) should make numerous little systems analyses, say about the characteristics of light bulbs. In retrospect, it seems to me that I would spend so much time trying to improve my decisions that I would never get the opportunity to enjoy the results of my increasingly wise choices. Quite seriously, though, it is important to keep such decision-making costs in mind when evaluating information markets, the marginal worth of information, and the real impacts of government-required information.

I am not by any means opposed to all regulation of advertising and information flows, but it should be based on realistic appraisals of the alternatives. The case for intervention is stronger, I believe, the greater the cost of information to the consumer, the greater the damage in case he makes a mistake, and the smaller the gains to enterprises from selling useful information. Several of the examples mentioned by Professor Pitofsky are items that are purchased infrequently, and the gains to firms from selling useful information may be comparatively low. Funeral services, for instance, are not regularly recurring purchases for the individual, and one might anticipate information trouble. The gains from selling helpful information will also be low where existing regulations impair the functioning of the market. The eyeglass industry is a well-documented example and one that is mentioned by Professor Pitofsky.[2] The regulation needed here may be deregulation or antimonopoly action. Another situation in which the rewards from selling information may be low is the blood industry, in which the wholesalers (hospitals) are usually nonprofit organizations. Such organizations have difficulty in profiting from probes to discover what information it would be rewarding to buy or to sell. Labels identifying the sources of blood may well

[2] Lee Benham and Alexandra Benham, "Regulating through the Professions: A Perspective on Information Control," *Journal of Law and Economics,* vol. 18 (October 1975), pp. 421-447.

provide an improvement over the existing situation. Warning labels on psychoanalysts and group-therapy leaders might be worth considering. In this case, all three factors mentioned above are pertinent: the costs to consumers of getting information about the product are unusually high, the damage done if one makes a poor choice may be large, and licensing requirements inhibit the selling of useful information.

In addition to favoring changes in government policies in such situations, I will mention (just to show that I am not inflexible) that I would approve several restrictions on advertising. Too often, as in the case of eyeglasses, restriction of advertising harms consumers by inhibiting competition or entry or innovation (even if it benefits them in other ways). In my judgment, however, a complete ban on singing commercials (or even on all commercials in the middle of programs) would benefit the average consumer without significant side effects. I am confident that managerial ingenuity could convey any pertinent information without bursting into song; enforcement costs should be relatively low; and the dynamic qualities of our economy could be preserved—at least to the degree that existed during the innovative periods in our history before singing commercials.

More seriously, I may favor one restriction—pushing antifraud actions and raising penalities for fraudulent advertising—more than Professor Pitofsky (or Professor Nelson) would. In his paper, Professor Pitofsky properly notes that, in deciding how far to go, one should weigh enforcement and other costs against the benefits; but one sometimes neglected benefit of each prosecution is the spillover contribution to a fraud-deterrent atmosphere—by increasing the perceived likelihood of fraud being severely penalized and by reducing the cost to firms of supporting informal ethical codes. Extra deterrence would prevent inefficient exchanges and, by reducing transaction costs, stimulate additional trades that are efficient. Thus, the benefits of antifraud actions exceed the *direct* damage prevention implied by stopping a particular fraudulent endeavor.

In a perfectly working market, of course, firms and households could not sell misleading information any more than they could sell glass crowbars. In reality, though, various kinds of transaction costs make it possible for some ventures to profit from deception; and I agree with Professor Pitofsky that frequently it is not profitable for competitors to devote advertising budgets to counteradvertising. Up to a point, "permanent" firms wish to have false claims policed (to increase the credibility of *their* advertising), but individual firms are unlikely to do it themselves because of the free-rider problem. (My colleague, John H. Moore, tells me that before the establishment of the Federal Trade Commission, major firms were begging for some kind of arrangement to police false advertising. If they could get government to do it, that would cost the firms less, and probably lend more credibility to advertising, than would forming an association to do it themselves; so they were all for the FTC.) Fortunately, courts usually can, at nonexorbitant cost, draw a workable line between deception and "puffing"; and government can be expected, when assigned part of the policing task, to carry out this kind of mission with some degree of success.

Government runs into greater trouble, it seems to me, when we ask it to decide what additional information should be required. As noted before, I would concede that here, too, some intervention is probably economical. (If I could see how to do it, I would especially like to see the government regulate the government's output of information. I would like to see warning labels on a number of government outputs and more candid information about nuclear waste storage, the nicotine content of our farm programs, and the fat content of innumerable budgets.) By and large, however, government regulations cannot be expected to help consumers dramatically, for legislators and bureaucrats are rewarded mainly for whatever actions and wealth-transfers can attract free-rider voters.

It is hard to figure out just what the political process puts pressure on regulators to do, but it seems pretty clear that regulators are seldom rewarded by consumers for catering to overall consumer interests. It is not surprising, therefore, that the regulatory agencies often consider or require warnings that can hardly be worth the cost. Consider, as illustrations, the warning not to drink the acid from automobile batteries or the once-proposed warning labels—debated last year—on poinsettia plants and mistletoe sprigs. It is not surprising that agencies sometimes want each of us to pay for everyone else's information. For example, sources of all fats may have to be listed for all foods, even though not everyone keeps a Kosher kitchen, few of us are even willing to sacrifice ice cream or fried eggs, and specialty foods are well publicized for those who *do* wish to be Kosher or to count cholesterol. It is not surprising, moreover, that regulations sometimes help inhibit the production of information, for example, the prices of doctors' services or the reporting of occupational disease by employers. Such shortcomings, stemming mainly from the incentive difficulties, make me less sanguine than Professor Pitofsky about recent regulatory efforts, such as ad substantiation and required disclosure.

I would like to reemphasize a point that has been made by others—that government-induced advertising is often of dubious value. I happen to be in the market for a new car, and I have been reading these claims about the new brake systems that will not "fade"—information that would presumably not be presented if the new brakes were not required.

I was appalled to realize that I have been zipping around town all these years with fading brakes. When I read *Consumer's Research Magazine* though, I found out that the nonfading brakes mainly enable you to change from *very* high speeds to sudden stops several times in, say, ten minutes. If you are that kind of driver, you need to know the firms' claims about having improved brakes. But, if you are an ordinary driver, this is rather useless information that manufacturers are being "induced" to present.

Another possible drawback of the government's expanding role in regulating information flows is that we may be tackling too much. Having the government appear to protect us seems likely to deter individual consumers from seeking, evaluating, and utilizing information themselves, though inevitably this has to be a vital input in consumer protection. Pervasive regulation may also drain off too much of our citizen monitoring capacity and legislative policy-making capacity. Again, while I do not know how to design an improved system, I am uneasy lest we fiddle while Rome burns.

Assuming that government regulation of labels and advertising does bring some of the above difficulties, I would like to emphasize that dubious actions need not come about because congressmen or regulatory personnel lack intelligence or diligence or compassion for the consumer. Many apparent anomalies occur because, once the decision to regulate is made, enforcement costs and decision-making costs "force" regulators to use meat-axe categories, intricate definitions, and crude proxies. As mentioned previously, however, the main trouble is that the political process does not gear regulators' actions to the overall interests of consumers. In terms of the figure of speech I am using this year, regulators inevitably march to a different drummer.

PART TWO

ADVERTISING AND THE FIRM

TOWARDS A THEORY OF THE ECONOMICS OF ADVERTISING

Lester G. Telser

Introduction

Advertising remains a challenging problem for economic theory for several reasons. First, the ordinary assumption that tastes are given does not serve us well for advertised products. We are forced to pay attention to the effects of what people know about products that they buy. The simplifying assumption of elementary economic theory focuses attention on price alone for commodities of known virtues or vices. To understand advertising we must reckon with the fact that a person's stock of knowledge about goods and services influences his preferences. It is, therefore, useful to assume given tastes only if the stock of knowledge is given. Under these circumstances, when the stock of knowledge changes, the theory that takes this into account will furnish better predictions of behavior.

Second, although advertising is a joint product that goes together with some physical good or service, it is not literally tied to the good or service. To illustrate, buttons and coats are normally tied together to make a joint product. Since different coats are made with different numbers of buttons, one can calculate a derived demand for buttons and a derived demand for coats separately. In these respects alone there is no substantial difference between advertising and coat buttons. The distinction lies in this. When someone buys a coat he pays for both the coat and the buttons. With advertising this is not generally true. There are people who may receive the benefits of advertising messages without facing the burden of paying for the advertising. There are also people who pay for the advertising when they buy the advertised good or service who do not necessarily benefit from the advertising because whatever information it contains is redundant to these buyers. This, however, begs the question of why they do not buy some equivalent good or service that is not advertised at all or is less advertised and in

I wish to thank Yale Brozen, Milton Friedman, Harry Johnson, Sam Peltzman, and George Stigler for their helpful comments on an earlier draft of this paper. I assume responsibility for all errors herein.

either case is sold at a lower price. Therefore, the indirect form of paying for advertising raises the question of whether there is some departure from that form of marginal cost pricing that we associate with a competitive market.

Third, advertising is the major source of revenue for the broadcasting industry, including both radio and television. The advertising receipts pay for the entertainment that broadcasting companies furnish the public. This entertainment is a free good to the radio or television audience, but not to those who provide it. Moreover, it would be an error to say that it costs the broadcasting company nothing if one more person turns on his radio or television set. This is an error in the same sense that it is an error to say that it costs a railroad nothing to operate a commuter train with some empty seats, or that it costs a restaurant nothing to have some empty tables. In all of these cases there is a random variation of demand, and it is generally less costly for those who satisfy this demand to hold some reserve of unused capacity rather than to attempt to meet the demand exactly. Similarly, the cost to the broadcasting industry depends on the expected audience size rather than the actual audience size. To attract a larger audience on average, the broadcasting company will usually incur a larger total cost. The addition or subtraction of a single member of the audience does not affect this cost. Having noted this does not solve the problem. Business firms normally try to get customers to pay directly for what they buy. In the example of the commuter train, commuters pay some amount for their tickets. Why is it, then, that in the case of the broadcasting industry, the entertainment is paid for by the firms advertising their products rather than the members of the audience, who benefit directly from the entertainment? Does this constitute an example of market failure?

A similar, though less extreme problem is present for the newspaper and magazine industry. In these industries the companies usually derive a substantial portion of their revenue from their advertising receipts. Newspapers and magazines that carry no advertising seldom seem capable of surviving. Unlike the broadcasting companies, newspaper and magazine publishers do not furnish their products to the readers at a zero price. Yet it is true that the readers generally do not pay for all of the benefits they derive from the magazines and newspapers.

Some forms of entertainment attract a substantial audience, yet are not used to convey advertising messages jointly with the entertainment they furnish. Motion picture theaters are one example. Rarely do motion picture theater screens in the United States show any advertising except for refreshments and notices of coming attractions, though in some Western European countries advertising is common in the motion picture theater. Books are another example. Except for advertising of other books on the dust jackets, there is seldom any advertising in a book. Why do books and magazines differ with respect to their usage of advertising?

We see forms of entertainment wholly, partially, and not at all supported by revenue from advertisers. An acceptable theory of the economics of advertising should be capable of explaining these differences.

Fourth, it must be recognized that advertising constitutes only one of several methods of promotion. The choice of which of the competing methods to use depends on the cost and effectiveness of these competing modes. A widely used and frequently bought product is usually more suitable for promotion by means of advertising than one infrequently bought by a few. This is apart from other considerations that may dictate the choice among alternatives. A contact by a salesman has a higher marginal cost and probable return than one by a television advertising message. A profit maximizing firm takes this into account in deciding whether to use salesmen or television advertising to promote its products. It is, therefore, easier to understand the differences in the advertising intensities among products in terms of a general theory of promotion or communication than by means of a special theory designed to explain advertising alone.

Fifth, there is a challenge to economic theory to see whether a conventional supply and demand analysis can furnish useful insights about the prevalence of advertising. At first sight the usual analysis of this type does not seem to apply to advertising. In the typical application of supply and demand, we assume a market with buyers on one side and sellers on the other. There is a known commodity and the only relevant fact for the participants in the market is the product price. Either a buyer or a seller can decide what to do on the basis of the price because by hypothesis the qualities and attributes of the product are known. The equilibrium in the market is described by the intersection of the supply and demand schedules. This equilibrium has several interesting properties. In particular the equilibrium results in exchanges from the sellers to the buyers such that the final owners of the goods are those who value them the most. The exchange results in a reallocation of the goods among the participants giving the maximal net gain for the group as a whole. The market clearing price represents the marginal benefit to the buyers and the marginal cost to the sellers. Hence the equilibrium quantity of goods exchanged equates the marginal cost to the marginal benefit. The pursuit of individual gain by the participants in the market results in an equilibrium that cannot be improved upon by recontracting among any subgroup of participants in the market. An important question is, therefore, whether similar results can apply to advertising.[1]

Advertising as a commodity seems to differ from the kinds of goods and services to which the ordinary supply and demand framework is applied. Advertising messages appear to go to people whether or not they want them. There is no separate market for advertising messages, such that the equilibrium quantity of advertising messages equates the marginal benefit of the advertising messages to the marginal cost. Before the recipient of an advertising message receives the message, he does not even know what information, if any, the message will contain. There is a paradox here. If the recipient did know in advance the contents of the advertising message, then it would be worth nothing. It is essential that the message be unknown in advance to the recipient so that the recipient will value the message. How much value depends on a complex set of circumstances. However, this is not a problem peculiar to advertising messages or information generally. It must be granted that it is often the case that a buyer obtains a commodity of unknown value in advance and, nevertheless, the buyer can decide how much he is willing to pay for it.

The situation for the sender of advertising messages also differs from the simple situation that a seller confronts according to supply and demand analysis for a known commodity. The sender of the advertising message, who can be regarded as the seller, does not know in advance what he will receive in exchange for giving the message to the recipient. The advertising message is costly to the sender and he does not wish to waste his resources. He does not wish to convey messages to people who will find them of no value. Therefore, the advertiser has an incentive to convey messages where they will benefit him the most by their effect on the recipients. Other things equal, the advertiser would like to send his messages to precisely those people who act as if they most value the messages. The analysis does resemble that which applies to the exchange of goods of known quality. It is in the interest of the seller to contact those who most value the good. One of the major questions is whether the existing mechanisms and institutions do work in the case of advertising as if there were a market for advertising messages with an equilibrium quantity and price of advertising messages having the same properties as those in the familiar analysis of a market equilibrium going back to Alfred Marshall. In certain favorable circumstances advertisers can contact potential cus-

[1] For a detailed analysis of market exchange along these lines, see Lester Telser, *Competition, Collusion, and Game Theory* (Chicago: Aldine-Atherton, 1972), chapters 1 and 2.

tomers willing to buy advertising messages and pay explicitly for these messages, for example, catalogues and price lists. When such messages command a positive price in the market, they need not be tied to the compensatory provision of entertainment.

The problem of buying or selling something that turns out to be a disappointment is not peculiar to advertising. It is pervasive. It is most prominent when the commodity is a form of information such as advertising. Even when we buy a bar of soap or a can of soup we do not know in advance whether or not the product will deliver the satisfaction that we expect. A seller faces a similar problem. At the time he makes the investment and other preparations for the manufacture and sale of a product, he does not know whether things will turn out the way he thought they would. Therefore, there are many cases where the exchange of commodities depends on the expectations of the participants in the market, who may be disappointed.

Summing up, a useful theory of the economics of advertising should consider the following phenomena:[2]

- Advertising as a form of communication competes with other forms of communication.
- Advertising is a product supplied jointly with some physical good or service, but is not physically tied to the good or service. Not all of the receivers of advertising messages pay for the advertising. Only those who actually buy the advertised good or service pay for the advertising.
- Advertising is a major source of revenue for certain entertainment industries, especially radio and television broadcasters.
- The market for advertising messages is implicit. It is not directly

[2] This paper elaborates the theory I presented in "Supply and Demand for Advertising Messages," *American Economic Review*, vol. 56 (May 1966), pp. 457-466. The earlier paper gave an analysis of the supply and demand for advertising messages that took explicit account of the cost of collecting revenue from the sale of advertising messages directly from the advertiser to the receivers of advertising messages. As Barnett pointed out in his discussion, the theory should also take into account the benefit of the entertainment that is furnished the receiver of the advertising message if it comes via television or radio. See Harold J. Barnett, "Discussion of the Economics of Broadcasting and Advertising," *American Economic Review*, vol. 56 (May 1966), pp. 467-470. I would also like to correct a misconception in Steiner's discussion of my earlier paper. There is a demand for advertising messages by potential customers of the product. There is also a demand for advertising messages from the advertising media by the sellers of products, who, in turn supply advertising to their potential customers. See "Discussion of the Economics of Broadcasting and Advertising," *American Economic Review*, vol. 56 (May 1966), pp. 472-474. Obviously, the supply and the demand for advertising *do* differ.

visible to the casual observer in the same sense that a tourist in Chicago could see the Chicago Board of Trade.

- Neither the sender nor the receiver of advertising messages knows the value and possibly the cost of the message in advance.

Communication as a Transaction

Advertising and the other methods of sales promotion constitute a form of communication. It is, therefore, useful at the outset to consider the pertinent aspects of communication.

A communication between two parties resembles an economic transaction. The sender of the message expects a benefit from his action that is to some degree greater than the cost. Similarly, the receiver of a message expects a benefit from the message that is greater than the cost of receiving it. Thre must be a mutual benefit or the communication will not occur. Both parties, though, may be disappointed by the actual outcome of the communication. It is essential to recognize that the expectation of a benefit is necessary, otherwise the communication will not be sent or it will not be received. This immediately raises the question of manipulation. The sender of a message wants it to affect the recipient in a way that will benefit himself. In this sense there must be "manipulation." This is not the same as coercion. The receiver of the message is under no compulsion to do what the sender wants. Even if the receiver of the message does not do what the sender wants him to do, that is, if he does not buy the sender's product, he still incurs a cost by spending his time on the advertising message. He would not be willing to bear this cost without compensation. Therefore, the cost of receiving useless advertising is made more palatable by accompanying it with compensation in the form of entertainment. It would be more difficult for the senders of advertising messages to obtain an audience if they did not provide some such compensation. We are led to ask whether it would be possible to accomplish these ends at a lower total cost.

The sender of a message ordinarily wants to obtain a response. When two people talk with each other face to face, the lag between sending a message and receiving the response is very short. Before this face-to-face conversation can occur, the two parties must find each other and arrange for a meeting. The pertinent issues are fairly obvious. Two friends can arrange a meeting since they know each other. For two strangers this is more difficult. To communicate, at least one of the parties must find the other. This process has a cost, the amount of which depends on the circumstances. The delay between sending a message and receiving a response is associated with a cost. The cost of the delay is lower if the parties are in personal contact, but the total cost, including the cost of making a contact, may be higher. The lower the cost of delay between the sending of a message and receiving a reply, the larger may be the cost of locating the recipient and arranging for the necessary closed loop communication. Finally, the actual transmission of the message, once contact is made, has a cost. Broadcasting a large number of messages to an audience of unknown people may have a lower unit cost per message and a higher cost of obtaining a response from the intended recipients than alternative modes of communication. Therefore, in choosing a medium for communication, the parties will take into account the total cost and presumably select that mode for which the total cost is the least.

Other dimensions of the communication are also of importance. In face-to-face communication the two parties are in personal contact. A sequence of messages goes back and forth between the two parties. Each message is an appropriate response to its predecessor. The messages are tailor-made for the occasion. The sequence of messages terminates when one of the parties believes that the marginal benefit of another message is less than the marginal cost. Put differently, the two-way communication between the two parties is a voluntary exchange like a transaction between a buyer and a seller. After some mutually satisfactory agreement is reached, the transaction is consummated and the process ends. The same thing happens with two-way communication between the two parties.

We may imagine that each party initially has his own particular stock of knowledge. As a result of the sequence of messages between the two parties, each will have a different stock of knowledge. That is, each will know things that he did not know before. Moreover, one may say that the communication will end when at least one of the parties has acquired an actual stock of knowledge equal to his desired stock of knowledge. The demand by each party for information in the communication transaction depends on the gap between that party's desired and actual stock of knowledge. Voluntary communication between the two parties begins because, for each, the actual stock of information is less than the desired stock. They expect the messages and responses to increase the actual stock of knowledge up to the point where it equals the desired stock. When this happens for at least one of the parties, the contact will break off.

This abstract way of thinking about communication is useful for understanding promotion. A potential buyer's demand for information or knowledge about a product depends on the difference between what he knows and what he wants to know. He may already know more than he wants to know. If so, he does not want additional information. In face-to-face communication it is fairly easy for the parties to exchange the desired messages because they can ask each other questions, elicit responses, fill in the gaps in their stock of knowledge. This is not so easy to do when there is a time lag in closing the communication loop. Most advertising does entail a long delay between the sending of the message and the receiving of the response. This has important consequences.

The sender of the advertising message often does not know precisely who will receive the message. He may know only some general characteristics of those who are likely to receive the message. Therefore, the particular messages transmitted by the advertiser will try to strike a common denominator. The advertiser will attempt to design a message that will add something to the actual stock of knowledge held by the unknown audience of potential recipients. The message will not necessarily serve that purpose optimally for any individual member of the audience. For some members of the audience the contents of the message may be utterly useless either because they already know about the product and do buy it or because they already know about the product and do not wish to buy it. The advertiser faces the problem of measuring the response to his messages only after some delay, by monitoring the sales of the product.

Advertising that is a joint product with television and radio entertainment—so that the audience receives compensation for the advertising messege in the form of entertainment—implicitly has a negative market-clearing price. This means that to the receivers of the advertising message, the messages are a bad for which they must be paid as an inducement to receive the messages.

However, there are also those to whom the advertising messages must be a good. These are the people who do buy the advertised products. The advertisers must receive some return from their advertising or they would not incur the cost of the advertising. Those who buy the advertised product pay for the advertising as a joint product with the physical good that they purchase. Therefore, there is a derived demand for the advertising messages by those who buy the advertised good. This by itself is not a sufficient reason for the claim that for these receivers of the advertising message, the messages are a good for which they are willing to pay.

In order to reach the latter conclusion, it must also be true that the same goods are available at a lower price without the advertising. If this is true then those who buy the advertised good do in fact reveal that they have an implicit demand for the advertising message, represented by their willingness to pay a positive price for it. For such buyers it must be true that it is cheaper for them to buy the advertised good and pay a higher price than to buy the less advertised good at a lower price. This follows becuse the relevant price is the total cost including the cost of finding and evaluating the less advertised good.

There is another implication of this argument. For those with a relatively large stock of knowledge about the product, the additional benefit of the advertising message is slight. The benefit is largest for those with the smallest stock of knowledge about the product initially. Therefore, the seller of the product has some incentive to offer it to the steady customers or to the repeat buyers at a lower price than to the newer buyers. This may explain why some more heavily advertised products give customers a lower price for the second purchase than for the first. The coupon enclosed in a package and the premiums given to those who collect a number of labels are examples.

Other considerations are also pertinent. Sellers of new products may give away free samples. This does not contradict the theory. In these cases the free samples are themselves a form of advertising message that conveys information to potential users of the product. The seller offers free samples in the expectation that some users will become regular customers of the product. In Nelson's terminology [3] this is a way of advertising experience goods.

The theory herein also predicts that a heavily advertised established product will not have a large proportion of its total sales going to steady customers unless these customers can buy the product at a lower price than the new customers. Put differently, a heavily advertised, unchanged, and established product that does not offer lower unit prices to repeat customers must be one that has a relatively small proportion of its total sales going to such customers. It must have a high turnover of its clientele.

There are also circumstances when the advertising of products may lower prices. This may occur if the advertising lowers the cost of search and increases the elasticity of the demand curves facing the sellers. Evidence on the advertising of the price of eyeglasses has this interpretation.[4]

Given the price per message, the demand for communications or messages is an increasing function of the difference between the desired

[3] Phillip Nelson, "Advertising as Information," *Journal of Political Economy*, vol. 82 (July/August 1974), pp. 729-754.

[4] For a detailed discussion see Lee Benham and Yale Brozen, "Advertising, Competition and the Price of Eyeglasses" (Washington, D.C.: American Enterprise Institute, 1975). For a mathematical analysis of the relation between advertising intensity and the product price see Lester Telser, "Advertising and Competition," *Journal of Political Economy*, vol. 72 (December 1964), pp. 537-562.

and the actual stock of knowledge held by the potential recipient of the messages. It follows that new, unfamiliar products tend to be more advertised than old products.

Widely used products are more likely to be advertised on radio or television programs that can attract a large audience. The relation is reciprocal. The existence of widely used and frequently bought products creates the kinds of radio and television programs that will attract the desired audience. It is misleading to look at the nature and quality of mass appeal radio and television programs without simultaneously considering the nature of the products, the advertising revenue from which supports these programs. This is to say that it is the existence of the widely used products that explains the widely viewed and listened to programs.

For some products general purpose messages are not suitable. The potential buyers will want communications that can answer their questions and furnish information particular to their situation. A minimal delay between the sending and the receiving of messages will better serve the purposes of both parties. If so, personal communication, despite its higher cost, will yield a higher net benefit. Therefore, it will be preferred by both parties.

Another important factor in the communications process is the cost of locating suitable recipients for the message. If this is low, then personal contact may promise the highest net return. For example, personal promotion is very important in the promotion of prescription drugs. This is so for two reasons. First, the physician often has specific questions that general purpose advertising cannot readily answer. Second, the cost of locating physicians and making personal contact with them is low compared with the cost of locating, and contacting the users of, say, cigarettes.

The cost of locating the appropriate recipients of advertising messages explains the existence of some specialized magazines and newspapers. These attract a particular audience that lowers the cost to those who wish to transmit advertising messages to them. Consequently, the advertising revenue helps pay for these publications. The readers receive a compensation for the advertising in the form of a lower price for the publications, which is made possible by the revenue the publishers receive from the advertising. To those readers of the publication who are not potential customers the advertising message is not a good ex ante. The advertising messages *are* a good ex ante to *some* readers of the publication—those why buy the advertised products. (It is not only to specialized publications that these arguments apply; they are equally valid for all publications that contain advertising.) The support that these publications obtain from their advertising revenue gives their readers a compensation for the advertising to the extent that the price of the publication is lower with the advertising than it would be without.

Advertisers are willing to support only those publications that can attract an interested audience, one with at least some members who will respond to the advertising message by buying the advertised product. In this way those who buy the product reveal a benefit that they derive from the advertising messages. The advertiser and the publisher both have a strong incentive to design the publication to attract an audience requiring as small a compensation as possible for the presence of advertising in the publication. Stated in a positive way, the publisher and the advertiser would like to attract the largest possible audience that will derive an actual benefit from the advertising in the publication. It is not in their interest to repel readers with the advertising. To the extent that the advertising is repellent, the price of the publication goes down, and the subsidy that is necessary to attract readership goes up.[5] Nor is this all. Some publications contain advertising of enough value to the readers that they may be willing to pay a positive price for the

[5] The only reliable data I have giving figures on the amount of the subsidy going from advertisers to newspapers and magazines are fairly old. To the extent that the advertisers pay to newspapers and magazines an amount that is in excess of the cost of the advertising to the newspapers and magazines, there is a subsidy of the editorial and other nonadvertising content in these publications. Consequently, there is subsidy to the buyers of newspapers and magazines. This is of the same form as the subsidy going to the viewers of television and the listeners of radio.

Borden reports that for a sample of twenty-three daily newspapers, 65 percent of the income came from advertising and 35 percent from circulation. However, only 35 percent of the total expense was incurred by the advertising in the newspapers while 65 percent of the total expense was the result of the nonadvertising content of the newspapers. Borden concludes that "After the expenses attributable to advertising had been allowed for, approximately one-half of the revenue was available to support the elaborate newspapers that were published, to be sold to readers at the low price of 2 or 3 cents for daily papers and 10 cents for Sunday papers" [Neil H. Borden, *The Economic Effects of Advertising* (Chicago: Richard D. Irwin, 1942), pp. 925-926]. Hence there is a subsidy in the case of newspapers.

For magazines Borden reports that "a substantial number" operate with little or no advertising revenue. There are also magazines offered at no charge to selected lists of potential readers. These do contain advertising and are most common in certain trade and business fields. Borden also believes that the readers of some mass circulation magazines do value the advertising in these magazines judging from the evidence given by surveys of readers. It would seem that elimination of the advertising would reduce the circulation of the magazines even if the price of the magazines did not change. Borden estimates that in 1935, 55 percent of the magazine content was reading matter and 45 percent was advertising. The latter contributed 55 percent of the revenue and 45 percent of the linage. Borden concludes that "from one-fourth to one-third of the advertising revenue [of magazines] of 1935 may have been considered a net contribution to publication" (p. 930).

advertising—that is, they would not pay as much for the publication if it lacked advertising.

This analysis throws light on some of the questions that were posed at the outset. Why is it that books are seldom used as an advertising medium? To be a suitable medium there would have to be a positive association between the demand for the product being advertised and the readers of the book. A book with very broad appeal and large sales would appear to be a suitable carrier of advertising messages for a widely used product. The most obvious choice of a product to advertise in a popular book is a similar book. Therefore, this theory would predict that we would find detective stories advertised in mystery novels, historical romances advertised in historical romances, and mathematics text books advertised in mathematics text books.

This theory also predicts that motion pictures (and refreshments) would be advertised on the screens of motion picture theaters. Theater programs contain advertising messages that appeal to the audience in the theater. This explains, if indeed it requires explanation, why certain kinds of restaurants advertise in theater programs.

The more repugnant the advertising messages are to the audience to whom they are directed, the larger the compensation that the audience as a whole will require in exchange for receiving the advertising message. To repeat, communication is a transaction that will not occur without benefits to both parties. If one of the parties transmits messages that the other party will not find useful per se, then the party transmitting the message will find it necessary to compensate the receiver of the message. Therefore, television programs supported by advertising revenue must entertain the audience. Indeed, it may well be that television programs that carry advertising messages must be more entertaining than those that do not carry advertising messages. Because the whole audience may not derive much benefit from the advertising messages, there is all the more reason for the television program to be entertaining. This implicitly measures the quality of the entertainment by the size of the audience it attracts. It is, accordingly, a popular measure of entertainment. It is not, however, the measure of entertainment that Aristotle advocates in his *Poetics*.

Public television by this argument is less popular because it has so much less advertising. If the television viewers valued the advertising messages more than they seem to at present, then commercial television programs might be designed to attract a smaller audience. Paradoxically, this smaller audience would contain a larger proportion of buyers of the product, and it would be of greater financial value to the advertiser. The advertiser does not necessarily seek the most popular program. He seeks the program that will attract that audience which will be most likely to find the advertising message beneficial. Beneficial means that the advertising message results in purchases of the product. Advertising cannot compel people to do things against their will. The purchase of an advertised product is a voluntary act in the same sense that the purchase of any product or any act of communication is a voluntary act between two parties.

When people say that the advertising messages do not confer a benefit on the receivers of the messages, there is a sense in which this assertion is correct according to the arguments given above. The pill must have a sugar coating or the patient will not take it. The entertainment in the radio or television program, the editorial content of the newspaper, the fiction in the magazine—these are the sugar coatings on the pills, the advertising messages. Yet, this is not the whole story. The advertiser would not supply the pill at all, sugar coated or bare, unless some people in the audience behaved as if the advertising message were useful. These are the people who buy the product as a result of the advertising. The sugar coating is only necessary as a cost of delivering the message to that portion of the audience who do not behave as if the message is beneficial.

It follows that if the members of the audience already know about the product in one way or another, then they are less likely to derive a benefit from the advertising message. Their current stock of knowledge about the product not only coincides with their desired stock, but also it coincides with the desired stock from the point of view of the advertiser. The advertiser has as little desire to waste his resources as anyone else. He does not wish to transmit messages to those who will find them redundant.

One may also raise the objcction that an advertising message containing a lie may better serve the interest of the advertiser than one that tells the truth. In this treatment of communication as a transaction between two parties, what determines the truth content of the messages exchanged? Those who receive advertising messages presumably know that the source of the messages is an interested party. The messages have a bias toward suppressing the unfavorable and emphasizing the favorable evidence. In this sense a lack of objectivity is inherent in advertising messages and is discounted, to a greater or lesser extent, by the recipient. If the short run gain from a distortion of the truth were large, then the temptation to lie would be strong indeed. However, the very strength of the inducement to lie calls forth its own antidote. Those circumstances that imply the largest immediate gain from lying are also those that would make the buyer most cautious in accepting the claims of the advertiser. In general, continued use of the product by the customer is the most effective guardian of the truth. An advertiser who makes outrageous claims would find it more costly to obtain repeat purchases. The pursuit of his self-interest tempers his desire to sacrifice the prospect of long term gains for the sake of larger short term gains. A low real interest rate encourages more truthful advertising.

The Market in Advertising Messages

Given that communication is a voluntary transaction between two parties, it follows that the quantity and price of advertising messages reflect an equilibrium of supply and demand in the market for advertising messages. The special circumstances about advertising lead to complications in the details but do not affect the main conclusions derived from an analysis of a market equilibrium for any commodity.

The supply of advertising messages comes from the sellers of products. The larger the quantity of advertising messages that they wish to convey, the larger is their total cost. Whether or not the marginal cost of advertising messages goes up as the quantity transmitted increases is an empirical question about which we have little solid evidence. It may be, however, that the average cost per advertising message is a decreasing function of the quantity so that the marginal cost is below the average cost. If so, the supply curve of advertising messages would be negatively sloped. Even if this were true, it does not necessarily imply that the producers of products that are advantageously advertised have a natural source of monopoly, since there may be offsetting factors that raise product costs for other reasons. For example, the costs of production may rise rapidly enough to offset possible economies of scale in the transmission of advertising messages. Hence product supply curves may be upward sloping even if the supply of advertising messages is downward sloping. A downward sloping supply of advertising messages does not imply that no stable equilibrium can exist in the market for advertising messages. A stable equilibrium can exist if the marginal benefit of advertising messages falls more rapidly than the marginal cost as the number of advertising messages increases. This does not seem implausible.

Although there may be no explicit market for advertising messages, an implicit market exists. There are several reasons for this assertion. First, those who benefit from the advertising pay for it when they buy the advertised product. The implicit price of the advertising is revealed in the market by the difference between the prices of advertised and unadvertised products with the same physical characteristics. Those who derive no benefit from the advertising messages per se receive a compensation in the form of the entertainment that is frequently provided as a joint product with the advertising message. Even if all the products in a given class are advertised to about the same extent, it does not follow that consumers lack a choice. As long as sellers can furnish consumers with joint products containing the components in different proportions, the observation that all products in a given class are advertised to the same extent may mean only that consumers of the product have very similar tastes. It does not follow that consumers with dissimilar tastes cannot make their demands felt in the marketplace. The incentive of sellers to obtain profits will incline them to gratify a demand if they believe it will be profitable to do so.

The circuitous way of paying for advertising is not an uncommon phenomenon in other sectors of the economy. It is generally but not always true that those who benefit from a good are also the ones who pay for it. Similarly, those who incur the cost of furnishing the good rarely do so out of benevolence. They too will require compensation if they are to continue supplying the good. There is often a practical problem of locating the beneficiaries and measuring how much they are willing to pay for various amounts of the good. This is learned from experience and often from trial and error. Those who deal most closely with the buyers may be in the best position to estimate the level and intensity of demand for a product. They often must do so in advance of sales. They transmit orders to their suppliers based on their estimates of the demand. The actual outcome generally differs from the expected outcome. Some prospective customers may decide that they do not wish to buy the product at the price that the seller thought they would be willing to pay, and others, who were not expected to, buy the product. Therefore, the seller and the actual buyers share the cost and the returns from the operation as a whole. The resemblance between this process and the implicit market for advertising messages is apparent.

Some who do not receive the message may still buy the product. Not all those who receive the messages derive any benefit from them. In either instance, the sender of the advertising message incurs "unnecessary" costs. These costs can be seen to be unnecessary after the fact but they are not unnecessary before the fact. Taking into account the costs of attracting an appropriate audience for the advertising messages, the sender of the advertising message chooses that mix of communications channels that will accomplish his purpose at the least total cost. He must make his choices on the basis of his available evidence, knowing that there will necessarily be departures from his plans and hopes. This general phenomenon does not distinguish advertising from other commercial activities.

The products that are advertised on radio and television are evident. In many cases the manufacturer of the product is the source of the advertising message; however, there are important examples where the major source of the advertising is the retailer instead of the manufacturer. For these products the retailer acts as an agent on behalf of the buyer. The buyer has more frequent contact with the retailer than he has with the individual products that he seldom buys. Consequently, it is the reputation of the retailer in which the buyer has confidence. The cost of this reputation may not appear in the official statistics reporting advertising outlays. It is nevertheless an important source of knowledge for the consumer. A consumer in Chicago, for instance, can usually have confidence in a product that Marshall Field sells without knowing much, if anything, about the product itself. The consumer can acquire a stock of knowledge about the reliability of various retailers. It is this knowledge rather than knowledge supplied by manufacturers that will guide his choice in many cases. Competition among retailers of equal reliability can serve the purpose of keeping the prices of the goods they sell close to marginal cost, which includes the cost of deserving the reputation that the consumer places in the seller.

The stock of knowledge that each person has about those with whom he deals is a form of specific capital. The individual acquires this stock of knowledge at some cost. The size of the acquired stock depends on the cost of acquiring it and on the expected returns from that stock. The equilibrium stock is such that its marginal cost equals its marginal return. Although the stock is not consumed with use, it does change with the passage of time because some of it becomes obsolete. The appearance of new products and the disappearance of old products, the entry of new sellers and the disappearance of old sellers, changes in existing products, and changes in the terms of sales all cause some of the existing stock of knowledge to disappear. In order to maintain his stock of knowledge at the desired level, the individual invests his resources in acquiring new knowledge. The cost of this investment is not necessarily a cash outlay. An individual acquires knowledge at the expense of alternative activities. In this sense there is a cost of maintaining the stock of knowledge at the desired level. For individuals whose time is costly, receiving advertising messages may be the cheapest source of information.

The return that an individual obtains from the stock of knowledge he has acquired depends on the choice he makes based on this knowledge. The stock consists of specific information about sellers and products. Therefore, it inclines the individual to repeat acts that led to satisfactory results and to desist from acts with unsatisfactory results. The existence of this stock of specific knowledge leads, therefore, to repeat purchases of satisfactory products. Since there is a cost of acquiring new information that would lead to change, there is a tendency toward inertia. Advertising can lower the cost of acquiring knowledge about products. Therefore, it can reduce inertia.

This argument should throw some light on the role of advertising. Advertising does not directly lead to repeat purchases. Because it exposes the individual to alternatives, advertising is a primary tool for the introduction of new products. The amount of the advertising expenditure does not depend only on the initial purchase it may attract. If the advertiser believes that the buyer will like his product, then he can expect to make a sequence of sales to the buyer over time. Therefore, the cost of the advertising can be spread over a longer period, and it is worth undertaking more advertising for a product that is good enough to generate repeat sales. The investment in advertising can be amortized like a capital outlay if the advertising message accomplishes its purpose and the product is satisfactory. In any case, it is consideration of the long run that determines the level of the advertising outlay.

It is also an implication of this argument that continued advertising of the same product is necessary only insofar as the buyers' desired stock of knowledge about the product exceeds their actual stock of knowledge. This results when people forget about the product and when new buyers enter the market. From the point of view of the advertiser, the actual stock of knowledge about the product equals the sum of the stock of knowledge in the possession of the individual buyers. When a buyer forgets about the product, this means that some knowledge about the product disappears. When a new potential buyer enters the market, he may have less knowledge about the product than the seller would like. The continued advertising of the established product corresponds to outlays on the repair and maintenance of physical plant and equipment that are designed to keep these assets at the desired level. Therefore, advertising outlays will be higher for those products with larger streams of new potential customers and higher rates of forgetting about the product.

Some may describe this differently. A potential new customer usually knows less about available products than do the old customers. Such a new buyer may believe that the most popular products, those with the largest market shares, must be satisfactory to the largest number of experienced buyers. If the new buyer thinks he is like these experienced buyers, then he is led to make the same choices as they would, at least initially. The new buyer does not know which products have the largest market shares. Lacking this direct information, he may judge the popularity of the products by the volume of their advertising. The most advertised product, by this argument, must be the one with the largest sales. Hence the volume of advertising serves as a signal of the acceptability of the product. Even if new buyers reason this way, they need not be mistaken if they can judge for themselves whether or not the commodities they buy are satisfactory. Unless they can make this judgment, it is difficult to understand why they would wish to use the choices of others as a guide for their own purchases. In any case, this mechanism does imply the following two conclusions. First, there will be a tendency for advertising outlays as a percentage of sales to remain constant over time, provided the set of available products remains the same and the number of incoming customers remains constant. If these conditions obtain then it also follows that the market shares of the products will tend to stay constant over time.

Conclusions

With appropriate modifications, the apparatus of supply and demand can furnish useful predictions about the market for advertising messages. Since the advertising messages are not a good for all who receive them, the implicit market clearing price for the advertising messages is negative. This means that those who receive advertising messages must be given remuneration for doing so. This remuneration is not a cash payment. It is a compensation in kind in the form of entertainment furnished to the recipients of the messages. People would not watch television unless there were amusing intervals between the commercials. The entertainment is paid for by the advertisers. They would not do so unless at least some recipients of the advertising messages treat them as a good. That these recipients act as if the advertising is a good is shown by their purchases of the advertised product. There is the further implication that the knowledgeable buyers of the advertised product may have the opportunity of paying a lower price for repeat purchases of the advertised product. In this way they can avoid some of the cost of the advertising. Hence those who buy the product as a direct result of the advertising are the most likely to pay for the advertising.

What people buy depends on what they know. Preferences are not given; they depend on the stock of knowledge. Since it is costly to acquire knowledge, buyers obtain a return from the knowledge they acquire by applying it in their purchase decisions. Therefore, there is a tendency for them to repeat actions that their experience has shown to be favorable and to desist from actions that proved unfavorable. This leads to inertia on the part of consumers. This inertia raises the return to the maker of an acceptable product who, by advertising, can bring it to the attention of a consumer. Although advertising can increase the propensity to buy a product for the first time, it cannot induce repeat purchases unless the consumer finds the product to be acceptable. This implies that heavily advertised products will be subject to more careful quality control by the manufacturers. Knowledge is a form of capital. One cannot understand advertising without recognizing how it works as a capital asset.

These views of advertising also throw light on the future of pay television and video discs. Neither will much affect the television broadcasting industry as it exists today. As long as it is true that certain consumer products will be widely used, it will pay to have popular television programs that will carry commercials about these products. Paradoxically, the more distasteful the advertising, the more likely it is that popular television programs will be broadcast at no charge to the viewing audience. Neither pay television, cable television, nor video discs can change this. The market mechanism works with a powerful force to give the viewers the advertising they want at a negative price.

Some qualification is necessary. Pay and cable television enable small markets to attract programs that will cater to them. Such programs do not often appear on commercial television financed by advertising receipts. Hence the diversity of television entertainment is likely to increase if pay and cable television are allowed to flourish. What we can expect in television resembles what we now find in magazines and newspapers.

OPTIMAL ADVERTISING: AN INTRA-INDUSTRY APPROACH

Michael E. Porter

Discussion of advertising's roles—as informer, persuader, facilitator of competition, deterrent to competition, villain or savior to the media—and influence on social values has filled many volumes. In fact, a recent review of the literature on just a few of these roles fills a whole book.[1]

Despite this attention to the effects of advertising, we have very little in the way of an operational theory of the optimal level of advertising by the firm. Dorfman and Steiner's 1954 paper presented a model of the determination of optimal advertising in a simple world where a monopolist faced a demand curve dependent on price and advertising outlays.[2] While this model is logically correct, it is nonoperational since the parameters that underlie the advertising elasticity of demand are unknown. Neither do we know the shape of the advertising cost function. Further, Dorfman and Steiner's model cannot easily be extended to cover advertising competition among firms, which should affect the revenue productivity of individual firm advertising outlays.

Other approaches to the optimal level of advertising of the firm have sought to relate it to various aspects of the firm's environment. A body of literature has developed on the relation between advertising and seller concentration, represented by papers in this conference.[3] This literature reflects the view that advertising levels will be affected by the patterns of competition among firms as determined by concentration. Other analyses have proposed that firms' advertising levels are affected by the varying cost of supplying information to differently situated

---

[1] James M. Ferguson, *Advertising and Competition: Theory, Measurement, Fact* (Cambridge, Mass.: Ballinger Publishing Co., 1974).

[2] Robert Dorfman and Peter Steiner, "Optimal Advertising and Optimal Quality," *American Economic Review*, vol. 44 (December 1954), pp. 826-836.

[3] See Part 4 in this volume. For a survey see also, Michael Porter, *Interbrand Choice, Strategy and Bilateral Market Power* (Cambridge, Mass.: Harvard University Press, 1976), James M. Ferguson, *Advertising and Competition*, chapter 5; and Stanley I. Ornstein, *Advertising and Concentration* (Washington, D.C.: American Enterprise Institute, 1977).

buyers.[4] Still other studies have investigated the receptivity of buyers to advertising information as a determinant of firms' outlays on it.[5]

While these approaches all reflect relevant characteristics of the firm's advertising decision, they have been pursued largely independently. In addition, two other characteristics of the historical approach to studying the firm's advertising decision pose serious limitations on its usefulness. First, advertising has in large part been treated as homogeneous, with no account taken of differences among the advertising media. Second, the firm's advertising decision has been analyzed independent of the other elements of its competitive strategy, such as the width of its product line, rate of new product introduction reflecting its research and development outlays, et cetera. All these limitations are reflected in prior tests of the cross-industry incidence of advertising.

This paper will seek to make a contribution towards reducing these theoretical and empirical deficiencies. I shall summarize a theoretical framework, drawn from a recent study of market power and interbrand choice in consumer good industries, for modeling the optimal level of advertising of the firm. The framework suggests why previous attempts to explain advertising levels have obtained ambiguous results. I argue that analysis of the size and composition of advertising outlays of firms within a single industry allows unbiased tests of some important determinants of the firms' optimal advertising outlays while holding others constant. Data on firms in the canned and frozen foods industry permit some exploratory empirical tests of the size and composition of firm advertising that provide tentative support for my hypotheses.

Optimal Advertising Levels for the Firm

The optimal advertising level of the firm can usefully be viewed as the result of the equilibrating reactions of individual transactors to parameters of the information markets they face, and the clearing of the market as a whole.[6] The firm's decision to supply advertising is derived from the buyer's demand for information to make his choice among competing brands of the product. The *buyer's information equilibrium* determines the size and composition of his investment in gathering information about brands from the various sources available, including the

[4] See, for example, Lester G. Telser, "Advertising and Competition," *Journal of Political Economy*, vol. 63 (December 1964), pp. 2-27.

[5] See, for example, Phillip Nelson, "Information and Consumer Behavior," *Journal of Political Economy,* vol. 78 (March/April 1970), pp. 311-329.

[6] For a more comprehensive discussion, see Michael Porter, *Interbrand Choice, Strategy and Bilateral Market Power,* chapter 5.

advertising media. The determinants of information equilibria for buyers in the market are important inputs to the determination of the seller's outlay on advertising. The other main input is the seller's cost function for disseminating information messages (such as advertising) to buyers. The buyer's demand for information and the seller's cost of disseminating messages jointly determine the *partial equilibrium of information outlays for the individual seller.* Finally, advertising outlays of individual sellers interact in the market, so that the revenue productivity of one seller's outlays depends on the outlays of competing sellers. In addition, patterns of mutual dependence recognition among sellers influence the degree to which advertising competition occurs. The *market equilibrium of information outlays* reflects the reconciliation in the market of individual sellers' advertising preferences.

Buyer Information Equilibrium. The buyer has access to numerous sources of product information: personal experience, salespersons, advice from friends, physical comparison of competing brands, independent technical information (for example, *Consumer Reports*), advertising in the various media, and so on. He invests in costly information to make the optimally informed choice of the brand of a product that best meets his needs.[7] Each source provides information about differing sets of product attributes and involves differing acquisition costs to the buyer in time and utility.[8] In addition, each information source is of different "quality," where perceived quality increases with the source's flexibility in adapting information to the buyer's particular preferences or needs, the expertness of the source about the brand and the product, and the likelihood that the source's information is colored by objectives (economic or otherwise) that may conflict with the buyer's.

A product will possess a set of product attributes, and buyers can be viewed as having a utility ranking of these attributes. This ranking of product attributes will vary across products (for example, in some products taste is ranked high, for others it is unimportant), as will the desire of the buyer to make an informed choice. As products vary in

[7] Conventional demand theory focuses on the choice among the products of different industries. Here I highlight the choice among brands of a given product (interbrand choice) as a central determinant of advertising.

[8] Much has been said about the relationship of advertising to the entertainment or information media in which it is sometimes embedded. From the firm's viewpoint, the importance of this jointness is largely in influencing the buyer's utility cost of acquiring the message. Jointness of advertising with media content may decrease both the objective and subjective cost of acquiring the advertising message, perhaps below zero. The rational advertiser has the incentive to make the ads themselves as entertaining as possible for the same effect.

cost and other utility-affecting attributes, the optimal investment in information designed to increase utility by selecting the best brand will, in general, change. Combining this with the differing utility costs of the array of information sources and their varying strengths in informing about particular product attributes, it is clear that not only the buyer's optimal outlay on information but also the portfolio of sources he selects will differ from product to product.

Partial Equilibrium of Information Outlay for the Single Seller. The seller faces buyers who select their strategies for gathering information as outlined above. The buyer demands messages from the various sources; the seller controls some of these messages directly (advertising), others indirectly (presentations by the independent retailer's salespersons), and others not at all. The cost of supplying or influencing messages to buyers varies by information source. Unit prices for transmitting a message vary among information sources, as do the sources' efficiencies in placing their messages before potential buyers of the particular product. For example, the cost per message of a salesperson's presentation may be higher than the cost per reader of a magazine advertisement. But the salesperson only makes this presentation to carefully selected (or self-selected) potential buyers, while the magazine advertisement is placed before many persons not interested in the product at the time. Thus the number of messages placed before potential buyers per dollar of outlay on sales promotion varies among the media. Since the density of potential buyers, the frequency of their appearance in the market, and the ease with which they can be identified all vary among products, this efficiency ratio also varies among products for a given medium.

The prices of messages sent via the various information sources, including the advertising media, are central data in the firm's optimization process. If they could discriminate freely in price, the media could set prices to different advertisers to capture all the rents that advertisers derive from the transmission of messages via the media. However, the media supply their services in markets that are to some degree competitive. This is reinforced since their production costs are highly fixed with the publication or broadcast of the medium itself, leading to strong pressures to cut prices to fill advertising space or air time. In addition, a given quantity of information service is priced the same to all advertisers, so that price discrimination does not eliminate the variation of information source efficiencies among products. Another important issue in media pricing is whether or not competition among media eliminates their differing efficiencies to different advertisers. Given the diversity of advertisers' situations, this would require elaborate price discrimination that we do not observe.[9]

The responsiveness of buyers to messages from information sources and the cost per message to potential buyers jointly determine the seller's optimal outlay on a given source, assuming no reactions of competing firms. Equilization of marginal returns from outlays on each information source controlled or influenced by the seller characterizes his optimal portfolio of information, of which his outlay on advertising will be a major part.

Market Equilibrium. The presence of competing sellers can affect the revenue productivity of information outlays by the firm. Competing outlays may reduce the response of buyers to messages of the firm. In addition, recognition of mutual dependence in the market limits the extent to which sellers will bid up advertising outlays competitively. Thus the firm's choice of an information portfolio as well as the level of outlays will be altered by the presence of competitors. Mutual dependence recognition may also be reflected in sellers' choices of diverse portfolios of information to minimize the competitive duplication of messages and the consequent reduction in their revenue productivity. Seller concentration and other structural determinants of oligopolistic rivalry will therefore influence the level of information outlays in a market and perhaps their composition as well.[10]

Business Strategy and Information Equilibrium. Because the seller's choices of certain decision variables can influence the buyer's strategy for gathering information, the system described above is a simultaneous one. The firm jointly sets the price of its product, its quality, the breadth of its product line, research and development outlays that determine the rate at which it introduces new or improved products, et cetera. I term the vector of decision variables that yield the overall posture of the firm to its buyers the firm's *marketing strategy.*[11] The marketing strategies of competing firms determine the array of brands the buyer faces,

[9] The centrality of media pricing behavior and the competition among media to the economics of the firm's advertising decision suggest that this area should receive much more research attention than it does.

[10] Advertising may be carried beyond the point where its marginal revenue productivity with buyers equals its marginal cost if it can erect barriers to entry or affect the market power of sellers vis-à-vis adjacent stages of production or distribution. See Michael Porter, *Interbrand Choice, Strategy and Bilateral Market Power*, chapter 5.

[11] For a discussion of the concept of firm strategy and its influence on market competition, see Michael Porter, *Interbrand Choice, Strategy and Bi-lateral Market Power*, chapter 4.

the rate at which they change, the frequency with which product innovations are introduced, et cetera. All these affect the optimal level and composition of the buyer's outlay on information and the responsiveness of buyers to the various information sources. For example, increasing the rate of brand turnover may increase the dispersion of utility levels expected by the buyer from choice of different brands, and hence the amount and character of information he will seek. The resulting differences in the responsiveness of buyers to information will affect the portfolios of information outlays sellers choose.

Variation in Advertising Rates among Firms. The equilibrating process that determines the firms' information outlays, including outlays on advertising, suggests the following implications for the variation in advertising rates among firms. First, the perceptions of mutual dependence, the characteristics of the product, and its set of buyers—all of which are parameters of the buyers' and sellers' equilibrating process—vary across industries. The demand for messages from each information source, the cost of placing messages from each source before potential buyers, and the level of competing messages will consequently vary. Therefore, the level of advertising (as one information source) and the portfolio of advertising media chosen will vary, in general, across industries. Insofar as firms operate in different industries, their advertising behavior will vary (holding other elements of marketing strategy besides advertising constant).

Second, in a given industry, buyers will be diverse in their rankings of attributes and their utility cost of gathering information from different sources. Intra-industry buyer heterogeneities increase the diversity of efficient information sources and may lead to different portfolios of information outlays by firms serving different segments of this buyer group. In addition, the message cost of different information sources will vary for differently situated firms. For example, the small firm serving a regional market will face greater leakages in the use of a national medium than the large national firm. These message cost differences will lead to variation in the portfolios being adopted by different firms. Thus, within a given industry, the level and composition of information outlays, including the level and composition of advertising, will vary across firms.

Third, the level and composition of advertising will vary as the elements of firm marketing strategy other than advertising vary. The firm seeking to be a product innovator through frequent product changes, for example, will engage in heavier advertising than the firm seeking to compete on an unadvertised, rock bottom price basis. This will be true both across industries and within a given industry. These three sources of variation in firm advertising behavior become central to the empirical examination of the incidence of advertising.

Estimating Advertising Rates across Firms

An implication of the discussion above is that the factors that determine the variation in optimum advertising rates across firms are numerous, reflecting the complexity of the equilibrating process and the full range of marketing strategy choices potentially available to the firm. A number of studies have sought to explain variations in advertising among firms. These studies have related industry-wide ratios of total advertising to sales to various independent variables such as seller concentration, unit price of the product, total industry sales, the number of products sold by the industry, demand elasticity, a dummy variable for durable goods, and growth in demand. The most attention has been lavished on the relation of advertising to concentration. Studies relating the two without further controlling variables have generally found either no relation or a very weak one. But this is not at all surprising given the many determinants of optimal advertising levels described above, and their great variation among industries. Tests of the advertising-concentration relation are likely to be overwhelmed by biases due to omitted variables, which make the usual tests of the significance of the concentration variable unduly conservative.[12] Those investigations of the advertising-concentration relation that have produced significant results have controlled either explicitly or unwittingly for some of the determinants of advertising based on characteristics of the product or buyer.[13]

Peter Doyle and P. K. Else claim to have explained substantial percentages of the interindustry variation in ratios of advertising to sales.[14] Unfortunately, however, both include *industry* sales as an independent variable, for which there is only a weak theoretical justification and which is linked to the advertising-to-sales ratio through an identity relation that tends to produce the negative coefficients actually obtained. Doyle's model illustrates another difficulty of explaining variations in advertising rates among industries in that it includes a dummy variable measuring product price. This variable is included on the appropriate

12 J. Kmenta, *Elements of Econometrics* (New York: Macmillan Publishing Co., 1971), pp. 392-395.

13 Michael Porter, *Interbrand Choice, Strategy and Bilateral Market Power*, chapter 5, contains a fuller discussion of these results.

14 Peter Doyle, "Advertising Expenditure and Consumer Demand," *Oxford Economic Papers*, November 1968, pp. 394-416; and P. K. Else, "The Incidence of Advertising in Manufacturing Industries," *Oxford Economic Papers*, March 1966, pp. 88-110.

hypothesis that a low unit price reduces the cost to the buyer of an unsatisfactory purchase decision and leads him to utilize less expensive sources of product information such as advertising. This would imply an inverse relation between unit price and advertising rate. However, there are other elements that are important in the determination of optimal firm advertising rates that are linked to product price: (1) product price is also a rough inverse proxy of frequency of purchase; (2) many low-priced products (food items, cosmetics, toiletries, et cetera) are purchased by the majority of consuming households; and (3) price is a proxy for the intrinsic complexity of the product and hence the range of product attributes that the buyer values. Thus, the statistical relation between advertising rates and unit price of the product is not sufficient to identify the underlying model. This problem afflicts many other statistical measures of determinants of advertising rates that have been utilized.

The inescapable conclusion is that explaining the variation in advertising rates among industries is an extremely difficult problem, leading generally to low coefficients of multiple determination (that is, to an explanation of only a small fraction of the variation in advertising) and low levels of significance of coefficients (that is, explanatory variables whose effect on advertising is not signicantly different from zero).[15] Even statistically significant coefficients are often difficult to interpret unambiguously because they can support more than one hypothesis. Statistically successful tests have generally used a sample of industries selected to hold constant some of the determinants of the equilibria described above. For example, H. M. Mann, J. A. Henning, and J. W. Meehan, Jr. have provided a statistically successful test of the advertising-concentration relation that uses a sample of heavily advertised low priced consumer nondurables.[16] Douglas Greer identified certain product categories that capture some elements of the firm's advertising decision and that yield, variously, a significant and insignificant quadratic (inverted-U) relationship between advertising and concentration.[17] John Cable, who has recognized a number of the influences on the advertising decision, correctly notes the difficulty of the empirical problem raised by the numerous influences on optimal advertising levels, and the importance of sample selection as a control.[18]

[15] See, for example, a recent test by Comanor and Wilson, *Advertising and Market Power* (Cambridge, Mass.: Harvard University Press, 1974), pp. 150-153.

[16] H. M. Mann, J. A. Henning, and J. W. Meehan, Jr., "Advertising and Concentration: An Empirical Investigation," *Journal of Industrial Economics*, November 1967, pp. 34-45.

[17] Douglas F. Greer, "Advertising and Market Concentration," *Southern Economic Journal*, July 1971, pp. 19-32.

[18] John Cable, "Market Structure, Advertising Policy, and Intermarket Differences in Advertising Intensity," in *Market Structure and Corporate Behavior*, Keith Cowling, ed. (London: Gray Mills Ltd., 1972), pp. 105-124.

Variation in Advertising Behavior within Industries

To address the problem of devising an empirical test that will contribute to our understanding of the determinants of firms' advertising rates, I will focus on the variance in individual firm advertising rates within a given industry, rather than the variance of average advertising rates across industries. The limitation of the sample to one industry provides a control for a large number of factors that determine optimal advertising rates. The nature of the product, the product's price, and the buyer population are all held nearly constant. Structural market characteristics influencing oligopolistic rivalry, including market concentration, are held constant. Market growth and overall market elasticity of demand are similarly controlled for in this procedure. What may vary within the industry are firms' choices of overall marketing strategies, affecting the level and composition of advertising that they choose. These strategic differences will be reinforced by internal heterogeneity of buyers. In addition, differently situated firms will face differing costs per message of utilizing the various advertising media. Thus the variation in advertising behavior within an industry should allow us to focus on the technology of advertising media and the relation between marketing strategy and advertising choices as they affect both the level and composition of advertising.

Within an industry, firms will differ in the volume of sales and the geographic territory in which they sell. Marketing strategies can vary in the breadth of the product line offered, the number of different brand names attached to items in the line, the rate of new brand introduction, the price and quality levels of the products, and numerous other dimensions. If buyers' utility functions are heterogeneous and firms are differently situated, there is no reason why the firms' approaches to marketing should become identical over time.[19]

Advertising and the Scale of the Firm. In a recent paper, I argued that the various advertising media will have differing "effective threshold" levels of outlays and that, as a result, the position and shape of the cost function relating dollar outlays on media to messages placed before

[19] Strategy differences can be taken as the result of random drawings or can be linked to differences in the sustainable capabilities or strengths of firms in an industry. The cause of the strategy differences is not central to my argument, which addresses the relation between observed strategy differences and advertising behavior. For my view of the genesis and stability of strategy differences among firms in an industry see Michael Porter, *Interbrand Choice, Strategy and Bilateral Market Power*, and Richard E. Caves and Michael E. Porter, "From Entry Barriers to Mobility Barriers: Conjectural Decisions and Contrived Deterrence to New Competition," *Quarterly Journal of Economics*, May 1977, pp. 241-261.

potential buyers will differ across media.[20] Briefly, the effective threshold or fixed minimum level of spending on a medium is dependent on its geographic divisibility, its rate structure, the presence or absence of zoned or regional editions, economies of repetition, and the absolute dollar outlays required for effective repetition levels. I concluded that national media such as magazines and especially network television have greater effective threshold levels of outlay than local media such as newspapers. Spot television ads (television ads purchased for showing on individual stations rather than the network) fall somewhere in between. This is because the economies of message repetition and indivisibilities of the unit of advertising purchased make the required minimum absolute outlay on spot television larger than on newspapers and because television stations generally reach a larger minimum audience size than could be obtained through a local newspaper. Regional magazines appear similar to spot television.

Although the characteristics of the product and its buyers strongly influence the optimal mix of media, when we control for these by looking within an industry firms' media choices should be strongly affected by their sales volume and by the geographic market they serve. The more regional or local the market served, the more likely is the firm to use media with lower effective geographic thresholds, such as local newspapers and spot television, in order to minimize leakages. For a given geographic market, the smaller the firm's sales volume, the more are these same media favored in order to minimize diseconomies. Small firms may also be more likely to utilize national or regional magazines that reach a very specialized audience, with the specialization of the audience reached by the medium offsetting its broad geographic scope. Large national firms, conversely, will find it optimal to take advantage of economies of national media such as network television and national magazines, easily vaulting the required minimum effective outlays.

Given the economies of scale accompanying high effective threshold media, the effect of the firm's sales volume on its ratio of *total* advertising outlays to sales is ambiguous. Within an industry, the outlays required for a given volume of advertising decline relative to sales, as the firm can increasingly utilize efficient national media. However, a firm's marketing strategies may change with relative scale, or the firm may increase advertising volume as its sales increase. Thus the advertising inefficiencies of small firms may or may not show up in higher rates of advertising outlays relative to larger firms.

[20] Michael E. Porter, "Interbrand Choice, Media Mix and Market Performance," *American Economic Review*, vol. 66 (May 1976), pp. 398-406.

Advertising and Firm Marketing Strategy. With many elements of the structural environment of the firm controlled by restricting our focus to a single industry, how might variations in marketing approach among profit maximizing firms affect the level and composition of their advertising? Anticipating the empirical tests which follow, I focus on the breadth of line, number of brand names, and rate of introduction of new products to the firm's line.

Controlling for sales volume and the number of brand names, the level of the firm's advertising outlays may increase with the breadth of its product line. Firms may offer broad lines to take advantage of complementarities in demand among related items and thereby to reduce the cost of promoting the full line versus the sum of the costs of promoting the individual items. But the marginal item will always require additional information outlays, so that if there are more items in the line the seller must transmit more information to buyers, other things being equal. The net increase in advertising costs of the full-line seller is balanced by the promotional economies and by any enhancement of product differentiation that may result from having the full line.

Breadth may also affect the composition of advertising. For a given advertising outlay, the producer with a narrow line will have either greater message repetition per item in his line, or more time or space allocated to each item in the line per message, than the producer with a broad line. Holding the firm's sales constant, if there are indivisibilities in the response of buyers to advertising messages or economies in the repetition of messages, there may be diseconomies as the number of items in the product line increases, offsetting in part the promotional economies of the full line and increasing the tendency for advertising to increase proportionally to sales as breadth of line increases. These would be most serious where the buyer desires information on the individual item rather than the items under a common brand as a group.

The repetition or message size diseconomies of a broad line would be minimized by choosing relatively cost efficient media and by choosing print as opposed to electronic media. Print media may be read by the buyer over a variable time period, and a variety of items can be listed or pictured in a printed ad, whereas an electronic advertisement is tightly constrained by the announcing and viewing time. The economies of message repetition are probably also less for print media than for the electronic media, since a given print ad can be reread repeatedly while the electronic ad cannot. Thus we may expect to find firms with broad product lines heavier users of print media where lower repetition is not so important, other things being equal, especially national magazine advertising that may have relatively low message costs per potential buyer. Breadth may also be associated with the use of local or regional media where different parts of the line can be emphasized in different areas. Finally, breadth could be associated with print media where the choice of publication, based on audience characteristics, allows the advertiser to reach buyers who value broad line complementarities. These arguments would suggest the use of spot television or magazines versus network television.

Controlling for the firm's sales volume, the number of brand names should also be positively related to advertising levels. Firms may employ multiple brand names for historical reasons such as past acquisition of branded producers in their industry (Consolidated Foods), or in order to allow different items in their line to adopt different advertising themes. Multiple brand names for the same items in the line also signal multiple marketing approaches—another way of saying that the firm is targeting its efforts toward multiple market segments or niches. If there are indivisibilities in establishing a brand name requiring some threshold level of advertising for each one adopted, more brand names should require greater total advertising outlays for a given level of sales. The greater outlays are balanced by the greater product differentiation that may result from narrow segment choice.

Firms with multiple brands will seek to minimize the disadvantages of reduced message repetition on each brand for a given sales level. This again suggests greater use of print rather than electronic media. If multiple brand names suggest multiple market segments, it would seem appropriate to use media that allow ads to be tailored to local areas (local or regional media) or that allow the seller to select specialized audiences (magazines).

Rate of introduction of new brands or of new items to the product line should be positively associated with advertising levels. Two studies have found that high levels of advertising are associated with high rates of introduction of new brands.[21] Both showed that advertising rates for cigarettes increased as producers increased the pace of new brand introduction. The indivisibilities in promoting a brand name, discussed above, are sufficient to establish this conclusion. The effect would be reinforced by diseconomies in the establishment of a steady-state stock of advertising goodwill in the early phase of the introduction of new items. Threshold spending required for the new item to gain buyers' attention may increase required advertising outlays. The higher outlays

[21] M. A. Alemson, "Advertising and the Nature of Competition in Oligopoly over Time: A Case Study," *Economic Journal*, June 1970, pp. 282-306; Lester Telser, "Advertising and Cigarettes," *Journal of Political Economy*, October 1962, pp. 471-491.

of the innovating firm are balanced by the greater product differentiation and potential for market share increases it may thereby enjoy.

The introduction of new products, controlling for sales volume, should increase the use of media with low cost per buyer message, such as network television, to minimize start-up diseconomies. Electronic media may be utilized to stress through repetition the theme of newness. The firm following the innovation approach generally portrays this common theme to all its buyers, and network television would be favored since the new product theme is constant nationwide. This is in sharp contrast to media choice following the market segmentation approach.

Empirical Tests

I selected the canned and frozen food industry to test these propositions about the variation in the level and composition of advertising within an industry. The industry was selected for a number of reasons. First, and most importantly, it contains a relatively large number of firms that are both publicly held, so that annual reports and other data are available, and not importantly diversified, so that the data is unbiased by interindustry differences in the parameters of the firm's advertising decision. These are perhaps the most stringent limitations that were imposed upon the industries that were considered. Second, firms in this industry differ greatly in size and, as a result, most forms of advertising are used by at least some industry members. Third, the product line sold by industry members is quite homogeneous in terms of its unit price levels, retail distribution patterns, and the population of buyers served.

A variety of data was assembled for a sample of fourteen firms in the industry for the years 1967–1968. A detailed description of the sources of these data, the reasons for the choice of time period, and the construction of the variables used in the study is contained in a technical appendix to this paper. The tight constraints on the sample size in the study are an unavoidable characteristic of research design confined to a single industry instead of the cross-industry designs usual in industrial organization. Given the limited degrees of freedom and the restriction of the empirical examination to one industry, the results of the study must be interpreted with caution.

The following variables were used in the study (the sources of data and construction of the variables are described in the Technical Appendix):

SALES The firm's sales volume corrected to remove sales outside the U.S. market, averaged over 1967–1968.

LGSALES	A dummy variable with the value of 1 if the firm's sales are $100 million or more and 0 otherwise.
BREADS	A discontinuous measure of the breadth of the firm's product line, divided by its average sales (*SALES*).
BRANDS	The number of different brand names advertised by the firm, averaged over 1967–1968, divided by its average sales (*SALES*).
INNOV	A dummy variable measure of the rate of new introductions to the firms' product line over the period 1967–1968.
ADVERT	The total outlays by the firm on advertising in all media in the United States, 1967–1968.
NETADV	The total outlays by the firm on network television advertising in the United States, 1967–1968.
MAGADV	The total outlays by the firm on magazine advertising in the United States, 1967–1968.
SPOTADV	The total outlays by the firm on spot television advertising in the United States, 1967–1968.
SUPLADV	The total outlays by the firm on advertising in national newspaper supplements in the United States, 1967–1968.
NEWSADV	The total outlays by the firm on local newspaper advertising in the United States, 1967–1968.

From these variables were computed the ratio of advertising in each medium to total media advertising and the ratio of total advertising outlays to sales (*A/S*).

Table 1 presents the level and composition of advertising outlays for the fourteen firms in the sample. *A/S* ranges from 0.14 percent to 7.54 percent, while the composition of advertising outlays varies markedly as well, especially with respect to network television, magazine, and newspaper advertising. Thus the data strongly affirm the fact that the level and composition of firm advertising varies within industries. The data themselves also strongly support the notion of a high effective threshold for network television advertising, because no firm with annual sales less than $150 million advertises in this medium.

Table 2 presents multiple regression equations explaining the variation in *A/S* among firms in the sample, and Table 3 presents some selected correlations among included variables. The first result of note is that firm sales have little effect on *A/S*.[22] The tendency, if any, is a negative relationship, although the simple negative correlation between

[22] The result was not affected by various alternative nonlinear specifications of the sales variable.

Table 1

THE RATE AND COMPOSITION OF ADVERTISING OUTLAYS IN FOURTEEN CANNED AND FROZEN FOOD FIRMS: 1967–1968 AVERAGES

Company	Average Sales ($ thousands)	A/S (percent)	Share Network Television	Share Magazines	Share Spot Television	Share Local Newspapers
1	$980,281	.54	.279	.115	.469	.128
2	741,586	3.91	.361	.292	.269	.077
3	439,228	1.57	.147	.395	.290	.157
4	325,516	1.17	.428	.021	.488	.059
5	320,676	3.60	.342	.031	.598	.025
6	257,056	2.53	.417	.061	.194	.225
7	245,666	1.42	.014	.195	.461	.340
8	157,795	3.99	.459	.052	.320	.036
9	74,525	1.64	.0	.206	.514	.225
10	43,355	1.46	.0	.373	.0	.627
11	37,505	.62	.0	.0	.413	.586
12	23,534	.14	.0	.637	.363	.0
13	21,523	1.58	.0	.271	.469	.260
14	15,853	7.54	.0	.426	.318	.204
MEAN	263,370	2.26	.175	.220	.369	.211
STANDARD DEVIATION	280,720	1.88	.187	.183	.148	.188

the two variables is small. However, the firm's strategy variables have a striking effect on the rate of advertising the firm chooses. The number of brand names the firm advertises per dollar of sales is always positive and highly significant. The rate of introduction of new items to the product line is also positive and highly significant. Breadth of line divided by sales volume is erratic. It is significant and negative in some runs, positive in others, though its omission reduces the coefficient of determination R^2 (fraction of the variation in A/S explained by the regression), suggesting that it is not an irrelevant variable. The problem may be multicollinearity (interdependence between supposedly independent variables), since the correlation between *BRANDS* and *BREADS* is high and *BREADS* has a positive simple correlation with A/S. Various alternative interactive specifications of breadth of line and number of brand names tested were less successful than the linear formulations.

Table 2

MULTIPLE REGRESSION EQUATIONS EXPLAINING ADVERTISING-TO-SALES RATIO IN FOURTEEN CANNED AND FROZEN FOOD COMPANIES

	Intercept	*SALES* (market share)	*BRANDS*	*BREADS*	*INNOV*	R^2	CORRECTED R^2
1.	.02433[a] (3.285)	.6352 (.330)				.009	−.074
2.	−.001114 (.213)		310.21[a] (5.354)		.02603[a] (4.027)	.774[a]	.698
3.	.002526 (.371)	.3623 (.335)	434.16[a] (6.734)	−210.09[b] (2.232)	.02564[a] (4.917)	.861[a]	.804
4.	.004204 (.954)		434.42[a] (7.059)	−226.18[b] (2.929)	.02562[a] (5.147)	.862[a]	.821

Note: Figures in parentheses are *t*-values. The significance of the regression coefficients is tested using a one-tail *t* test, and the significance of the coefficients of multiple determination is tested using the *F* test.

Coefficients of sales are multiplied by 10^8 for ease in reporting.

[a] Indicates coefficient is significant at the 99 percent level.

[b] Indicates coefficient is significant at the 95 percent level.

[c] Indicates coefficient is significant at the 90 percent level.

Table 3

SELECTED CORRELATIONS AMONG INDEPENDENT VARIABLES IN FOURTEEN CANNED AND FROZEN FOOD COMPANIES

	A/S	*BRANDS*	*BREADS*	*INNOV*
SALES	−.09[a]	−.47	−.65	.12
BRANDS	.61	1.00	.73	−.45
BREADS	.20		1.00	−.34
INNOV	.28			1.00

[a] For n = 14, a simple correlation of 0.52 is statistically significant at the 95 percent level.

The results, though they must be qualified by the presence of a collinear data set, strongly support the arguments presented above about the determinants of overall advertising levels. In addition, the included variables explain a large proportion of the interfirm variation of A/S.

Table 4 presents a simple correlation matrix of the composition of firm advertising outlays, firm sales, and measures of the firm's marketing strategy. While few of the simple correlation coefficients are statistically significant, perhaps because of the low degrees of freedom, the correlation pattern is generally supportive of my earlier arguments. Large sales volume is strongly associated with use of network television advertising and to a lesser extent spot television advertising. A large number of brand names relative to sales volume is associated with the use of print

Table 4

SIMPLE CORRELATIONS BETWEEN MEDIA COMPOSITION AND FIRM SALES AND MARKETING STRATEGY

	Percent Network Television	Percent Spot Television	Percent Magazines	Percent Local Newspapers
SALES	.54[a]	.17	−.22	−.37
LGSALES	.81	.13	−.47	−.49
BRANDS	−.51	−.05	.38	.18
BREADS	−.64	.13	.57	−.03
INNOV	.52	−.03	−.22	−.40

[a] For n = 14, a simple correlation of 0.52 is statistically significant at the 95 percent level.

Table 5

MULTIPLE REGRESSION EQUATION EXPLAINING THE MEDIA COMPOSITION OF ADVERTISING IN FOURTEEN CANNED AND FROZEN FOOD COMPANIES

Dependent Variable	Intercept	*SALES*	*LGSALES*	*BRANDS*	*BREADS*	*INNOV*	R^2	CORRECTED R^2
1. Percent Network Television	.08093 (1.298)	.3566E–6 [b] (2.202)					.288 [b]	.229
2. Percent Network Television	–.2364E–7 (.001)		.3060 [a] (4.811)				.659 [a]	.630
3. Percent Network Television	.02732 (.433)	.2963E–6 [c] (1.975)				.16219 [c] (1.906)	.465 [b]	.367
4. Percent Network Television	.3034 [a] (5.005)				–2853.8 [b] (2.898)		.412 [b]	.363
5. Percent Network Television	.2454 [a] (4.274)			–1734.1 [c] (2.071)			.263 [c]	.202
6. Percent Network Television	–.01283 (.107)		.2733 [b] (2.344)		8.609 (.007)	.07269 (.969)	.688 [a]	.594
1. Percent Newspaper	.3170 (4.392)		–.18620 [c] (1.950)				.241 [c]	.177
2. Percent Newspaper	.5360 (4.186)	–.4578E–6 [b] (2.238)			–2841.4 [c] (1.995)	–.1792 [c] (1.909)	.460 [c]	.298
3. Percent Newspaper	.7466 (6.860)		–.53304 [a] (5.326)		–5134.9 [a] (4.350)		.721 [a]	.670
4. Percent Newspaper	.7542 (6.952)		–.49676 [a] (4.718)		–5083.8 [a] (4.326)	–.07161 (1.057)	.749 [a]	.674

1. Percent Magazine Advertising	.2572[a] (3.648)	−.1429E–6 (.780)				.048	−.031
2. Percent Magazine Advertising	.1681[a] (2.779)		1264.9 (1.434)			.146	.075
3. Percent Magazine Advertising	.1067[c] (1.687)			2503.3[b] (2.436)		.331[b]	.275
4. Percent Magazine Advertising	1.077[a] (4.475)		2285.6 (.855)		−.5463[c] (1.832)	.383[c]	.271
5. Percent Magazine Advertising	.1130 (1.274)			2461.9[c] (2.155)	−.01022 (.106)	.332	.210
1. Percent Spot TV and Magazines	.2857 (3.190)	3613E–6[b] (2.244)	−1180.9 (1.292)	5676.0[a] (4.058)		.664[a]	.563

Note: Figures in parentheses are *t* values. The significance of the regression coefficients is tested using a one-tail *t* test and the significance of the coefficients of multiple determination is tested using the *F* test.

[a] indicates coefficient is significant at the 99 percent level.

[b] indicates coefficient is significant at the 95 percent level.

[c] indicates coefficient is significant at the 90 percent level.

media, especially magazines. Breadth of line relative to sales volume is strongly related to use of magazine advertising. Breadth of line and a large number of brand names relative to sales are associated with low use of network television. A high rate of new introductions to the product line, on the other hand, is strongly associated with network television advertising and negatively associated with use of print media.

These conclusions are supported by the multiple regression analysis in Table 5.[23] *LGSALES* is a powerful determinant of the percentage of network television adopted by the firm. The discontinuous measure performs better than *SALES,* suggesting that the use of network television is subject to a threshold beyond which further increases in sales do not necessarily increase the share of advertising allocated to it. *INNOV* performs reasonably well with the expected positive sign, and its low significance may well be due to multicollinearity.[24] The other variables are not generally significant in determining the share of advertising allocated to network television.

SALES and *LGSALES* have a strong negative influence on the percentage of advertising on local newspapers, consistent with the view that local newspapers have low effective threshold. *LGSALES* and *BREADS* entered together yield the strongest results; however, *BREADS* has a strong negative influence on local newspaper shares, while *INNOV* has a negative but not strongly significant influence (though again it is affected by collinearity). In equations for both the percentage of network television and percentage of local newspaper, a large percentage of the interfirm variance is explained.

The equation for the percentage of magazine advertising is only modestly significant, with *BREADS* exerting the only significant influence in the expected positive direction. When the percentage of spot television is added to magazine advertising, however, the statistical results improve. *SALES* is positive and significant, consistent with my hypothesis that these media have higher effective thresholds than local newspapers. *BREADS* is also positive and strongly significant, suggesting that broad-line firms avoid high threshold network television but also avoid relatively cost inefficient local newspapers. Whether spot television or magazine advertising has a higher effective threshold is ambiguous and dependent on the nature of the specific magazines utilized by the firm. Hence it is perhaps not surprising that the two together could be explained more successfully than either individually.

[23] Because of the relation among the dependent variables in the media share equations, the coefficients for common independent variables in the different equations are related. However, the assumptions of ordinary least squares are not violated.

[24] The simple correlation between *INNOV* and *LGSALES* is 0.46.

The results from Table 5 might be translated as follows into the language of marketing strategy. Within an industry, large firms make use of the cost effectiveness of network television, while small firms are pushed to local newspapers. Firms with high *BRANDS* or *BREADS* seem to be following a strategy of pursuing multiple market segments, whether they be geographic or product based. The firms segmenting their markets avoid network television, with its common messages beamed nationwide, in favor of spot television or magazines where messages may be better tuned to the target segments. The spot TV advertising messages themselves as well as the brand names advertised can differ by geographic area, and magazines can be selected with the target audience in mind. Innovating firms use electronic media to stress the dominant theme of newness and choose network television to take advantage of economies in repeating this common theme nationwide. Thus the media have differing capabilities for information transmittal which show themselves in tandem with their cost differences.

Conclusion

In view of the limited degrees of freedom and the confinement of attention to a single industry, my results can be taken only as exploratory. These qualifications aside, however, it does appear that the level and composition of firm advertising varies systematically among firms within industries. This variation seems to be consistent with the hypothesis that the firm's marketing strategy variables, of which advertising is one, are simultaneously determined. In addition, the evidence on variations in media composition is consistent with differences among media in their effective threshold levels of outlay and in their flexibility in addressing different advertising themes.

The results support the complex view of the firm's optimal advertising level presented in earlier sections. Translated into an interindustry context, they suggest that controls for the full array of firms' decision variables will be necessary to permit isolating the influence of individual decision variables. This proposition pertains not only to advertising, but also to pricing behavior and the determination of product quality and rates of outlay for research and development as well; and thus the concept of simultaneous strategy determination has wider significance for research in industrial organization.

Finally, it is hoped that the use of methodologies focusing within an industry will be stimulated by this study. Such methodologies can often prove to be a powerful way of studying individual firm behavior and avoiding the difficulties of controlling for industry variables. The difficulty inherent in such methodologies is, of course, the lack of data. This and other recent studies [25] have demonstrated, however, that some data are available, though not served up in neatly bound Census volumes. A combination of careful sample selection and the use of intra-industry data may allow us to unscramble the difficult questions about advertising that are the subject of this volume.

Technical Appendix

The sources of data for the study are as follows. Lists of publicly held leading firms in the canned and frozen food industry in 1967 and 1968 were taken from the *News Front Directory of 25,000 Leading U.S. Firms.* Other leading firms in the industry were identified using the Dun and Bradstreet *Million Dollar Directory* for the years 1967 and 1968. Unfortunately, all the firms that were not publicly held either proved too small to be included in the sources of the advertising data (to be described below), or their annual sales volume was not publicly available, so that advertising to sales ratios could not be computed.

For the publicly held firms identified from *News Front*, data on total advertising outlays by media were obtained from two sources. *National Advertising in Newspapers* (American Newspaper Publishers Association) contained data on annual outlays on advertising in U.S. local newspapers by firms that had spent $25,000 or more on that medium in the year. For each firm included, expenditures on newspaper advertising were given by separate brand name, so that it was possible to obtain a count of brand names advertised in this medium. *National Advertising Investments* (Leading National Advertisers, Inc.) contained data giving annual U.S. advertising outlays on network television, spot (local station) television, magazines, and national newspaper supplements, for firms that had spent $25,000 or more on all these media combined in the year. Again data were available by brand name of the firm, so that a count of brand names advertised in these media was obtained. Both advertising sources were based on a survey of a substantial majority of the subject media.

The years 1967 and 1968 were selected for the study for several reasons. After 1968, a number of firms in the canned and frozen food industry were acquired or merged with other firms, reducing the already limited number of degrees of freedom. Before 1967, the sources of the advertising data lacked the strategic breakdown between network and

[25] For example, see H. H. Newman, "Strategic Groups and the Structure-Performance Relationship: A Study with Respect to the Chemical Process Industries," (Ph.D. Dissertation, Harvard University, 1973), and W. J. Adams, "Corporate Power and Profitability," (Ph.D. Dissertation, Harvard University, 1973).

spot television advertising. Thus although longer period averages for the dependent and independent variables in the study would have been desirable in insuring that the observed relationships were stable and structural rather than transitory, the nature of the data precluded using a longer period.

Data on firm outlays on media besides the ones listed were not available. Other significant advertising media are network radio, local radio, outdoor (billboard) advertising and direct mail advertisements. The first three are relatively unimportant in terms of total media outlays (see *The Outlook for Newspapers*, American Newspaper Publishers Association, 1974); direct mail is more substantial in aggregate estimates of advertising outlays, but is subject to few if any indivisibilities that would increase the effective threshold level of advertising through this medium. In addition, there was no evidence that food manufacturers made much use of the medium. The included media represented a substantial majority of total media advertising outlays, and thus the omission of the lesser media was not felt to affect seriously the conclusions of the study.

The media data covered only the actual media cost, excluding the cost of preparing the advertisement itself. However, data from various sources suggest that preparation costs usually represent only a small fraction of media cost. To the extent that the ratio of preparation costs to media costs does not vary systematically among firms (which might be expected), the omission of preparation costs would not affect the statistical results.

Matching the leading firms and the sources of advertising data yielded fourteen firms for which complete data were available. For these fourteen firms, a variety of other data were collected. First, annual income statement and balance sheet data were available both from company annual reports and from *Moody's Industrial Manual* for the years covered by the study. Data on annual firm sales were taken from these sources. Since the data on advertising covered only the U.S. market, and some of the firms in the sample had sales abroad that were consolidated in the total sales figures, various strategies were employed to estimate the percentage of total foreign sales for each firm. In some cases the company annual reports or securities registration statements (SEC Form 10K) disclosed this percentage for the years under study. In these cases sales could be adjusted directly. For somewhat more than half of the firms, however, these data were not disclosed for 1967 or 1968. For these firms, data disclosed in later years and extrapolation were utilized to estimate foreign sales in 1967–1968. All firms disclosed at least a closely approximated figure for foreign sales by 1971–1972. The percentage of foreign sales in the earliest year available was then adjusted for changes since 1967–1968 based on growth in operations abroad versus domestic operations as discussed in the firms' annual reports. Annual reports in the 1967–1972 period, while not disclosing absolute foreign sales, generally disclosed the annual rate of growth of foreign sales. Working backward from the first year in which the absolute foreign sales were disclosed, it was possible to approximate the percentage of foreign sales in 1967–1968. Reported sales in 1967 and 1968 were adjusted by the percentage of foreign sales to yield *SALES*, or domestic sales.

BRANDS was computed from the count of advertised brand names taken from the advertising sources as described above. For each year, the number of brand names of the firm was taken to be the *greater* of the number of brands determined from counts taken from the two advertising data sources. The number of brand names was averaged over the two years of the study and divided by the firm's sales volume to yield the variable used in the analysis.

A measure of the breadth of the firms' product lines, *BREADS*, was developed from study of company annual reports and registration statements. Each company disclosed the items in its product line. They were divided into the following lines consistent with the manner in which the industry appeared to classify products: canned vegetables, canned fruit, frozen vegetables, frozen fruit, canned fruit juices and drinks, canned soups, frozen prepared dinners and dishes, canned speciality foods, snack foods, canned meat, frozen meat, and other. A dummy variable was constructed measuring the number of these lines in which the firm had products, and divided by the firm's sales volume.

A dummy variable measure of the rate of introduction of new items to the firm's product line, *INNOV*, was also developed based on study of the firms' annual reports and other data. It is accepted practice in the industry to discuss products newly introduced that year in the annual report, often with a count of new items introduced. Based on these data, firms could be relatively easily grouped into two categories: those which introduced a substantial number of new items during 1967–1968 and those which introduced none or a very small number. This classification was the basis for a dichotomous dummy variable. It was assumed in this procedure that if firms frequently introduced new items they would disclose this with substantial fanfare to their stockholders. The assumption seems accurate given accepted practice in the industry.

COMMENTARIES

David M. Blank

I think both papers are very stimulating and suggestive, and I have only a few brief observations. First, on Dr. Porter's paper, I have the impression that the appropriate line of demarcation is between television and print rather than between national media (network television and magazines) and local media (spot television and newspapers). Dr. Porter stresses the opposite conclusion, but I defer to the reader to determine whether my impression is correct, that is, whether most of the variables work rather differently for the television media than they do for the print media.

Turning to Dr. Telser's paper, there are two comments I would like to make. First, Dr. Telser suggests at several points that those who buy the products advertised pay for the advertising. This is an old and in my view unsatisfactory idea.

Let me refer, for a moment, to the Steiner study; it is a singularly good example of the point I am trying to make. Steiner reported that toy manufacturers discovered that national advertising, particularly on Saturday morning network television, provided an extraordinarily efficient way to increase sales.[1] The result of that advertising and of the preselling of toys, was the introduction of a new kind of retail operation, in which retail margins and prices were aggressively slashed. Now, I do not know how the people who bought those toys after the advertising was introduced by the industry paid for the advertising. Indeed, it appears that if there had been no advertising, they would have paid more.

Second, Dr. Telser not only discusses and concerns himself with various relationships within the advertising market, but extends his analysis to the relationship between the advertising market and the entertainment market. He goes even further by strongly suggesting that it is the demands or needs of the advertising marketplace that bring about certain kinds of TV programs and certain kinds of magazines and magazine articles.

I think that stretches things a little far. I think that advertising has a profound and significant role to play in the economic marketplace,

---

[1] Robert L. Steiner, "Does Advertising Lower Consumer Prices?" *Journal of Marketing*, vol. 37, no. 4 (October 1973), pp. 19-26.

but to envisage everything that it touches to be in effect determined by advertising, extends the argument far beyond any reasonable belief.

Let me, for example, read a sentence from the end of Dr. Telser's paper. "As long as it is true," he says, "that certain consumer products will be widely used, it will pay to have popular television programs that will carry commercials about these products."

If we assume that certain consumer products will be used widely for some indefinite period, I infer that popular television programs will be with us for a long time. I think that is true, but I do not think it is true because of advertising. I could rewrite that sentence to read, "As long as it is true that certain consumer products will be widely used, it will pay to have popular magazines that will carry advertisements about those products."

Presumably when *Life, Look,* and *Collier's* were around, that would have been an intuitively correct statement, as it is now about television. But, *Life, Look,* and *Collier's* are no longer around. And they have disappeared, not because of changes in the advertising market, but, rather, because of changes in the entertainment market. I would strongly urge against extending the argument about advertising too far.

I think the reason it would be incorrect to overlook the importance of the other markets, particularly the entertainment market in which these media play a role, is that the value of the entertainment to consumers is in many ways significantly larger than the value of the advertising to advertisers.

When I entered this industry I was given an analogy of how peculiarly television is positioned. It was the suggestion that the baseball industry would certainly be very different if the teams could not charge admission—if the New York Yankees could obtain revenue only by billboards in the outfield. That is really what the television industry is all about.

The new competitors in television have found ways of establishing different pricing mechanisms, and I think it is an open question exactly what will happen in that competition. I do not think that the existence of national advertising will determine the results.

It is useful to recall that the radio industry was created and funded for a fair period by people who wanted to sell radio sets rather than by advertisers. The television industry was, to a very significant extent, created and funded in its beginning by people who wanted to sell television sets rather than those who wanted to sell advertising. The introduction of color television had very little to do with the role it would play in the advertising market, although it did have a lot to do with the way in which consumers would react to television programs and the rapidity with which they would buy color television sets.

Thus, I am suggesting that advertising has an important enough role to play on its own. Let us not try to extend its influence further than we should.

Gerard R. Butters

The central thesis of Telser's paper, as I have read it, is that an economist's bag of tools can work to explain advertising much as his tools work in more conventional areas of application. I think that one can agree with that position without resolving such difficult issues as whether or not, for example, a particular magazine's existence is explained solely on the basis of the advertising contained in it.

I agree with Telser that supply and demand analysis works, as long as one puts in a few basic twists. In particular, in the context of TV, radio, and some print media advertising, one must recognize that advertising is often provided at a negative price, in the sense that people pay attention to advertising only because they are subsidized with entertainment for doing so. With this in mind, one can operate with supply and demand curves much as usual.

For example, one can say that the introduction of cable TV, a form of entertainment which competes with broadcast TV, will shift the demand curve for broadcast TV to the left, and will result in a lower quantity of advertising provided at a lower (more negative) price. This is a very ordinary economic argument. What is controversial is how great this shift will be. It appears that Professor Telser's impression was that the shift in quantity would be slight, whereas Mr. Blank's impression was that it very well may be large. This is a disagreement on orders of magnitude, not on the kinds of tools which ought to be applied to such problems.

I agree more generally that when viewed as *positive* analysis—analysis that attempts to explain and predict advertising behavior, but not necessarily to evaluate it as good or bad—economic reasoning does apply successfully to many existing practices. It does explain, I think, why advertising is the predominant form of promotion in some industries but not in others. It helps to explain the existence and functions of specialized forms of the media. It explains the choice of products to be advertised in each of the media. It explains why new products are advertised more than old ones.

Although I agree that positive economic analysis can be applied successfully to this area, I think that we economists must admit we do not have as strong a theory of advertising as we would like. In most of the literature on the subject—I am certainly not singling out the work of Professor Telser—much of the analysis is in the form of after-the-fact rationalizations of commonly observed events. This makes it easy to nit-pick on the grounds that an alternative rationalization would be just as appropriate. Indeed, I will take the opportunity to nit-pick in this fashion with regard to two points in the paper.

First, with regard to the example of prescription drugs versus cigarettes, I submit that Telser has the right answer, but for the wrong reason. I think that prescription drugs are promoted by salesmen not because it is cheaper to locate physicians than it is to locate cigarette smokers—I am sure I can locate more cigarette smokers here than physicians—but simply because there is a much larger gain per doctor visited. This is true because a doctor acts as an agent for many ultimate buyers of drugs and therefore influences a large volume of sales. More fundamentally, the drug market supports such intermediaries, and the cigarette market does not, because (1) subtle differences in product are of much more consequence to drug consumers than to cigarette consumers, and (2) the conveyance of information of such a discriminating sort requires interactive communication between experts.

Secondly, with regard to Telser's discussion of advertising in books, I agree that it is reasonable that books are used to advertise other books of a similar nature; but this does not answer the question that he posed: Why do books carry so little advertising compared with other media? If paperback best sellers happened to include a substantial amount of advertising of commonly consumed products, I think this could be even more simply rationalized.

My main disagreement with Professor Telser, however, is not on the matter of positive analysis, but on the matter of normative analysis. For ease of reference, let me sketch out the main line of his argument. He starts with the axiom that consumers will act in their own best interest, given a particular state of knowledge. From this axiom, he concludes that if consumers change their behavior in response to an advertisement, they must be better off, at least in some statistically expected sense. A consumer may, on occasion, be fooled; but, on average, he will be better off. It follows next that the interests of sellers and consumers generally coincide; this is because both gain if and only if the consumer changes his behavior in response to the ad. Finally, as a result of this common interest, he concludes that sellers will be motivated to supply advertising in the cheapest possible way, taking into account both their own costs and the pain to consumers in viewing unwanted ads. In summary, those who benefit most from ads tend to get them and those who are most proficient in providing ads tend to send them.

Although there is some truth in each stage of the above argument, each also has potential flaws. First, the initial axiom may be wrong.

It is commonly believed, but nearly impossible to prove, that advertising acts in some insidious persuasive fashion that goes beyond the mere provision of knowledge. I have nothing new to add to this perennial topic of debate.

Secondly, the subsequent arguments depend on the assumption that the consumer has the freedom of choice to receive or not to receive promotional messages. This is true with respect to TV, radio, and most print advertising—the consumer can always shut off his TV—but it is not true with respect to billboards and door-to-door salesmen.

Third, the commonality of interest between seller and buyer extends only to information which would induce the buyer to purchase a particular seller's commodity. As a result, even if we assume that sellers do not lie or distort facts, they certainly do not have an incentive to present the whole truth in a form convenient to the buyer. The fundamental reason why this is true is not a property of advertising in particular, but rather a general characteristic of the economics of information.

There are two properties of information that limit the degree to which it can be bought and sold like any other commodity. One property, stressed by both Professors Telser and Porter, is that if one is purchasing information, one cannot ascertain its value before purchase. A more important property, to my mind, is the public good nature of information. Unlike the case of ordinary goods, the use of information by one individual may not reduce its usefulness to others. This fact makes it more difficult for a collector or disseminator of information to be adequately recompensed for his services. This is because once he gives or sells information to a few individuals, these individuals may in turn give or sell the same information to all other interested parties, thus undermining the market for the original supplier of information.

These arguments are well recognized when applied to the case of general scientific knowledge and technological innovation. Government officials sponsor research, enact patent laws, subsidize universities, and otherwise attempt to correct for the weak incentives present in the private market to develop information of this sort.

In the context of consumer goods industries, this line of argument would suggest that governments should either collect and disseminate information about common household goods or subsidize other endeavors of this nature, such as the publication of *Consumer Reports*. Instead of policing the advertising campaigns promoting leading pain-relievers, the Federal Trade Commission might conduct its own advertising campaign stressing such facts as (if I am correct) that all aspirin is alike, and that no other nonprescription pain-killer has been shown to be more effective than aspirin.

Now, once the government gets into an area like this, we have a whole new set of problems, which I do not want to discuss. This has been done in the morning session, and I would be needlessly repeating the arguments. But I do want to point out that the public good nature of information can be used as a justification for some of the forms of government intervention discussed earlier.

Turning now to Professor Porter, I find that I am very much in sympathy with the substance and approach of his paper, especially the first section. We need to think of markets not only in terms of demand characteristics and costs of production, but also in terms of the technology of information transfer. In this regard, the differences between the various forms of the media are very important.

In particular, I agree with Porter that interindustry studies of advertising are fraught with difficulty. The fact that industries with high reported profit rates tend to have high advertising to sales ratios does not imply any specific causal relationship between advertising and profits. At this level of aggregation, little of practical value is forthcoming. Even if it could be established beyond doubt that in some vague sense "imperfections" in the advertising market are responsible for "excessive" profits in certain industries, such a result would not have any clear policy implications. How would we know whether a proposed policy change would ameliorate or exacerbate the unspecified "imperfections"?

If, on the other hand, more detailed analysis were to establish, for example, that the difference in profit rates is attributable mainly to, say, the difference in network and spot TV advertising rates, then there would be considerable hope that specific policy proposals could be intelligently evaluated. Other work by Professor Porter points in this direction; and although I am by no means a partisan of his position, I think it deserves close attention.

Turning to the empirical side of Porter's paper, I find two aspects of his work impressive. The first is his success in locating and collecting a set of data that is not subject to the biases and difficulties inherent in the use of Census data, SEC data, and other sources often used in cross-industry studies. The second is the high values of R^2 that he obtains in his regressions.

If I have any criticism, it is that the sophistication and complexity of the theoretical part of his paper go far beyond what seems necessary to interpret the empirical results. For example, in the regressions of advertising/sales on sales, brands/sales, and product lines divided by sales, the positive coefficients may be interpreted simply as an indication that those firms whose brands or product lines are on a small scale need to use more expensive local or specialized media, and this is why their advertising to sale ratios are high. This one effect seems to explain nearly all of Porter's results. The fact that so simple an explanation goes as far as it does, however, must on balance be considered a virtue.

Julian L. Simon

My central comment bears on both Telser's and Porter's interesting papers as well as upon much other research on advertising: writers tend to discuss advertising mostly as a monolithic phenomenon. Thus, Telser's paper is titled "Towards a Theory of the Economics of Advertising," suggesting a single, all-embracing theory. And Porter seeks "an operational theory of the optimal level of advertising." (In the bodies of their papers, however, both Professor Telser and Professor Porter do attend to the variety of types of advertising.)

I wish to urge that instead of talking of advertising as a single phenomenon, we should consider various kinds of advertising separately. I believe this to be crucial in (1) preventing us from falling into error in our thinking about advertising; (2) keeping us from getting involved in fruitless arguments about whether Advertising with a capital A does or does not have the effect, say, of raising prices, when in fact one kind of advertising will show one effect and another kind of advertising will show another effect; and (3) pointing us toward the key issues in advertising. We ought to remember that the advertising in an industrial tool catalog has little in common with the television advertising for Tide.

One reason that talking about advertising as a single entity is misleading is that we inexorably think about *television* advertising, which really is quite unrepresentative of advertising as a whole. Thus, Telser concludes with the statement, "The market mechanism works with a powerful force to give the viewers the advertising they want at a negative price." That is a very interesting idea, and it has considerable truth for television advertising. But for the vast bulk of advertising, that observation does not fit.

Let us consider some figures: In 1975, television accounted for 19 percent of the $28 billion advertising in measured media plus "miscellaneous," and radio accounted for another 7 percent—in total, a quarter of the total measured media.[1] There is also much advertising *not* included in the $28 billion total—many brochures, packages, casual posters, window displays, university catalogs, and so on. And personal selling—which Telser properly considers part of the relevant universe of interest—is three or four times as much as all advertising. Television

[1] *Advertising Age*, December 29, 1975, p. 34.

and radio advertising therefore constitute perhaps 6 to 9 percent of all promotion. Hence, for *most* promotion it is not true that the receiver pays a negative price, even though it is true for television advertising. The newspaper advertising reader reads willingly, and he therefore pays a positive price in time, as does the reader of direct mail.

Again, my point is that TV advertising—which is often thought to represent all advertising—is a small and unrepresentative part of all promotion. Television advertising certainly is a legitimate subject for theorizing. But I believe that we should theorize about television advertising separately from other kinds of advertising.

Another drawback of talking about advertising monolithically is that it points us away from interesting and important policy issues. Television advertising is the least important kind of advertising economically, except for its role in supporting television. Whether TV advertising exists or does not exist affects practically nothing in the economy. But in contrast, the Supreme Court decision about drug advertising may be *very* important to consumers.[2] Yet one usually does not think about store window advertising of drugs when one thinks of Advertising with a capital A. And one certainly never thinks of classified advertising for jobs and employees, which is among the most important branches of advertising. A tax or other social decision that affects the quantity of classified advertising could be disastrous.

Another drawback of thinking about advertising as an entity, and then focusing on television advertising as representative, is that doing so draws our attention away from the romantic and economically exciting aspects of advertising—the promotion of new products. As Telser noted, products are advertised more when they are new than when they are old, because there is more news to convey about them when they are new. And this news can produce amazing results—as it did for Milton Reynolds when he introduced the ball-point pen to the United States after World War II. Without advertising, Reynolds's adventure would have been impossible—and ball-point pens would have taken much longer to become cheap and widely used. But this sort of advertising situation is neglected when we talk about advertising in general, and about TV advertising as its representative.

Turning to Professor Porter's paper, I am glad he studied differences in behavior among firms rather than differences among industries. I am convinced that trying to explain differences in advertising as a percentage of sales across various industries is mostly a waste of time because of the differences in the natures of products and situations.

---

[2] See Virginia State Board of Pharmacy v. Virginia Citizens Council, Inc., 425 U.S. 748 (1976).

Rather than trying to explain the *level* of advertising in one industry and another, it is much better to tackle the matter by asking how changes in demand and cost and number of entrants—over time or within the same industry—lead to changes in the level of advertising.

As to Professor Porter's finding that there is little or no relationship between sales and the advertising-to-sales ratio—I believe it. Looking at IRS data for sizes and classes of firms in all reported industries about twelve years ago, George Crain and I found a general lack of relationship.[3] In about half the industries, the relationship between sales and the advertising-to-sales ratio was positive, and in the other half of the industries the relationship was negative.

One reason why a relationship between a firm's sales and its advertising-to-sales ratio is not found may be the use of the advertising-to-sales ratio as a variable. I am inclined to believe that, in general, this ratio is not a meaningful measure of "advertising intensity" or of anything else, because of its systematic interaction with price and quality, which are almost always left out of the analyses.

Now two minor remarks:

(1) This part of the volume deals with advertising and the firm. Much of the empirical work on advertising has related the firm's characteristics to its advertising, especially when studying the effects of concentration. In my judgment this has been a mistake, because advertising works at the level of the *brand*, and many firms, such as liquor and cereal sellers, offer several brands (although apparently less so in the canned and frozen food industry studied by Porter). The observed relationships for firms and brands can be quite opposite; for example, in many markets the number of firms is decreasing while the number of brands is increasing. And I found that, in all the markets for which I could get data, the concentration in brand advertising was decreasing even though the concentration in firm advertising was increasing.[4] This suggests that advertising is not implicated in a trend toward firm concentration, and it illustrates the point that studies of advertising should tend to look at brand behavior rather than firm behavior.

(2) Both Telser and Porter mentioned returns to scale in advertising, and Telser suggested that the matter is in doubt. I do not agree. The studies surveyed in my 1970 book strongly support the proposition that there are no increasing returns or economies of scale.[5] The second advertisement does not pull as many responses as the first. A full page

---

[3] See Julian Simon, *Issues in the Economics of Advertising* (Chicago: University of Illinois Press, 1970), Appendix B.

[4] *Ibid.*, pp. 231-235.

[5] *Ibid.*, pp. 3-22.

ad does not produce twice as many sales as a half-page ad. Even allowing for discounts, the second $10,000 does not produce as many sales as the first $10,000. The effect is most pronounced where the data are best—in the mail-order business—where it was obvious to me when I had a mail-order business, just as it was to Shryer when he wrote about it at length and with great sophistication in 1912.[6]

In closing, I wish to repeat the plea that we study the various kinds of advertising separately, paying attention to the important theoretical and social differences among them. But I am enough of a realist about economic science to recognize that the intellectual excitement comes from broad propositions rather than from detailed truths and that this plea can therefore be at best a slight nudge.

Thomas A. Wilson

I shall first discuss Telser's theoretical paper, then review Porter's empirical work, and close with some speculations on the possible effects of the development of pay TV and the extension of cable TV.

I find Telser's analysis to be somewhat confused and inconsistent. The confusion in the paper is due to Telser's partly recognizing that advertising is, in an important sense, a joint product with the media content, while at the same time holding to his earlier view that advertising is a joint product with the advertised good. This inconsistent approach is a source of many difficulties. For example:

(1) Telser recognizes that the implicit price for advertising to the consumer is negative and equal to the subsidy to the media content. Yet he also states that the implicit price for advertising is positive and equal to the difference between the price of the advertised and unadvertised product.

(2) At various points Telser argues essentially that there is a derived demand for advertising from the buyers of the product—as if advertising were equivalent to an input required for production. Yet the usefulness of any information provided by advertising is *prior* to the purchase decision; hence the demand for advertising is not logically derived from a consumer's demand for the product.

(3) Telser states that an implication of his analysis is that repeat buyers get the product at the lower price. This does not appear to be the situation for most heavily advertised convenience goods. However,

[6] William A. Shryer, *Analytical Advertising* (Detroit: Business Service Corp., 1912).

Thomas A. Wilson was visiting professor of economics, University of California, Berkeley, at the time of the conference.

it would in any case indicate that advertising is a joint product with the advertised product only for new buyers.

Advertising and the advertising product are not in joint supply in the usual sense of that term, since there is no technical interdependence between the product and the advertising. They are also not in joint demand, since one can "purchase" the advertising (typically at a zero or negative price) without purchasing the product itself. The acquisition of information—of which advertising contributes a part—logically precedes the purchase decision; hence, advertising is an input into the information process before the purchase decision.

Advertising is a joint product, however, with the content of the advertising media, since there is a technical interdependence between advertising and the content of the carrying media. Because the consumer of the content of the media cannot easily avoid exposure to the advertising they are also a joint product on the demand side. An adequate theory of the economics of advertising must therefore recognize the existence of two separate but related markets—the market for advertising messages and the market for advertised products.

As Peter Steiner originally pointed out in discussing Telser's earlier paper on the "Supply and Demand for Advertising Messages,"[1] there are two relevant demand curves in the market for advertising messages—the implicit demand by the ultimate recipients of the messages, and the operational demand by the firms purchasing the messages. The fact that advertising is provided to the consumer at a negative price indicates that the volume of advertising exceeds what the consumer would freely choose at a zero price. While transaction costs may explain why producers rather than consumers pay for most advertisements, they do not explain why producers' demand for advertising at a positive price exceeds consumers' demand at a zero price.

Note that the subsidy involved is not simply the difference between the total costs of the media package including the advertising and the price paid by the consumer, nor the difference between the cost of the content and the price paid by the consumer (since the consumer may be prepared to pay something for the advertising). In the case of both print and broadcasting media, unallocable joint costs may be involved. Since print media are sold to consumers, it is not clear that all print media that carry advertising are necessarily subsidized by it. In the case of broadcasting media, however, where the consumer pays nothing for the package, there is clearly a subsidy involved.

---

[1] *American Economic Review*, vol. 56 (May 1966), pp. 457-466; see P. O. Steiner's comment on pp. 472-475. See also W. S. Comanor and T. A. Wilson, *Advertising and Market Power* (Cambridge: Harvard University Press, 1974), pp. 8-21.

Why is the producers' demand for advertising greater than what consumers would willingly choose to consume at a zero price? The following factors are relevant.

(1) The consumer takes into account the disutility associated with receiving advertising, whereas the producer may ignore it wholly or partly—for example, I may refuse to consume advertising at a zero price because of the time cost to me—but if it is intermixed with media content such that I must consume it in order to get the content (and have no option of buying the content directly), I will consume it and hence be more likely to purchase the producer's product. In other words, although there may be a positive benefit to the consumer from the message, it may be less than the disutility experienced by the consumer in receiving it. This effect reflects conditions in the market for advertising messages, due to monopoly power, legal restrictions, and technological conditions, that prevent perfect competition. In one important market—newspapers—the bulk of the markets in this country are monopolistic or duopolistic. In another market—television—legal restrictions and technical difficulties prevent the direct sale of the media content, and the limitation of the spectrum means that most markets are highly concentrated.

(2) The consumer will ex ante attach a lower value to his exposure to persuasive or misinformative advertising than will the producer. However, since this topic is covered in the part of this volume on advertising as information,[2] I will not consider it further, and hence will assume that advertising does convey information.

(3) The benefit to the advertiser depends on his price cost (excluding advertising) margins, and hence this benefit increases with the market power of the producers of the advertised product. If advertising increases attainable price cost margins, this reinforces the effect.

I conclude that the demand for advertising by producers is therefore not necessarily simply derived from consumers' demand for information. This would occur only where both the media and the product markets are sufficiently competitive (in the sense that price is equal to normal costs in the long run, and no legal restrictions are placed on product combinations and charges).

As noted earlier, there is little reason to suppose that all media markets are sufficiently competitive. What does the available empirical evidence indicate about the state of competition in product markets? In consumer goods markets, the majority of empirical studies confirm

---

[2] See, in particular, the papers by Phillip Nelson and Sherwin Rosen and the comments by Yehuda Kotowitz in this volume.

the hypothesis, developed in the seminal work of Joe Bain,[3] that intensive advertising is an important source of entry barriers in a number of industries. This issue is so important to the analysis that I will briefly note the more pertinent studies.

The main objection to the argument that the strong positive empirical relationship between advertising and rates of return indicates that advertising is a source of market power, is that this relationship could be a mere reflection of accounting biases—a statistical artifact attributable to the prevalence of inappropriate accounting practices. This view persists[4] despite evidence that adjusted rates of return (to correct for these biases) continue to show a strong positive relationship with advertising, and other more direct evidence (not based on rates of return analysis) that advertising is a deterrent to new entrants. In the former category I refer to the studies by Weiss,[5] and to the relevant chapter in the recent book by Comanor and myself.[6]

Perhaps the studies that analyze entry more directly are as important as these analyses utilizing adjusted rates of return. In a recent paper, Orr[7] found that net rates of entry into Canadian manufacturing industries were significantly and negatively influenced by advertising intensity and other entry barrier variables derived from Bain's analysis. In another recent paper, Stonebraker[8] found that entry risk was an important determinant of profitability and that entry risk was positively related to advertising intensity. We therefore conclude that the available evidence is more consistent with the hypothesis that advertising contributes to entry barriers than with the alternative hypothesis that there is no effect.[9]

---

[3] J. S. Bain, *Barriers to New Competition* (Cambridge: Harvard University Press, 1956).

[4] See, for example, Yale Brozen, "Entry Barriers: Advertising and Product Differentiation," in H. J. Goldschmid et al., eds., *Industrial Concentration: The New Learning* (Boston: Little, Brown & Co., 1974), pp. 115-137. See also the comments by Harold Demsetz, in Part Four of this volume.

[5] L. W. Weiss, "Advertising, Profits, and Corporate Taxes," *Review of Economics and Statistics*, vol. 51 (November 1969), pp. 421-429.

[6] Comanor and Wilson, *Advertising and Market Power*, pp. 169-195.

[7] Dale Orr, "The Determinants of Entry: A Study of the Canadian Manufacturing Industries," *Review of Economics and Statistics*, vol. 56 (February 1974), pp. 58-66.

[8] R. J. Stonebraker, "Corporate Profits and the Risk of Entry," *Review of Economics and Statistics*, vol. 58 (February 1976), pp. 33-39.

[9] Two recent papers by Bloch and Ayanian reach opposite conclusions. See H. Bloch, "Advertising and Profitability: A Reappraisal," *Journal of Political Economy*, vol. 82 (March/April 1974), 267-286; R. Ayanian, "Advertising and Rate of Return," *Journal of Law and Economics*, vol. 18 (October 1975), pp. 479-506. However, the empirical results reported in both of these papers are vitiated by the use of inappropriate techniques to estimate the depreciation rates for advertising investments.

Because of monopoly conditions in some media markets and legal restrictions in others, and because of evidence that advertising is an important source of entry barriers in product markets, we can therefore conclude that neither requirement for a one-to-one correspondence of the two demand curves in the market for advertising messages holds—in other words, the producers' demand curve cannot be derived directly from the consumers' demand curve for information without additional information on competitive conditions in the product and media markets.

The analyses of both Porter and Telser suggest that the choice of media and the relative importance of advertising and other methods of marketing and promotion will vary greatly from product to product. The advantages of direct selling for products where buyers are few and readily identified should mean less relative reliance on advertising in those markets. The advantages of print media, with their greater flexibility (in terms of cost) and selectivity should lead them to be the preferred marketing media for firms with specialized products, for firms that are smaller, and for firms that must convey a great deal of information in their ads (such as detailed price information or complex product specifications). Broadcast media, and particularly network TV, have advantages for established or new brands in broad national markets, and for larger firms because of the larger threshold costs involved in using these media.

These hypotheses are borne out in Porter's empirical work on the canned and frozen food industry. Porter finds that the proportion of advertising accounted for by network TV is significantly related to size, as is the percentage devoted to spot TV.[10] New product introduction also appears positively related to the use of network TV advertising —while not statistically significant at conventional levels, the odds on a positive effect are better than twenty-to-one. Newspaper advertising, on the other hand, is significantly and negatively related to firm size, and positively related to the breadth of the product line.

An unresolved question in Porter's empirical work is whether the firm size is really a masked geographic scale effect—in other words, is there a size effect per se or an apparent size effect because large and small firms sell in different geographic markets (national versus regional or local)?

A similar issue is whether the type of products sold varies systematically with size—for example, small firms may tend to specialize in canned specialty foods. In this case the size effect could be a proxy

---

[10] While Porter does not report separate equations for spot TV, the above conclusion may be inferred from the equations for magazine advertising and magazine advertising combined with spot TV.

for product mix effect. Porter controls for overall breadth of product line, but not for the variation of the composition of the product line. These results—while hardly definitive in view of the size and scope of the sample—are nevertheless sufficiently interesting to make one hope that Porter and others will test these hypotheses using data for other firms and other industries.

Let me now consider the effects of existing commercial TV arrangements on TV content and on the characteristics of the market for TV advertising. I will also speculate on the effects of development of pay TV and the extension of cable TV, assuming that FCC regulations do not strangle pay TV at birth and cable TV in its infancy.

The present arrangements preclude the use of TV to contact specialized audiences because of the high fixed cost of TV time, the finiteness of the spectrum, and the inability to charge the specialized audience for any portion of these costs. Hence, programming under present commercial TV arrangements of necessity has to try to attract as broad an audience as possible. This is in contrast to the situation in the printed media, where diverse magazines thrive in the marketplace by catering to different audiences and by varying the relative importance of their user charges. It is also in dramatic contrast to movie theaters where the full cost of the entertainment is paid by the consumer and where advertising, as Telser correctly points out, is mainly used to promote other movies.

The consequence of the present arrangements is that TV advertising involves high threshold costs, largely precluding its use by smaller firms or firms in specialized markets. Hence, TV advertising is dominated by the advertising for broad market convenience goods such as detergents, headache and other bodily remedies, convenience foods, cosmetics, and so on.

Indeed, we could conclude that, at present, the market for TV messages works powerfully to give consumers advertising that they do *not* want at a zero price. It does this through the heavy subsidization of the media content. In the case of TV, the requirement of a tied sale, with no charge to the consumer, leads to oversubsidization by advertisers and precludes specialty programming. As demonstrated by Porter here and in another recent paper,[11] large threshold costs are imposed on advertisers using these media. Pay TV would permit a greater variety of programming with mixtures of user charges—varying from the present zero charge (with advertising carefully mixed with the media content) to partial charges with either less or more specialized advertising, to

[11] Michael E. Porter, "Interbrand Choice, Media Mix and Market Performance," *American Economic Review*, vol. 66 (May 1976), pp. 398-406.

100 percent user charges. Thus, and not suprisingly, the removal of legal barriers and the implementation of technological innovations would enable the market to perform better. Whether this would be sufficient to reduce significantly the anticompetitive effects of large-scale advertising by established producers, as revealed in the empirical studies cited earlier, remains to be seen, and clearly must be left to future researchers to resolve.

PART THREE

ADVERTISING AS INFORMATION

ADVERTISING AS INFORMATION ONCE MORE

Phillip Nelson

The central proposition of an article I wrote in 1974 on advertising as information [1] was that advertising was simply information—that all the major features of advertising behavior could be understood in terms of advertising's information function. The article has not produced an endless stream of reformed, ex-advertising haters. The Federal Trade Commission still operates inconsistently with that proposition. For example, a recent FTC ruling requires celebrity endorsers of a brand actually to use the brand.[2] Evidently my case was not sufficiently convincing. It is the purpose of this paper to provide a more convincing case—theoretically and empirically—for the position that advertising is information.

Most people are willing to accept the proposition that advertising contains information about qualities, such as price or the way a dress looks, that a consumer can determine before his purchase of a brand—in my terminology, search qualities. There is no similar agreement about advertising's information role for qualities, such as the taste of a brand of tuna fish, that a consumer discovers only by actually purchasing and trying out a brand—experience qualities, I call them. Most economists share my skepticism about the credibility of experience good advertising. If believed, advertisers would have an incentive to extol the virtues of their brand whether or not those virtues exist. As a result, the advertising message for experience qualities can contain little information that is believable.

Many economists, however, balk at my contention that, even for experience qualities, advertising contains information—namely, the fact that the brand does advertise. This information is useful, since the more heavily a brand advertises, the more likely it is to be a better buy. (I call this indirect information in contrast to the direct information that is contained in the advertising messages for search qualities.) A celebrity endorsement is simply an efficient way to get consumers to remember

1 Phillip Nelson, "Advertising as Information," *Journal of Political Economy*, vol. 81, no. 4 (July/August 1974), pp. 729-754.

2 Federal Trade Commission, "Guides Concerning Use of Endorsements and Testimonials in Advertising," 16 CFR Part 255.

that a brand advertised or to look at the advertisement in the first place. Whether advertising contains useful indirect information or not is the issue. Are the "better" buys more heavily advertised than the "worse" buys?

Advertising and "P^*"

Before tackling that question a preliminary problem must be faced. What does one mean by "better" buys, given variations in the quality of products and in consumer tastes? I skirt this problem by breaking it into two parts. First, I assume that each consumer has an identical utility function, that is, an identical ordering of his preferences over the various goods that he may consume. There is, on this assumption, some utility-corrected price, P^*, that each consumer is willing to pay for a good at a given level of utility or satisfaction. The consumer's preferences for some goods may or may not depend in part on the quantity of other goods he consumes. Under one set of restrictions that might be imposed on his utility function, his consumption of one good will leave his preferences for other goods unchanged (so that P^* becomes a measure of price per unit of utility received). It is possible to avoid these restrictions but still determine how advertising affects P^* and, therefore, whether the most heavily advertised goods are the best buys.

To analyze the effect of advertising on P^* it is necessary to make the problem mathematically tractable. To do so I assume a particular demand function, the "translog" demand function. This function has the advantage of being fairly general and still easy to work with. In Appendix A the translog demand function is rigorously defined, and the relationship between advertising and P^* derived. There it is shown, roughly speaking, that if there are no economies of scale in advertising (that is, if given percentage increases in advertising do not yield larger percentage increases in demand for the advertised products), then advertising expenditures will be negatively related to P^*. This conclusion depends on certain other conditions as well, but, as Appendix A shows, these other conditions are likely to be satisfied. Even if they are not satisfied, their net effect is not likely to reverse the predicted relationship between advertising expenditures and P^*.

Quantity Demanded and P^*. Consider the *mutatis mutandis* demand curve: the relationship of quantity to P^* when the firm varies advertising expenditures with price in such a way as to maximize profits.[3] In con-

[3] Harold Demsetz, "The Nature of Equilibrium in Monopolistic Competition," *Journal of Political Economy*, vol. 67, no. 1 (February 1959), pp. 22-30.

trast to the ordinary demand curve, the *mutatis mutandis* demand curve is not everywhere negatively sloped. For this curve there is a negative relationship between quantity and P^* only when advertising expenditures are negatively related to P^*—roughly when there are no economies of scale in advertising (with economies of scale a large-selling brand increases the quantity demanded so much more efficiently by increasing its advertising expenditures that it finds it pays actually to increase its P^* relative to the smaller selling brands).[4] Hence, a demonstration that the *mutatis mutandis* demand curve is negatively sloped would be a demonstration that advertising and P^* are negatively related.

In "Advertising as Information" I made an incomplete case for the negative relationship between P^* and quantity. I showed, with the help of a note by Richard Schmalensee,[5] that with zero economic profits the *mutatis mutandis* demand curve must be negatively sloped. But the zero profit condition is not expected to hold over the whole range of observed quantities. Some firms are likely to have lower costs in producing what consumers wish than other firms. These firms with the lower costs are likely to be earning positive profits. What one can reasonably assume, however, is that the high cost producers are earning zero profits, so that the *mutatis mutandis* demand curve is negatively

---

[4] It would appear from Appendix A (equation A.10) that this is one other condition that will generate a negatively sloped *mutatis mutandis* demand curve, that is, when the advertising elasticity of demand ϵ_A is greater than the price of elasticity of demand ϵ_P (or more precisely if the numerator of equation (A.10) is positive. Since one expects α_3, α_4, and α_5 to be negative, ϵ_A has to be greater than ϵ_P for the numerator to be positive. However, the demand function of Appendix A merely shows the maximum quantity demanded that can be generated by a profit-maximizing combination of price and volume of advertising. It does not specify whether any given quantity so generated is consistent with long-run equilibrium. That latter requirement places additional constraints on the Appendix A equation. In particular the condition $\epsilon_A > \epsilon_P$ cannot hold in the long run. As text equation (1) shows, $\epsilon_A > \epsilon_P$ implies an advertising-to-sales ratio greater than one. To say the least, this would imply negative economic profits, a state of the world that cannot persist.

This argument would be decisive if we were absolutely sure that the sum of the effects of α_3, α_4, and α_5 was negative. No such certainty exists in economics. However, even if the sum of the α's effect was positive, we could reject the hypothesis that $\frac{dlnA}{dlnP}$ is positive when $\frac{dlnQ}{dlnP}$ is negative. That hypothesis implies that $\frac{dlnQ}{dlnA}$ is negative.

$$\frac{dlnQ}{dlnA} = \frac{dlnQ}{dlnP} \cdot \frac{dlnP}{dlnA}$$

A positive $\frac{dlnP}{dlnA}$ and a negative $\frac{dlnQ}{dlnP}$ implies a negative $\frac{dlnQ}{dlnA}$. But there is overwhelming evidence for a positive relationship between quantity and advertising.

[5] Richard Schmalensee, "A Note on Monopolistic Competition and Excess Capacity," *Journal of Political Economy*, vol. 80 (May/June 1972), pp. 586-591.

sloped at the lower end of observed quantites for the industry. (The low-cost producers tend to produce more than high-cost producers because a downward shift in the marginal cost curve results in an increase in production.)

What happens to this demand curve for larger quantities? The most obvious force at work will tend to make for a more negative relationship between P^* and quantity as quantity increases. One expects the quantity elasticity of demand with respect to advertising to decrease with increases in advertising. This is simply applying the general view with respect to scale economies to the case of advertising expenditures: that scale economies are gradually exhausted as firm size grows. In the specific case of advertising the payoff for switching to cheaper media as the size of markets grows will tend to be greater for the smaller brands. The smaller the advertising elasticity, the more negative the slope of the *mutatis mutandis* demand curve. Hence the *mutatis mutandis* demand curve is probably going to be more negatively sloped in the range beyond the zero profit equilibrium.[6]

[6] It is conceivable that other conditions would produce a positive relationship between P^* and quantity at a point sufficiently removed from the zero profit equilibrium position, though the available evidence suggests that these conditions are unlikely to be found: advertising-to-sales ratios within an industry neither systematically increase nor decrease with increases in brand size. See, for example, Julian Simon, *Issues in the Economics of Advertising* (Urbana: University of Illinois Press, 1970). If advertising-to-sales ratios are constant across brand sizes, the *mutatis mutandis* demand curve, once negatively sloped, cannot become positively sloped. As Schmalensee shows, a constant advertising/sales ratio implies a constant ratio between the quantity elasticity with respect to advertising and the quantity elasticity with respect to price. Suppose—contrary to what I want to prove—the *mutatis mutandis* demand curve began to slope upward after it sloped downward. Then there will be a set of pairs of points. Within each pair the points will differ in quantity demanded and in advertising expenditures but will have the same P^*. Take any of these pairs. Since price is the same for the two points, changes in ϵ_A and the price elasticity ϵ_P between the two points can occur only through changes in advertising expenditures. Assume the ratio of $\frac{\epsilon_A}{\epsilon_P}$ to be the same for the two points. Then the percentage change in ϵ_A between the two points must equal the percentage change in ϵ_P between the two points, $\frac{\Delta\epsilon_P}{\epsilon_P} = \frac{\Delta\epsilon_A}{\epsilon_A}$. From Appendix A equations (A.2 and A.3), this implies: $\frac{2\alpha_5}{\epsilon_A} = \frac{\alpha_3}{\epsilon_P}$. But if that condition holds the denominator of $\frac{dlnQ}{dlnP}$ (see equation A.10) is larger at the point in the pair associated with the larger quantity. Instead of switching to a negative sign, the denominator is a larger positive number because ϵ_A will be smaller at the point with higher advertising expenditures. Therefore, there cannot be a positively sloped portion of the *mutatis mutandis* demand curve following a negatively sloped portion. Even with the larger brands earning positive profits, one expects the *mutatis mutandis* demand curve to be negatively sloped, at least from the point of zero profits on. This should cover the bulk of brand choices facing the consumer.

How can one test the proposition that the *mutatis mutandis* demand curve is negatively sloped? A seemingly insuperable problem is involved in measuring P^*. There is no measure of utility that would allow one to construct a utility-corrected measure of price. This clearly prohibits a meaningful cross-sectional regression between price and quantity across different brands for a given product. Substantial uncontrolled quality variation would be involved. However, the time series regression of quantity on price for a given brand can be meaningful. Just choose a reasonably short time period during which no substantial product innovations took place. Under these conditions the brand's utility relative to other brands of the good probably has only a modest variation. To the extent that there is such variation it would bias regressions of quantity on price toward zero.

A regression of quantity on price that does not control for advertising or any other nonprice determinant of the quantity demanded is an estimate of the *mutatis mutandis* demand curve. For such a regression advertising is not held constant, but is allowed to adjust to price. If one included advertising as an additional variable, one would be estimating the ordinary demand curve.

Lester Telser provides estimates of the average price elasticity of the *mutatis mutandis* demand curve for four food commodities during the period 1955–1957: orange juice—5.7; regular coffee—3.7; instant coffee—5.2; margarine—3.0. Telser observed twenty-three individual brands with negative signs, and one with a positive sign.[7] The probability that this result could be produced by chance is less than .0001. The assumption that utility is constant is reasonable, given this time period and these products.[8]

The a priori case developed in the previous pages for a negative relationship between advertising and P^* seems fairly strong: advertising will be negatively related to P^* unless (roughly speaking) there are increasing returns to scale in advertising expenditures.

---

[7] Lester Telser, "The Demand for Branded Goods as Estimated from Consumer Panel Data," *Review of Economics and Statistics*, vol. 44 (April 1962), pp. 300-324.

[8] One problem with these estimates arises from their virtue—that utility is being held constant. Response to price holding utility constant need not be the same as response to P^*. Since information about utility is so much more difficult for the consumer to obtain than information about price, the market response to the two need not be the same. However, for our purpose this is no serious problem. While the difference between price and P^* can affect the magnitude of the estimated elasticity, it cannot affect the sign of the estimate. That sign depends on the advertising elasticity, not on the price elasticity. (See Appendix A, equation A.10.) Thus the Telser estimates are evidence that the *mutatis mutandis* demand curve is negatively sloped.

Are There Increasing Returns? William Comanor and Thomas Wilson certainly think so.[9] Direct tests for scale economies are likely to be highly unsatisfactory,[10] but one may obtain an indirect estimate of the advertising elasticity or examine certain other implications of increasing returns to scale in advertising.

The advertising elasticity is related to P^* elasticity by the following equation:

$$\epsilon_A = \epsilon_P \cdot \frac{A}{S} \tag{1}$$

where ϵ_A = advertising elasticity
ϵ_P = price elasticity
$\frac{A}{S}$ = the advertising/sales ratio

Given knowledge of the advertising/sales ratio, one can move from estimates of the price elasticity to estimates of advertising elasticity.[11] The real problem with using equation (1) to estimate advertising elasticities is that, as far as I know, Telser's work provides the only study of the price-quantity relationship on the brand level.[12] His price elasticity refers to a *mutatis mutandis* demand curve. ϵ_P in equation (1) is the price elasticity of the ordinary demand curve. As long as Telser's estimates are significantly negative, however, his elasticity is an upward biased estimate (in absolute terms) of ϵ_P.[13]

---

[9] William Comanor and Thomas Wilson, "Advertising, Market Structure, and Performance," *Review of Economics and Statistics*, vol. 49, no. 4 (November 1967), pp. 423-440.

[10] There is a serious simultaneous equation problem involved in the advertising/sales relationship. On the brand level, I know of no study that has overcome this difficulty.

[11] Of course, the former estimates are not without their simultaneous equation problem as well, but that bias should not be very serious in this case. It is not unreasonable to believe that the pattern of brand price changes does not originate primarily from shifts in the demand curve. Shifts in the demand curve result in changes in price only when marginal costs are not constant. If shifts in the demand curve were the dominant force at work, one would anticipate a significant trend in prices of a brand relative to the industry price as a brand gradually became more or less popular. The commodities for which brand price elasticities are available would not be expected to have wildly fluctuating popularity in demand. For the one brand for which Telser provides the evidence, the relative price of the brand had no apparent trend.

[12] Telser, "The Demand for Branded Goods," pp. 300-324.

[13] If the *mutatis mutandis* demand curve is negatively sloped, advertising is negatively related to price. We know it is positively related to quantity. Hence the expected value of the regression of quantity on price excluding advertising as a variable should have a larger negative value than the regression coefficient of the price term when advertising is included. Another source of upward bias in Telser's estimates is that, whereas ϵ_P refers to P^*, Telser's estimates were made in terms of price. When a consumer has no information about utility other than price, one

The IRS industrial category that contains Telser's products is miscellaneous foods, whose advertising/sales ratio was .041 in 1957.[14] Using the average of Telser's elasticities (4.4), the estimated advertising elasticity for foods is .18. Even if one uses the highest advertising/sales ratio for 1957—perfumes at .147—and assumes that the appropriate price elasticity is 4.4, the resulting estimate of the advertising elasticity is still less than 1; it equals .65.

One would expect high advertising/sales ratios to be associated with low price elasticities, whether or not advertising creates monopoly power. The evidence supports such expectations.[15] In consequence the .65 probably grossly overstates the advertising elasticity for perfumes, and this is our highest estimate. Table 1 records the results of using the procedure for all IRS industries.

Another approach to the issue of economies of scale in advertising examines the implications of such a phenomenon for the organization of industry. I ask only whether economies of scale in advertising exist over the range of actual output or not. A firm will decide to produce at an output level where there are economies of scale in advertising only if marginal nonadvertising costs (which include all costs of production and distribution other than direct outlays on advertising) are rising.[16]

does not expect any systematic relationship between price and quantity. When a consumer knows the utility, one would expect the same elasticity with respect to price and P^*. However, in the case of price variation for a brand over time, the consumer is in a position to get some information about utility without directly experimenting. He might know previous prices. (It is not surprising that firms frequently quote previous prices on a brand if the current price is lower.) This additional source of information should make consumers more responsive to price over time than to P^*, when P^* varies across brands.

I suspect these upward biases outweigh the downward simultaneous equation bias.

14 Lester Telser, "Advertising and Competition," *Journal of Political Economy*, vol. 72, no. 6 (December 1964), pp. 537-562.

15 Phillip Nelson, "Consumer Information and Advertising," in M. Galatin and R. Leiter, eds., *Economics of Information* (New York: Cyrco Press, forthcoming).

16 A necessary condition for profit maximization is that the second derivative of profits with respect to advertising, holding price constant, be negative.

$$\begin{aligned} \Pi &= PQ - C(Q) - A \\ \Pi'_A &= [P - C'_Q]\, Q'_A - 1 \\ \Pi''_A &= [P - C'_Q] Q''_A - C''_Q (Q'_A)^2 \end{aligned}$$

where Π = profits, $C(Q)$ = cost function, $'$ indicates the first partial derivative, and $''$ indicates the second partial derivative.

Π''_A is negative only if Q''_A is negative or C''_Q is positive. In the notation of the Appendix

$$Q''_A = \frac{Q}{A^2} \left[\epsilon_A (\epsilon_A - 1) + 2\alpha_5\right]$$

One does expect α_5 to be negative, but if (as seems reasonable) its magnitude is small compared to ϵ_A, an ϵ_A greater than 1 will "probably" generate a positive Q''_A.

Table 1
ADVERTISING ELASTICITIES OF DEMAND, 1957

Appliances	.14	Liquor	.11
Bakery	.12	Meats	.03
Beer	.30	Men's Clothing	.04
Books	.12	Millinery	.01
Carpets	.09	Miscellaneous Apparel	.05
Cereals	.21	Miscellaneous Foods	.18
Cigars	.10	Motor Parts	.03
Clocks and Watches	.25	Motor Vehicles	.04
Communications Equipment	.09	Motorcycles	.05
Confectionery	.16	Other Tobacco	.24
Costume Jewelry	.11	Paints	.06
Dairy Products	.08	Perfume	.65
Drugs	.45	Periodicals	.01
Footwear	.06	Petroleum Refining	.02
Furniture	.06	Professional and Scientific Instruments	.09
Furs	.04	Soaps	.35
Grain Mill Products	.07	Sugar	.01
Hats	.09	Tires	.06
Jewelry	.10	Wine	.19
Knit Goods	.05	Women's Clothing	.06
Leather Goods	.05		

Note: Calculated from equation (1), above, p. 138.

These other marginal costs can rise only if managerial diseconomies of scale outweigh the other possible economies of scale, since managerial diseconomies are the sole source of diseconomies of scale for nonadvertising costs. If, indeed, these other marginal costs are rising and the marginal advertising costs are falling, firms have an incentive to make firm size with respect to advertising larger and firm size for all other purposes smaller. This can be achieved by having several firms produce the same brand with these firms sharing the advertising costs. Something like this occurs in the case of franchise dealers such as McDonald's fast service restaurants. Another quasi-example is farmer cooperatives such as Sunkist Oranges. If there were no relationship between the advertising and other functions of the firm this process could be continued until there were no diseconomies of scale for the production and distribution functions of the firm. But there is a relationship between the two functions. Advertising McDonald's hamburgers would not be very useful unless it were a fairly standardized product. So the advertising unit requires a quality control unit, either by controlling the inputs that go into a McDonald's hamburger or by inspecting the operation of the individual units, or both. In consequence not all diseconomies of scale for other functions can be eliminated by reducing firm size for these other functions.

The special distribution of multifirm brands is evidence that either diseconomies of scale in other functions are limited to special areas or the quality control problem is very serious. The evidence shows only that there are diseconomies of scale in increasing the number of retail units managed by a single firm and that there are diseconomies of scale in agricultural production. Neither case is important for the standard advertised brand.

One can argue that the problem of quality control increases the cost of creating multifirm brands in the face of diseconomies of scale in other firm functions. (To argue simultaneously that advertising is brainwashing and independent of brand quality is to tread on slippery ground.) That same argument cannot be used to explain the opposite phenomenon: the multibrand firm. Suppose a firm were producing two different brands in the strongest sense of different brands: that consumers are unaware that the same company is producing both. Then the standard sources of possible scale economies in advertising will not operate as the company increases the number of brands it produces beyond one. There will not be a greater number of potential customers who can respond to the advertisement of either brand; the reputability or desirability of the product cannot increase with increases in the number of brands.

Another frequently mentioned source of scale economies is increased market power in the advertising market. It is alleged that there are volume discounts in television advertising. If this were so, it would appear that a multibrand company could get larger discounts than a single brand company, holding brand size constant.

The best empirical evidence suggests that there are no volume discounts in television advertising.[17] Even if there were, the volume discounts could not generate a multibrand company in the face of any other source of diseconomies of scale. There is a simple way for firms to take advantage of any volume discount without themselves growing—through their advertising agency. Firms could easily pool their resources through their advertising agencies to take advantage of them. The most

[17] James Ferguson, *Advertising and Competition: Theory, Measurement, Fact* (Cambridge, Mass.: Ballinger Publishing Company, 1974), p. 78; David Blank, "Television Advertising: The Great Discount Illusion, or Tonypandy Revisited," *Journal of Business*, vol. 41 (January 1968) pp. 10-38.

convincing evidence that power in the advertising market is not the reason for multibrand firms is the opposite behavior of many of these firms. Many firms use different advertising agencies for different brands. Under these circumstances there can be no power vis-à-vis the television industry in having more than one brand.

It seems fairly clear, then, that there cannot be economies of scale in advertising when one increases firm size by increasing the number of distinct brands. But one would expect diseconomies of scale for the other firm functions as the firm increased the number of brands, if these diseconomies of scale operated when the firm increased brand size. The source of such diseconomies is the managerial problem. If management is finding it difficult to coordinate activities at the brand level, it would appear likely that the addition of another brand would pose additional managerial burdens. It is true that the coordination problem is different in the two cases. There are greater possibilities of decentralization between brands than within brands. But it is also true that the standard source of economies of scale in production and distribution would operate more intensively within brands than between brands. Two brands are likely to require different production processes and, sometimes, somewhat different distribution patterns. To the extent that the firm takes advantage of possible distribution and production economies for more than one brand, decentralization by brand must be reduced. In short, the existence of multibrand firms is evidence—albeit imperfect—of economies of scale in nonadvertising costs.[18]

The multibrand firm is not just a rare exception to the rule of one brand for one firm. For most of the industries I examined, it is the dominant pattern. The results are presented in Table 2.[19]

---

[18] It is evidence that is in part self-destructive. The addition of brands motivated by economies of scale reduces these economies as far as any one brand is concerned. One would not expect the reduction to be complete. Even if it were, one would not expect this addition of brands to yield increasing marginal costs for the functions of a firm other than advertising.

[19] Data on sales by brand and company are generally not available. What I used instead were data on advertising expenditures in six media (magazines, newspaper supplements, national television, spot television, national radio, and outdoor advertising). Given the relative stability of the advertising-to-sales ratio discovered in other data, advertising expenditures should serve as an acceptable proxy for sales. The real problem with the data I used is that the brand by company data are given only within an industry, so that I had to use my general knowledge to identify some multibrand firms. There are probably other multibrand firms that have brands scattered in different industrial categories, so I have understated the number of multibrand firms by this procedure. I have used a broad definition of brand. All products with the same key word in the brand title are called the same brand. This eliminates any reasonable crossover from the advertising of one brand to another. For example, I have included Seagram's Gin and Seagram's Whiskey as the same brand, but have maintained that both are a different brand from Four Roses. This decision tends to understate the appropriate number of brands.

Table 2

MULTIBRAND FIRMS ADVERTISING AS A PERCENT OF THE TOTAL BY SELECTED INDUSTRY, 1972

Cigarettes	.9996
Cigars	.94
Dental Goods	.998
Furniture	.39
Laundry Equipment	.60
Liquor	.91
Perfumes	.76
Sauces, Gravies and Dips	.88
Shoes, Regular and Casual	.77
Shortenings and Oil	.90

Source: Leading National Advertisers, *National Advertising Investments*, 1972.

Shifts in Demand. Thus far this analysis has assumed that the variation in demand for brands has been generated by movements along a demand curve with both P^* and advertising varying. Variation in demand can also be generated by shifts in the demand curve. An outward shift in the demand curve will almost always produce an increase in advertising.[20] But what does that outward shift do to P^*? Only by answering that question can one determine what these shifts do to the relation between advertising and P^*.

One reason for shifts in demand curves is variation in tastes among consumers. Some brands will specialize in satisfying one set of consumer tastes while other brands specialize in satisfying other sets of consumer tastes. One expects the brand specializing in the tastes of the larger group of consumers to have the larger demand. This statement is not as self-evident as it appears on the surface. A greater demand can be satisfied either by a larger number of brands or by greater size per brand or by both. There is a tendency for both to go up as demand increases. This tendency has been confirmed between industries.[21] One would expect the same phenomenon to operate within an industry. As far as this source of variation in demand is concerned, an average con-

[20] In the Appendix A notation if the shift in the demand curve is an upward shift in α_0 (a multiplicative shift), the marginal product of advertising is increased at any level of advertising expenditure. If, on the other hand, the shift is an additive shift, there is no change in the level of advertising. Most of the forces I examine yield the multiplicative shift. I do examine one possible case of the linear shift.

[21] Gideon Rosenbluth, *Concentration in Canadian Manufacturing Industries* (Princeton, New Jersey: Princeton University Press, 1957).

sumer can predict that he will be better off trying the more heavily advertised brand. In other words, there will be a negative relation between advertising and utility-corrected price, where utility is now measured by the average utility of consumers.

The other major source of shifting demand curves is age of the brand. Part of the difference in demand by age is properly handled by treating advertising as a stock rather than a flow. But the appropriate stock concept is different from the point of view of the firm and the individual consumer. The individual consumer responds to the quantity of remembered advertising messages—that is, to the endorsement implied by heavy advertising—and this is the stock of advertising from his point of view. The firm, on the other hand, must add a measure of the number of direct and indirect repeat purchasers to the number of remembered advertising messages in order to compute the stock of advertising from its point of view. (The indirect repeat purchasers are those who respond to the recommendations of relatives and friends who were either directly or indirectly induced to try the brand by advertising.) Assuming that the advertising stock is defined from the individual consumer's point of view (that is, as the number of remembered messages), increases in the age of the brand will cause shifts in the demand curve by increasing the number of consumers who are directly or indirectly repeat purchasers of a brand. If the number of repeat purchasers is independent of the stock of advertising, then the increase in demand with age will have no impact on the volume of this stock. Whatever the impact on P^* of this increase, it produces no relationship between advertising and P^*.

However, one expects a positive relationship between number of repeat purchases and the stock of advertising. A consumer is more likely to remember that he tried an advertised rather than an unadvertised brand, so he is more likely to repurchase the former than the latter.[22] In consequence, the shift in the demand curve with age of brand increases the advertising stock by increasing the marginal product of advertising at any given level. The larger the number of potential repeat purchasers (those who would repurchase if their memory were jogged), the greater the advertising expenditure, holding the number of customers trying the brand for the first time constant. But this group of repeat purchasers will be greater the lower P^* when their last experiment took place. In consequence a negative relationship between advertising and P^* will be generated because one expects a positive correlation in P^*s period to period. In other words, the shift in the

[22] Nelson, "Advertising as Information," pp. 753-754.

demand curve with age of firm is a greater shift for firms that previously charged low P^*s. These will also be the firms that probably charge low current P^*s, because their utility-corrected costs are lower.

In addition to these effects of shifts in the demand curve that are generated by the particular source of the shift, there is a more general impact. Consider the relationship,

$$P^* = \frac{MC^*}{1 - \frac{1}{\epsilon_P}} \tag{2}$$

where MC^* = a utility corrected marginal production cost, where marginal costs are defined net of advertising, and ϵ_P = the elasticity of demand (in absolute terms) in the ordinary demand curve.

P^* will tend to go up or down or stay the same with outward shifts in the demand curve when MC^* is correspondingly rising, falling, or constant. As we saw earlier, the dominance of the multibrand firm strongly suggests that MC^* is not rising over the range of firm output. Hence P^* tends to remain constant or decline with outward shifts in the demand curve.

The consequences of variation in the elasticity of demand are not so unambiguous. A growth in brand size, *ceteris paribus*, will tend to give the firm a larger share of the market with a possible consequent reduction in the elasticity of demand. But all the other forces we have considered tend to increase demand elasticity with increases in brand size. If the larger brand sizes are generated by a higher portion of repeat purchasers, larger brand sizes are associated with higher demand elasticities. In the case of experience goods, the only consumers who can assess the utility of the good are those who have experienced the good or have been advised by others. Hence their demand curves are necessarily more elastic than those who are trying the brand for the first time.

If the larger brand size is generated by being in a subindustry with more potential customers, then the demand curve will be more elastic the larger the size of the brand. The larger sized brands will have more close substitutes than the smaller sized brands. It is not clear which of these forces will dominate in determining the elasticity of demand.

The actual quantities produced will be the result of some combination of movements along a demand curve and shifts in the demand curve. The former clearly produces a negative association between advertising and P^*. With one exception all the forces examined in connection with shifts in the demand curve do the same thing, and that exception does not appear to be an overwhelming force. One can predict, though not with probability equal to one, that advertising and quantity will have a negative relationship with P^*.

The Evidence. The most direct evidence of this phenomenon is the preference of consumers—independent of advertising—for the larger selling brands. As I showed in "Advertising as Information," brands are more likely to advertise that they are the best selling brand in their class than they are to advertise any other rank. This policy makes sense only if consumers believe that the best selling brand is likely to be the better buy.

A counterargument holds that most brands are too complicated for the consumer to evaluate. Because he cannot measure the utility of a brand no matter how many times he experiments with it, the consumer cannot derive any useful indirect information from advertising. In order to derive such information, he must learn something useful by experimenting. Advertising acts as an amplifier—increasing the impact of whatever consumers learn by repeat purchase and advice of others. But if there is no information to amplify, advertising cannot yield any useful indirect information.

The answer is that, while consumers might be unable to evaluate a few commodities, most consumers will be able to evaluate most commodities. Suppose the counterargument were true. Firms would use the cheapest possible ingredients subject to legal constraints. If all firms obeyed the law, there would be a tendency for the products produced to be uniform at the lowest possible level of quality. What actually occurs, however, is for the most part nonuniformity of quality among different brands. *Consumer Reports*, for example, finds quality variation in virtually all the goods it examines.

Of course, a tendency toward uniformity does not necessarily produce uniformity. A firm might use a more expensive ingredient now and then by mistake. But the counterargument does make one clear prediction: that there can be no systematic relation between quality and any other variable that is unrelated to firm mistakes. In particular, there can be no relation between advertising and the quality of brands. If consumers have some information, one predicts that advertising will be positively related to brand quality at least for those goods for which the price of advertised brands is higher than the price of unadvertised brands. In running such a test one does not have to worry about whether the quality difference is worth the price difference or not, because the ignorance model predicts no quality differences attributable to advertising whatsoever.

The evidence—admittedly minuscule—does indicate a positive association between advertised brands and quality when advertised brands cost more. Telser reports that for canned foods advertised brands are of higher grades (as measured by the U.S. Department of Agriculture) than are nonadvertised brands.[23]

Until more studies of quality variation and advertising are made, the chief argument against the ignorance hypothesis must rest on other grounds. If the consumer is able to tell on the basis of one or a few experiments the utility of a brand to him, frequency of purchase (or its rough inverse measure, durability) becomes an important determinant of his actions. The number of brands he samples and the extent to which he depends on others for advice will all be related to durability.[24] I find the predicted relation (a positive one) between *Consumer Reports* ratings and durability. I also find the predicted relation between concentration ratios (which move inversely to the consumer's sample size) and durability. Given this evidence, I find it hard to accept the complete consumer ignorance hypothesis.

Of course, one could argue that the consumer perceives only part of the consequences of his consumption. The indirect information obtained from advertising reflects only what is known by those who have already experienced several brands. That seems to be a useful contribution to the consumer information problem, even though it might not make a consumer fully informed.

Advertising as Information

In "Advertising as Information" I tested the theory of advertising as information by using it to predict the distribution of advertising by industry. According to this theory, information may be direct or indirect. If it is direct, any remembered advertising message beyond the first will be redundant. But if it is indirect, consumers will adopt a decision rule whereby a product is a better buy the more it is advertised, so that remembered advertising messages beyond the first will *not* be redundant. The return to the firm for providing additional advertising messages will be greater for indirect information than for direct information (at least where the marginal revenue curve of advertising is downward sloping), and advertising expenditures will be greater, the greater the importance of indirect information relative to direct information.

I argue that indirect information will be more important for experience qualities than for search qualities. Search qualities are defined as the qualities that a consumer investigates before purchase; experience qualities are the qualities that a consumer determines only

---

[23] Telser, "Advertising and Competition," pp. 541-542.

[24] Phillip Nelson, "Information and Consumer Behavior," *Journal of Political Economy*, vol. 78, no. 2 (March/April 1970), pp. 311-329.

after purchase. For search qualities, advertising provides direct information because consumers generally can believe the advertising message. For experience qualities the dominant information will be indirect because consumers do not necessarily believe the advertising message.

A consumer cannot afford to investigate all of the alternative qualities of the goods in the market. In order to make decisions about his sample size the consumer must make a utility assessment of these qualities. Suppose, then, that the consumer converts these qualities to some utility measure (the particular measure does not matter as long as he uses the same measure throughout). The utilities of all of the alternatives he faces for a particular good form a probability distribution. Having chosen whether he will search for or experience a given quality, the consumer is confronted with a probability distribution of the utilities of search qualities (his search distribution) and with a probability distribution of the utility of experience qualities (his experience distribution). Define R as the ratio of the variance of the experience distribution to the variance of the search distribution. One can predict that as R increases the amount of advertising expenditures will increase.[25]

I tested this prediction by classifying goods into experience and search categories and by then determining which category had the greater advertising/sales ratios. Although I tried to guard against arbitrarily classifying goods one way or another, the evidence would be much more convincing if it did not depend on personal judgments about how goods should be classified.

Fortunately, there is a way to avoid this problem. The relative importance of experience qualities to search qualities has implications for a whole host of market characteristics besides advertising expenditures. Instead of relating these market characteristics to the basically unobservable underlying variable R, I relate these market characteristics to each other. Given their relationship to the underlying variable, one can predict how these characteristics will relate to each other.[26]

---

[25] Nelson, "Advertising as Information" and "Consumer Information and Advertising."

[26] Suppose that we can specify the relation of two different market characteristics, y_1 and y_2 (advertising-to-sales ratios and concentration ratios, for example), to the ratio of experience to search variances R. In the linear approximation:

$$y_{1j} = \alpha_1 + \beta_1 R_j + \epsilon_{1j} \qquad (1)$$
$$y_{2j} = \alpha_2 + \beta_2 R_j + \epsilon_{2j}$$

If ϵ_{1j} is independent of ϵ_{2j}, then

$$r_{12} = \frac{\beta_1 \beta_2 \sigma_R^2}{\sigma_{y_1} \sigma_{y_2}} \qquad (2)$$

where r_{12} = the correlation of y_1 with y_2. Knowing the signs of β_1 and β_2, one can predict the sign of r_{12}, which is observable even though σ_R^2 is not.

Market Characteristics and Information. To some this testing procedure must seem unhappily indirect. Indeed, there are statistical problems produced by this indirectness. However, these problems are more than adequately handled through a combination of my procedure and the overwhelming importance of the information variables themselves. My procedure is to perform many tests by using many market characteristics. The market characteristics that I examine by industry in this paper are, in addition to advertising expenditures, (1) advertising media distributions; (2) concentration ratios; (3) expenditures on retail services; and (4) the spatial clustering of retail activity. These five characteristics generate ten tests (seven involving advertising variables). In addition, a durability variable provides four more tests. It is my conviction that the total impact of these tests provides strong support for the information hypothesis, much stronger support than a smaller number of direct tests would generate.

One of the problems with this approach is that it requires an analysis of the impact of R on a large number of market characteristics —an analysis that would take us far beyond the confines of this paper. Fortunately, that analysis is available elsewhere.[27] I give just a rough "feel" for the nature of the predictions made.

The media distribution of advertising. Define this distribution (M) as the ratio of advertising expenditures in magazines and newspaper supplements to total available advertising expenditures for a particular brand. (Newspaper advertising is not available.) This measure is a proxy for the value of advertising information for the consumers, since the value of the time consumers allocate to magazine advertising is greater than the value of the time they allocate to television and other media of which they are, roughly speaking, a captive audience. We have seen that changes in the search and experience variances have opposite effects on the number of advertising messages demanded by the consumer. In consequence the greater R—the ratio of experience to search variances—the more advertising messages a consumer demands. Hence an increase in R reduces the relative value to the consumer of the first advertising message compared with later advertising messages.

Define Y as the estimated value of M for the first dollar's worth of advertising on a given brand. From the previous paragraph one predicts that Y will decrease as R increases. It can also be shown that the average value of M for all brands in a given industry will decrease as R increases. Furthermore, durability will increase the value of ad-

[27] Nelson, "Advertising as Information" and "Consumer Information and Advertising." In simplified form in the former and in a more precise form in the latter.

vertising information to those consumers ready to respond to the advertising message—and hence will also increase Y.

Concentration ratios. Consumers influence concentration ratios by the number of brands of a good they sample and by the correlation of their choices with those of other consumers. If, for example, there were no correlation of their choices, the number of brands on the market would be unrelated to consumer sample size. If there were a perfect correlation, the sample size of the consumer would set an upper limit on the number of brands on the market. Increases in R decrease the number of brands a consumer samples and increase the correlation of a consumer's choice with other consumers. Sample sizes are reduced by increases in R because sampling by way of experience is basically a more expensive procedure than sampling by way of search (if search becomes too expensive one can always switch to experience). The smaller sample sizes associated with increases in R cause the market to deviate more from a competitive market in two important respects. (1) The variance will be larger in qualities about which all consumers agree, that is, more brands that all consumers do not like will be able to survive; and (2) the variance in qualities about which consumers disagree will fall. (This variance is greatest in competitive markets.) As R increases in an industry, therefore, consumers will find themselves agreeing with each other more frequently about which brands are good and which are bad. The market produces fewer brands about which consumer tastes differ and more brands about which consumer tastes agree. When one consumer's preferences are closely related with those of another, he will more likely follow the latter's advice in choosing the brands to be sampled. So both the decreased sample sizes and the increased correlation of one consumer's choice with another's increase the concentration ratio as R increases.

We can also show that increases in frequency of purchase (decreases in durability) increase concentration ratios by reducing the number of brands a consumer samples.

Gross margins. The retailer's gross margin, measured by the ratio of sales minus costs to sales for a particular good, is payment for services that are substitutes for consumer search expenditures. The demand for this substitute increases as the demand for search increases. Hence, increases in the search variance with their resulting decreases in R increase gross margins. Similarly increases in durability, by reducing total search, reduce gross margins.

Clustering. One source of clustering, defined as the ratio of retail sales of a good in central cities to sales in standard metropolitan areas with central cities, is the incentive of retailers to minimize the distance that consumers have to travel from one search to another. The returns to clustering increase as consumers search more. Hence, increases in the search variance and the resulting decreases in *R* increase clustering. Increases in durability increase the number of searches per experiment and hence will increase clustering.

Empirical Results

The theory yields predictions about the relationship of market characteristics to *R*. These results lead to predictions about the relationship of market characteristics with each other. The most relevant statistics to compare with these predictions are the partial correlations of the market characteristics, holding durability constant, since durability is an additional variable explaining the behavior of our market characteristics. Table 3 gives both the predictions and actual partial correlations of these market characteristics with each other. (Since partial correlations tend to overcorrect for the impact of the variable held constant, the simple correlations are presented as well.) The predictions are overwhelmingly supported by the observed correlations. All the correlations with the better measure of a variable are significantly different from zero in the predicted direction.

Similarly, in looking at the relationship of market characteristics with durability, one should control for the impact of the other market characteristics as proxies for the experience and search variances. These results are also recorded in Table 3. The partial correlations of durability with market characteristics have the predicted signs in each case. Some—but not all—of the observed correlations are significant as well.

The relationships predicted by the information variables are not only statistically significant; they seem to be fairly important. Suppose each market characteristic is regressed against all the other market characteristics, not including among the independent variables any measurement variant of the dependent variables. The resulting multiple R^2s would tend to understate the fraction of the variation in the dependent variable explained by the information variable, since random measurement errors operate to reduce correlations. In spite of this problem, the R^2s are quite substantial, considering that the data are cross sectional with narrowly defined industries. (See Table 4.)

There is a more severe test of the information hypothesis in the sense that fewer alternative hypotheses could generate the predictions. Each of the market characteristics can be considered an approximation of our information variable, *R*. Because of the error in measurement,

Table 3

PREDICTED AND ACTUAL CORRELATIONS

		1	21	22	23	24	25	26	31	32	4	5
2	Advertising Exp.											
	Predicted Sign	+										
21	*A/S* Simple	.269										
	Partial	.277										
22	A_1 Simple	.371	.319									
	Partial	.406	.318									
23	A_2 Simple	.167	.220	.168								
	Partial	.180	.219	.159								
24	*Log A/S* Simple	.341	.542	.466	.186							
	Partial	.368	.543	.454	.179							
25	*Log* A_1 Simple	.359	.338	.733	.169	.653						
	Partial	.397	.339	.724	.158	.645						
26	*Log* A_2 Simple	.353	.409	.657	.379	.663	.897					
	Partial	.407	.414	.644	.374	.656	.892					
3	Media Ratios											
	Predicted Sign	–		–								
31	$\overline{M}$ Simple	–.171	–.171	–.402	–.144	–.309	–.499	–.533				
	Partial	–.232	–.169	–.373	–.121	–.285	–.465	–.495				
32	*Y* Simple	–.201	–.148	–.283	–.143	–.242	–.331	–.384	.815			
	Partial	–.248	–.144	–.254	–.130	–.219	–.295	–.345	.802			

4 GM = Gross Margins											
Predicted Sign	−			−					+		
Simple	−.260	−.206	−.292	−.129	−.304	−.388	−.388	.531	.513		
Partial	−.311	−.204	−.262	−.115	−.283	−.353	−.348	.492	.482		
5 CL = Cluster											
Predicted Sign	−			−					+	+	
Simple	−.243	−.196	−.306	−.112	−.262	−.414	−.413	.547	.453	.734	
Partial	−.318	−.197	−.268	−.093	−.233	−.371	−.361	.492	.406	.712	
6 DUR = Durability											
Predicted Sign	+			?					+	−	+
Simple	.151	−.033	−.167	−.071	−.130	−.214	−.247	.313	.242	.251	.344
Partial	.303				−.118	−.156			.112	−.023	

The Variables

1 CON four firm concentration ratios 1967
2 advertising expenditures 1967
21 A/S = advertising/sales ratios
22 A_1 = advertising per brand with a narrow brand definition
23 A_2 = advertising per brand with a broad brand definition
3 M = media ratios: the ratio of advertising expenditures in magazines and newspaper supplements to total advertising expenditures in 1967
31 $\overline{M}$ = the average M for an industry
32 Y = the y intercept in the regression of M on A. I regressed M and A_1, on A_2, on A_1 and A_2, on cubic A_1, on cubic A_2, and on cubic A_1 and cubic A_2. I chose as Y_2 the intercept associated with the regression yielding the highest corrected R^2. If, however, that intercept was greater than 1 or less than 0, I used 1 or 0 respectively as my estimate of Y.
4 GM = gross margins: the ratio of sales minus merchandise costs to sales for the retailing of goods in the industry
5 CL = clustering: the ratio of retail sales of a good in the central city to sales in the standard metropolitan area
6 DUR = durability = 1 if good is a durable, 0 if good is a nondurable. Partial correlations holding durability constant. Exception: partial with durables and another variable hold all other variables constant. 186 Observations. For the 5 percent one-tail test the critical r = .120 for simple correlations, .121 for partials holding durability constant, and .122 for the partials with durability as one of the variables. For the 5 percent two-tail test, the corresponding critical r's are .143, .143 and .145.

Source: Nelson, "Consumer Information and Advertising." See it for a description of the data producing those correlations.

Table 4

MULTIPLE REGRESSIONS[a]

Dependent Variables		Independent Variables							
		Con	*Log A/S*	*Log A_1*	*Y*	*CL*	*GM*	*DUR*	Corrected[d] R^2
Con	*b*		.0199	.0360	−.0406	−.2443	−.1588	.1360	.2162
	t^b		(.217)	(2.00)	(2.23)	(.86)	(1.33)	(.681)	
	t^c		(4.35)						
Log A_1	*b*	1.6705			−.3848	−1.8176	−1.1544	−.3877	.2610
	t^b	(4.30)			(1.48)	(1.81)	(.90)	(2.12)	
Y	*b*	−.1006	−.0008	−.0303		.2744	1.3590	.0792	.2770
	t^b	(.86)	(.05)	(1.18)		(.95)	(3.85)	(1.51)	
	t^c		(1.47)						
CL	*b*	−.0401	.0052	−.0145	.0182		.7754	.0422	.5759
	t^b	(1.33)	(.095)	(2.22)	(.95)		(10.37)	(3.19)	
	t^c		(1.72)						
GM	*b*	−.0163	−.0040	−.0001	.0562	.4838		−.0033	.5754
	t^b	(.68)	(1.26)	(.02)	(3.85)	(10.37)		(.31)	
	t^c		(.96)						

[a] Notation as in Table 3.
[b] Testing the hypothesis that $\beta_{ij} = 0$. If $t > 1.67$ the associated regression coefficient is statistically significant.
[c] Testing the hypothesis that $\beta_{i(24)} + \beta_{i(25)} = 0$.
[d] The percentage of the total variance of the dependent variable which is explained by the independent variables (corrected for degrees of freedom).

Table 5

A COMPARISON OF ACTUAL AND ESTIMATED PARTIAL CORRELATIONS[a]

		Estimates[b]							
Correlation[c]	**Actual**	Coefficients[c]	Estimates	Coefficients	Estimates	Coefficients	Estimates	Coefficients	Estimates
1(25)	.397	1(32), 4(25)	.182	(25)(32), 14	.190	1(32), 5(25)	.227	(25)(32), 15	.231
1(31)	−.232	4(31), 1(32)	−.253	5(31), 1(32)	−.301				
1(32)	−.248	4(32), 1(31)	−.227	5(32), 1(31)	−.191	(25)(32), 14	−.260	(25)(32), 15	−.253
14	−.311	15, (32)4	−.378	15, (31)4	−.318	15, (25)4	−.303	1(32),(25)4	−.297
15	−.318	14, (32)5	−.262	14, (31)5	−.311	14, (25)5	−.327	1(32),(25)5	−.312
(25)(31)	−.465	(25)(32), (31)5	−.357	(25)(32), (31)4	−.301	(25)5, 1(31)	−.271	(25)4, 1(31)	−.263
(25)(32)	−.295	(25)5, 1(32)	−.289	(25)4, 1(32)	−.281				
(25)4	−.353	(25)5, 4(32)	−.440	(25)(32), 14	−.370				
(25)5	−.371	(32)5, 4(25)	−.297	15, (25)4	−.361				
(31)4	.492	(31)5, 14	.481	(31)5, (32)4	.584				
(32)4	.482	(32)5, 14	.397	(31)4, (32)5	.406				
(31)5	.492	(31)4, 15	.503	(31)4, (32)5	.414				
(32)5	.406	(32)4, 15	.493	(32)4, (31)5	.483				
45	.712	(32)4, 15	.618	14, (32)5	.509	(32)4, (25)5	.606	(32)5, (25)4	.486

[a] Partial correlations holding durability constant.

[b] Estimates based on the equation in note 28. For example, the first estimate appearing on the first line is $r_{1(25)} = \frac{r_{1(32)} \cdot r_{4(25)}}{r_{4(32)}}$. Those correlation coefficients that appear to be unusually large or small—$r_{1(25)}$, $r_{(25)(31)}$, r_{45}—are not used to estimate the other correlation coefficients.

[c] Subscripts conform to the notation of Table 3.

the coefficients of each of the measures should have the predicted sign even when they are all included in the sample multiple regression. The absolute values of both the t values (which measure significance) and the coefficients will be considerably lower in the multiple regression than in the simple regressions. The inclusion as independent variables of several measures of the same independent variable will produce that result. Table 4 records the multiple regressions of each market characteristic on the other market characteristics and durability. All of the signs are in the right direction.

There is one more exceedingly strong test of our theory. It is not only a test of the relevance of information variables in determining market characteristics, but a test of the precise formulation of the relationship we have been using and a test of whether R is the exclusive reason for the relationship between the market characteristics. If R is the exclusive reason for the relationship between market characteristics, one can predict the value of the correlation coefficients as well as their sign.[28] For most of the correlation coefficients R passes this test fairly well (see Table 5). The few exceptions can be easily explained.[29] All in all, this evidence strongly supports the theory that advertising is information.

Appendix A: Derivation of the Relationship between A and P*

Assuming a translog production function, quantity demanded (Q) is the following function of prices* (P) and advertising expenditures (A).

$$lnQ = \alpha_0 + \alpha_1\, lnP + \alpha_2\, lnA + \alpha_3\, lnPlnA + \alpha_4\, (lnP)^2 + \alpha_5\, (lnA)^2 \qquad \text{(A.1)}$$

The price elasticity of demand in absolute terms (ϵ_P) is given by:

$$\epsilon_P = -\frac{\partial lnQ}{\partial lnP} = -(\alpha_1 + \alpha_3\, lnA + 2\alpha_4\, lnP) \qquad \text{(A.2)}$$

The advertising elasticity of demand (ϵ_A) equals:

$$\epsilon_A = \frac{\partial lnQ}{\partial lnA} = \alpha_2 + \alpha_3\, lnP + 2\alpha_5\, lnA \qquad \text{(A.3)}$$

Schmalensee and others have shown that a firm that is maximizing profits will operate such that:[30]

$$\frac{A}{QP} = \frac{\epsilon_A}{\epsilon_P} \qquad \text{(A.4)}$$

---

[28] Given those conditions, equation (2) in note 26 generates the following relation between correlation coefficients.

$$r_{qk} = \frac{r_{iq}\, r_{jk}}{r_{ij}}$$

[29] Nelson, "Consumer Information and Advertising," forthcoming.

[30] Schmalensee, *The Economics of Advertising*, p. 22.

or

$$Q = \frac{-(\alpha_1 + \alpha_3 \, lnA + 2\alpha_4 \, lnP)}{\alpha_2 + \alpha_3 \, lnP + 2\alpha_5 \, lnA} \cdot \frac{A}{P} \qquad \text{(A.5)}$$

I am interested in determining the conditions under which $\frac{dA}{dP}$ will be negative, or the conditions when $\frac{dlnA}{dlnP}$ will be negative, since both these derivatives must have the same sign. When these conditions hold high *A*s will provide indirect information about low *P*s. Equation (A.1) can be made a function simply of *A* and *P* by substituting equation (A.5) into equation (A.1), or

$$lnA - lnP + ln[-(\alpha_1 + \alpha_3 \, lnA + 2\alpha_4 \, lnP)] - ln(\alpha_2 + \alpha_3 \, lnP + 2\alpha_5 \, lnA) = \alpha_0 + \alpha_1 \, lnP + \alpha_2 \, lnA + \alpha_3 \, lnPlnA + \alpha_4 \, (lnP)^2 + \alpha_5 \, (lnA)^2 \qquad \text{(A.6)}$$

Now take the derivative of equation (A.6) with respect to *lnP* defining $A' = \frac{dlnA}{dlnP}$:

$$A' - 1 - \frac{1}{\epsilon_P}(\alpha_3 A' + 2\alpha_4) - \frac{1}{\epsilon_A}(\alpha_3 + 2\alpha_5 A') = \alpha_1 + \alpha_2 A' + \alpha_3 A' \, lnP + \alpha_3 \, lnA + 2\alpha_4 \, lnP + 2\alpha_5 A' \, lnA \qquad \text{(A.7)}$$

Gathering terms and solving for A':

$$A' = \frac{dlnA}{dlnP} = \frac{1 - \epsilon_P + \frac{\alpha_3}{\epsilon_A} + \frac{2\alpha_4}{\epsilon_P}}{1 - \epsilon_A - \frac{\alpha_3}{\epsilon_P} - \frac{2\alpha_5}{\epsilon_A}} \qquad \text{(A.8)}$$

$\frac{dlnA}{dlnP} < 0$ if the numerator in equation (A.8) is negative and the denominator is positive. Look at the numerator. ϵ_p is necessarily greater than 1. One expects α_4 to be negative. This implies that the demand curve becomes more inelastic with decreases in price*. This is part of the conventional wisdom. It is also generated by Stigler's search model. [31] One expects α_3 to be negative. An increase in advertising expenditures should make the price elasticity of demand greater. As argued in the text, advertising jogs a consumer's memory about the brands he has already tried. He can, therefore, more easily repeat purchase the brands he likes and avoid the brands he does not like. Not everybody would be willing to accept this specification of α_3. Even with a positive α_3, it would be exceedingly unlikely that the numerator would be positive, since ϵ_p is likely to be substantially greater than 1.

The denominator in equation (A.8) is the critical term. Again, I expect, but others may not, α_3 to be negative. α_5—as I argue in the text—should be negative. Economies of scale are reduced, usually, as size increases. I argue in note 6 that even if α_3 is positive, one does not expect it to dominate over α_5 in equation (A.8). Therefore, as long as ϵ_A is less than 1, the demoninator of equation (A.8) will be positive. Under these conditions we expect $\frac{dlnA}{dlnP}$ to be less than 0.

In the analysis in the text two other total derivatives are of interest: $\frac{dlnQ}{dlnP}$ and $\frac{dlnQ}{dlnA}$.

$$\frac{dlnQ}{dlnP} = \frac{\partial lnQ}{\partial lnP} + \frac{\partial lnQ}{\partial lnA} \cdot \frac{dlnA}{dlnP} \tag{A.9}$$

$$\frac{dlnQ}{dlnP} = \frac{\epsilon_A - \epsilon_P + 2\alpha_3 + 2\alpha_5 \frac{\epsilon_P}{\epsilon_A} + 2\alpha_4 \frac{\epsilon_A}{\epsilon_P}}{1 - \epsilon_A - \frac{\alpha_3}{\epsilon_P} - \frac{2\alpha_5}{\epsilon_A}} \tag{A.10}$$

By the same arguments as already given one expects the numerator of equation (A.10) to be negative if $\epsilon_A < 1$. If $\epsilon_A < 1$ one expects the denominator to be positive. Hence if $\epsilon_A < 1$

$$\frac{dlnQ}{dlnP} < 0$$

$$\frac{dlnQ}{dlnA} = \frac{\epsilon_A - \epsilon_P + 2\alpha_3 + 2\alpha_5 \frac{\epsilon_P}{\epsilon_A} + 2\alpha_4 \frac{\epsilon_A}{\epsilon_P}}{1 - \epsilon_P + \frac{\alpha_3}{\epsilon_A} + \frac{2\alpha_4}{\epsilon_P}} \tag{A.11}$$

If $\frac{dlnQ}{dlnP}$ is negative and $\frac{dlnQ}{dlnA}$ is positive, $\frac{dlnA}{dlnP}$ must be negative.

Appendix B: Data Sources

The industrial classification scheme used in this article is dictated by the availability of advertising data. My basic source of such data is the Leading National Advertisers, *National Advertising Investments*, which provides information on advertising expenditures for all companies investing $20,000 or more in magazines, newspaper supplements, and network and spot television.[32] In addition outdoor advertising expendi-

---

[31] Phillip Nelson, "The Economic Consequences of Advertising," *Journal of Business*, vol. 48, no. 2 (April 1975), pp. 213-241.

[32] Leading National Advertisers, Inc., *National Advertising Investments* (Norwalk, Connecticut, 1967).

tures are provided. These expenditures are tabulated in a tape provided by the Federal Trade Commission. The data come by brand, company, and an LNA industrial code. In addition, the Federal Trade Commission assigned five- or four-digit Standard Industrial Classification codes to brands for which these codes could fairly unambiguously be assigned. In consequence, my industrial classification is a potpourri of nonoverlapping five-digit and four-digit SIC industries and some LNA industries.

Media Distribution of Advertising. The section on media distribution of advertising suggests that the measure of that distribution that would best serve as a proxy for value of advertising information to the consumer would be the ratio of advertising expenditures in all print media to total advertising expenditures. However, I do not have usable data on newspaper expenditures, other than newspaper supplements. In consequence I am forced to use as my measure M the ratio of magazine and newspaper supplement advertising expenditures to total advertising expenditures for the media I do have. Newspaper data would be difficult to use anyway because the substitutability of retail advertising for national brand advertising plays a much more serious role with newspaper advertising, the focus of retail advertising, than with any other medium.

One of the most serious problems in dealing with advertising by brands is defining a brand. For example, are Jade East After Shave and Jade East Cologne one or two brands? I used two different brand definitions. For one definition each LNA listing was called a brand. (This would make every Jade East product separately listed by LNA a separate brand.) For the other definition, all first names that were the same within the industry code were taken to be brands. (All Jade East products within a five-digit toiletries industry would be considered the same brand.)

Sales. I used as my measure the value of shipments for domestic manufactures in 1967,[33] plus the value of imports plus duties minus the value of exports in 1967.[34]

Concentration Ratios. I use four firm concentration ratios in 1967 (for my data the correlation between four-firm concentration and eight-firm

[33] U.S. Department of Commerce, Bureau of the Census, *Census of Manufactures*, 1967.

[34] U.S. Department of Commerce, Bureau of the Census, *U.S. Commodity Exports and Imports*, 1967-68.

concentration ratios was greater than .9) for five-digit industries.[35] In order to preserve comparability, where my industrial classification is either a four-digit industry or an LNA industry, I used the weighted average of the five-digit SIC concentration ratios. The weights are value added for each SIC industry.

Gross Margins/Sales. To obtain a sufficiently detailed series for my industries, I had to combine data from several sources. My basic data were gross margin/sales by major store types in 1971 from the U.S. Bureau of the Census.[36] To get more detailed industry breakdowns I used gross margins/sales by detailed categories for department stores in 1964–1965, drug stores in 1950–1951, and supermarkets in 1960.[37] The procedure I used reduced the impact of variation in dates or sources on the calculation of gross margins/sales.

Cluster. This was the one measure that I could not obtain data for in the detail to match the detail of my industrial code, though I managed to develop more detail than the data supplied at first sight. My measure of cluster for an industry is the ratio of retail sales for that industry in central business districts to sales in all standard metropolitan areas with central business districts in 1963.[38]

---

[35] U.S. Department of Commerce, Bureau of the Census, *Concentration Ratios in Manufacturing*, 1967.

[36] U.S. Department of Commerce, Bureau of the Census, *Retail Trade Report*, 1971.

[37] National Retail Merchant's Association, *Departmental Merchandising and Operating Results*, 1964-65; O. E. Burley, et al., *Drug Store Operating Costs and Profits* (New York: McGraw-Hill, 1956); "The Dillon Study," *The Progressive Grocer*, May 1960.

[38] U.S. Department of Commerce, Bureau of the Census, *1963 Census of Business Retail Trade Summary Statistics*, 1966, part 2.

ADVERTISING, INFORMATION, AND PRODUCT DIFFERENTIATION

Sherwin Rosen

Many discussions of advertising in both popular and professional literature are linked to the concept of product differentiation. One line of argument describes advertising and its concomitant product differentiation as manifestations of wasteful nonprice competition. Advertising and variations in product design are claimed to have a negative sum quality; though each seller undertakes advertising and other selling expenditures in the belief that his own market share will increase, market demand is not redistributed among sellers when all engage in these activities simultaneously. Resources that have more productive alternatives elsewhere in the economy are used up in a self-defeating effort to increase market share. The nonprice competitive aspects of advertising and product differentiation are seen as forms of economic warfare that increase costs, raise product prices, and reduce market demand overall, with few, if any, offsetting social benefits. Moreover, intense nonprice competition among sellers gives rise to a plethora of commodity varieties (many with unnecessary and useless frills that are costly but unproductive), wasteful duplication, and too many sellers—surely an indictment of competitive market systems and the idea of consumer sovereignty.

Whatever the merits of this line of argument, recent developments in economic research suggest that some reexamination of the issues may be desirable and fruitful. First, George Stigler laid the groundwork for a rigorous theory of the economics of information by showing that it pays to be somewhat ignorant: it is not rational to be completely informed when there are costs of obtaining information and costs of transacting.[1] The residual ignorance among market participants is sustained because it is too costly to remove through arbitrage some residual differences in product price and quality. In Stigler's model, advertising may convey genuine information about price and product

I am indebted to Michael Mussa and James W. Friedman for many helpful discussions. Some of the research underlying this study was supported by the National Science Foundation.

[1] George Stigler, "The Economics of Information," *Journal of Political Economy*, vol. 69 (June 1961), pp. 213-225.

quality dispersion that improves the overall efficiency of the market system and increases—not decreases—social welfare. Second, the concept of product differentiation has acquired a more precise meaning and many empirical applications through the development of a new approach to the determination of product price.[2] This is the so-called characteristics or hedonic approach, whereby prices of product varieties within a generic class are related to their characteristics or attributes.

In a previous paper, I constructed a theory of product differentiation in purely competitive markets based on many systematic empirical studies that have related differentiated product prices to product attributes.[3] The main idea is that differentiated products cater to different types of buyers. Product differentiation will therefore almost always be observed in the presence of buyer and seller diversity. If buyers' tastes for different aspects of the good are heterogeneous, competition impels sellers to seek out new markets and offer varieties of the product most closely matching the preferences of diverse customers. Even if buyers have homogeneous preferences, product differentiation may be observed in competitive markets so long as sellers are diverse, with some having comparative advantages at producing alternative attribute combinations. The natural outcome of this kind of competitive market is an optimal matching and sorting of buyers and sellers, with transactions consummated in the most economical way and with maximum value received by consumers. Simply from observing the results of the sorting process, that is, the prices and product varieties that actually obtain, it is difficult if not impossible to distinguish "excessive" from "optimal" product differentiation, at least without imposing a particular value system, perhaps one's own—or one in the manner of Consumers' Union—on the data.

One purpose of this study and of other recent contributions to the economics of advertising is to blend these two developments.[4] The main theme to be developed is that buyers and sellers are not necessarily matched correctly or efficiently in the presence of transactions costs, uncertainty, and ignorance. The social value of information and adver-

[2] See Kelvin Lancaster, "A New Approach to Consumer Theory," *Journal of Political Economy*, vol. 74, no. 2 (April 1966), pp. 132-157, and "Socially Optimal Product Differentiation," *American Economic Review*, vol. 65 (September 1975), pp. 567-585.

[3] Sherwin Rosen, "Hedonic Prices and Implicit Markets: Product Differentiation in Pure Competition," *Journal of Political Economy*, vol. 82, no. 1 (January/February 1974), pp. 34-55.

[4] For examples of these other recent contributions, see Phillip Nelson, "Advertising as Information," *Journal of Political Economy*, vol. 82, no. 4 (July/August 1974), pp. 729-754, and "Information and Consumer Behavior," *Journal of Political Economy*, vol. 78 (March/April 1970), pp. 311-329.

tising represents a more efficient sorting mechanism. Since information gathering and dissemination are activities inherently subject to some scale economies we can expect such expenditures to be undertaken by firms, especially if buyer search and product assessment costs are sufficiently large. If so, then some buyers may be able to specialize their range of search and assessment activities over a narrower range of goods, shop more efficiently, and obtain a better match between the most preferred characteristics and the availabilities of product types offered in the market. This is the real value of information, and it points up the sense in which advertising becomes a tie-in feature of alternative product varieties. Accurately transmitted information commands a high price in much the same way that persons offering superior marriage and real estate brokerage services receive larger incomes.

The next section briefly reviews the theory of product differentiation in competitive markets with complete information and sets up the basic framework of analysis. Subsequent sections examine the nature of competition in differentiated product markets, emphasizing the role of new goods for filling gaps in the available spectrum; the view that advertising may change buyers' perceptions of attributes embodied in differentiated product varieties; and some of the elements of the demand for information in such markets and their consequences for the economics of advertising. An appendix presents some new results on the value of attribute information to buyers searching over a class of heterogeneous goods.

Competitive Markets for Differentiated Products

The process by which advertising brings about matching of buyers and sellers may be understood by assuming initially that there is complete information and pure competition—conditions under which no advertising would take place.[5] Products within a generic class are assumed to be comparable in terms of their underlying, objectively measured characteristics or attributes. Each consumer decides on the best item to purchase by comparison shopping, that is, by weighing the market prices necessary to obtain more preferred attributes of the commodity against subjective valuations of those attributes. Different buyers purchase different varieties because they differ in tastes and incomes and because their subjective valuations of attributes differ. Sellers decide what varieties to offer in the market by comparing prices against costs. Some sellers may specialize by producing those varieties at which they

[5] See Rosen, "Hedonic Prices and Implicit Markets," pp. 34-55, for details and elaboration.

are most adept, depending on the technology required. But even if no specialized production knowledge across varieties is present, sellers will still offer different varieties in accordance with consumers' demands for them. Thus, product differentiation occurs even with perfect information and without advertising or "taste altering" expenditures.

Consider a class of goods that can be represented by some set of measurable characteristics. Individual product varieties are observed to be differentiated from each other according to the proportions in which they embody the various characteristics: each product variety offers a fixed package of characteristics, with characteristic proportions varying from one variety to another. Buyers value products not as ends in themselves, but as means of obtaining the characteristics embodied in them. It would appear that this kind of concept applies to most commodities actually exchanged in the real world. Houses are differentiated according to architectural style, number of rooms, lot size, quality of construction, locational and neighborhood advantages, and so on; different brands of toothpaste offer a variety of properties that involve taste, breath, stain removal, and tooth decay prevention; cold remedies vary in their aspirin content, presence of antihistamine, and shelf life, among other things. Readers can extend the list at will. Think of restaurants, automobiles, cameras, various clothing items, furniture, soaps and detergents, food products, graduate and undergraduate colleges, marriage partners, different kinds of jobs, characteristics of workers, and so on, ad infinitum. Clearly product differentiation is the rule rather than the exception in virtually all market exchange. In everyday life we often speak of variations within product classes as "quality" differences. The notion of product characteristics embodied in market goods gives a more precise meaning to the term necessary for analysis.

Denote characteristics embodied by goods of the type under consideration by the vector z, with components $(z_1, z_2, \ldots, z_m)$, where the first component of z represents one characteristic, the second component represents another, and so on through the mth component. By hypothesis each observed good in the market is described by numerical values of z. Suppose, for example, that a good embodies five characteristics $(m=5)$ and that the quantity of each characteristic embodied in that good is given as follows: $z_1=2$, $z_2=4$, $z_3=3$, $z_4=1$, $z_5=2$. Then $z=(2,4,3,1,2)$. The necessary data available to agents in this market consist of the number and variety of goods present and the prices associated with each of them. But since goods are uniquely associated with particular values of z and represent the way in which characteristics are transformed to consumption activity, it is a straightforward matter to transform observed prices of various items to *implicit* prices of observed characteristics. Let $p(z)$ represent the cost of obtaining the characteristics represented by z or, equivalently, the price of one unit of some good in which z is embodied. On this assumption, the available values of z and the corresponding prices of z both are identified with the product varieties that are offered by that market. The function $p(z)$ is illustrated by Figure 1, where the number of goods available is so dense that a continuum of varieties is available in the market. In Figure 1, z has only one component ($m=1$), and $p(z)$ is a simple curve. If z had two or more components, $p(z)$ would be a surface in a space with coordinates $z_1, z_2, \ldots, z_m$ and p.[6]

Throughout most of this paper the problem is further simplified by assuming that each customer purchases only one variety of whatever appears in the market, and does not find it possible or advantageous to combine several varieties into a new package that may not exist. This is consistent with the notion stated earlier that producers attempt to tailor their products to the preferences of various customers. It is easily rationalized on the assumption that the assembly of attribute packages is accomplished more efficiently in specialized, large-scale production processes than in small-scale piecemeal production at home. While it is possible to think of examples where assembly at home is more efficient than assembly "at the factory" (building up a wardrobe for instance), the assumption is very convenient and does not materially affect the analysis. It would appear that the problem in any practical case almost always can be redefined to make the assumption essentially true (for example, look at the separate markets for pants, shoes, suits, shirts, and so forth, as opposed to the market for total wardrobes).

An analytical statement of the comparison shopping mode of choice is summarized as follows. Represent each customer's tastes and subjective values by a standard neoclassical utility function with the z-components included as additional arguments:

$$u = U(c,z) \tag{1}$$

where c is a composite of the whole market basket of other consumption goods bought by the consumer and u is the utility index. Measure market prices relative to the basket c, so that the price $p(c)$ of c is unity. Then the buyer's choice is restricted by a budget identity.

$$y = c + p(z) \tag{2}$$

[6] I assume that products are continuously differentiated whenever it is analytically convenient to do so. This assumption is similar for the problem at hand to assuming infinitely divisible commodities in demand theory. It makes absolutely no difference to the logic of the argument if there are a finite number of products, though the mathematics are more complex. See examples below.

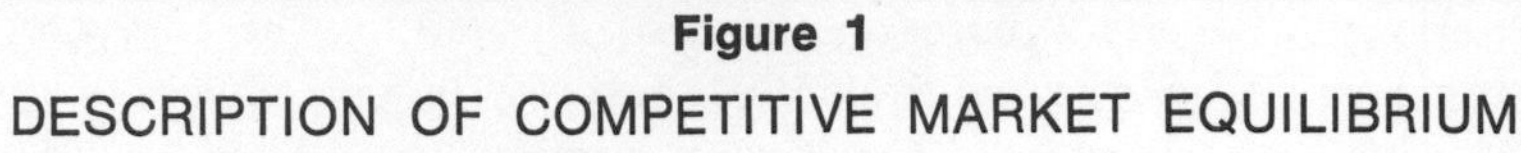

Figure 1

DESCRIPTION OF COMPETITIVE MARKET EQUILIBRIUM

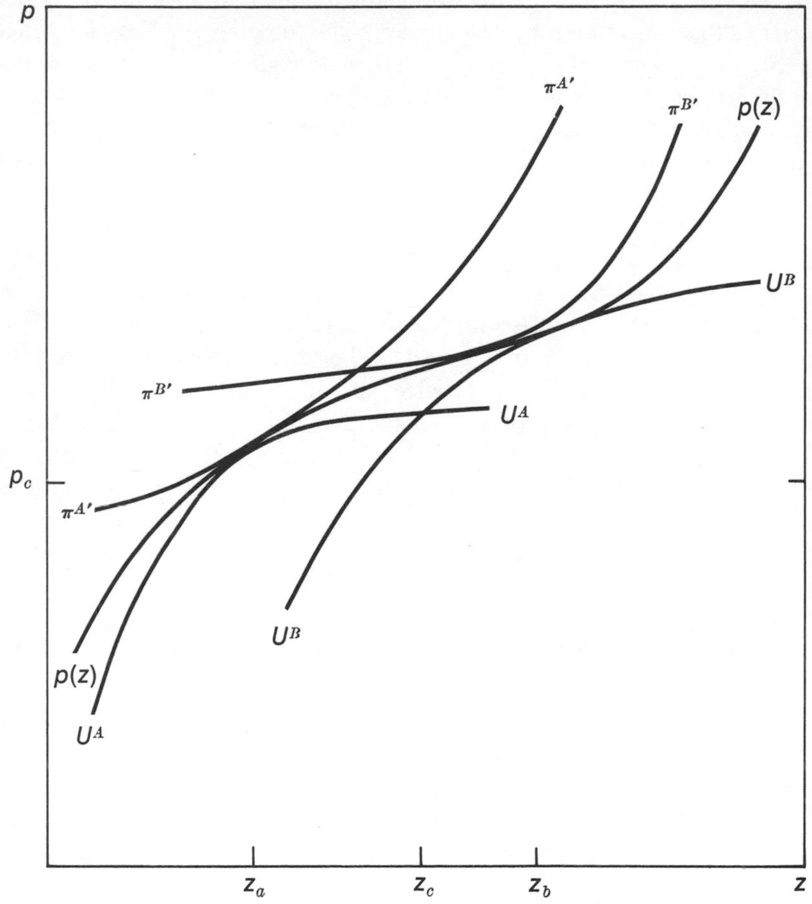

where y is income to be spent on other consumption goods, c, and on one of the differentiated products in question (an item offering a particular value of z). For more simplicity it is further assumed that buyers purchase only one unit of the differentiated product.[7]

The buyer's problem now amounts to the usual one of maximizing (1) subject to (2). Unlike the usual case in which the buyer chooses the optimal quantities of different goods, he is viewed here as having

[7] This assumption is also easily relaxed, but the resulting complexity would detract from the main point.

to allocate his income among product characteristics $z_1, z_2, \ldots, z_m$, which is achieved by purchasing the one market good that embodies them. The consumer buys additional units of any one characteristic by shifting purchases from a variety offering fewer units of the characteristic (or bundle of characteristics) to one that offers more units of it. When a purchase is made, the marginal condition

$$p'(z) = U_z/U_c \tag{3}$$

is satisfied, according to which the marginal subjective evaluation, U_z/U_c, of z equals its marginal cost $p'(z)$. Suppose the consumer contemplates a variety of the differentiated product offering some arbitrary value of characteristics, say z^0. What (3) shows is that in deciding whether to purchase the variety offering z^0, the buyer must compare it with varieties offering other values of z. For example, examine a variety with a slightly different value of z, say z^1. The characteristic differential between the two is $dz = z^1 - z^0$. The difference in price is $dp = p(z^1) - p(z^0) \approx p'(z^0)dz$, where $p'(z^0)$ is the change in price charged the consumer per unit change in the bundle of attributes embodied in z^0. The amount the consumer is willing to pay for the additional characteristics is $(U_z/U_c)dz$, where U_z/U_c is evaluated in the neighborhood of z^0. If this exceeds the amount that must be paid in order to acquire them, dp, then z^1 is better than z^0 and conversely if the inequality goes in the other direction. Which items turn out to be the best bargains depends not only on price, but on preferences as well.

An arithmetic illustration of the solution may be considered for the vectors $z^0 = (2,4,3,1,2)$ and $z^1 = (8,4,3,1,2)$. The vector z^1 embodies 6 more units of the characteristic z_1 than does z^0, while the quantity of every other characteristic, $z_2 \ldots z_5$, is the same. (The solution could be applied to the case in which z^1 embodies different amounts of two or more characteristics than those embodied in z^0, but it is simpler for illustrative purposes to consider the case in which it embodies more of only one.) Now suppose that when the consumer buys a good embodying z^0 he gains 10 more units of utility for every additional unit of z_1 consumed, that is $U_z=10$ (where the amounts consumed of $z_2 \ldots z_5$ are constant). Suppose also that $U_c=2$, that is, his utility rises by 2 for every additional dollar he spends on other goods. Then his marginal subjective valuation (U_z/U_c) of z is 5: he is willing to give up as many as 5 units of the composite market basket of other consumption goods (or since $p(c)=1$, \$5 worth of other goods) for each additional unit of z_1. If, for example, $p(z^0)=200$ and $p(z^1)=225$, so that $p'(z^0)=25/6 < U_z/U_c=5$, he will switch from z^0 to z^1, giving up \$25 worth of other goods in the process. The amount the consumer is willing to pay for additional characteristics is $U_z/U_c\ dz=(10/2)6=30$, whereas the amount that he must pay to acquire them is only $dp=p'(z^0)dz=25$.

A diagrammatic representation is obtained by noting that (1) and (2) together define a family of price-attribute indifference surfaces in the p-z plane.[8] Each member of the family of surfaces represents the combinations of demand prices and characteristic bundles that leave the utility index unchanged. Figure 1, where there is only one attribute, shows one member, U^A, of this family for customer A and one member, U^B, for customer B. A and B have different tastes. If the underlying utility function (1) has the familiar diminishing marginal valuation property whereby U_z/U_c falls as z rises, the price-attribute indifference surfaces have the concave appearance as illustrated. There is an indifference curve defined through every point of the p-z space for each person, and each person gains a higher level of utility as he shifts to a lower indifference curve, that is, as he shifts to higher levels of z and/or lower levels of p. Although the consumer always prefers more z at given prices, the market price function $p(z)$ constrains the maximum utility that can be achieved. Therefore, the maximum must be described by the value of z for which $p(z)$ and the indifference curves are tangent. In Figure 1, consumer A finds z_a to be the best choice, while customer B buys z_b. If A contemplated buying a good offering less than z_a, the incremental subjective value of more z would exceed its cost and that good would be nonoptimal. A similar statement, with the inequality reversed, holds for goods offering more than z_a, as described above. Similar logic holds for customer B.

The fact that the indifference curves for A and B are not congruent means that either their tastes or their incomes are not identical. If the z attributes are normal goods as economists use the word, then persons buying brands with more z tend to have larger incomes (for example, the rich buy Cadillacs more readily than those with lower incomes). This is a case of differences in marginal valuation caused by income differences in the usual manner of demand theory. But pure differences in tastes, whatever their cause, have exactly the same consequences on the varieties purchased. Finally, it may be true for some customers that the maximum utility achieved in the differentiated products market when the optimum variety is purchased is less than that obtained from doing without the product altogether. Such individuals do not buy any variety offered in the market.

[8] These are nothing other than the level sets of the indirect utility function conditioned on z.

Sellers' production decisions also are easy to describe in the simple case of nonjoint production. Each production establishment has a cost function

$$c = C(n,z) \tag{4}$$

where c is total cost, n is the number of items and z is the vector of design characteristics of the product offered in the market.[9] Pure competition implies that $p(z)$ is considered parametric for production and sales decisions. Each firm can sell all it wants of any variety without affecting the price because each seller is too small to add more than negligible weight to the market. The product actually produced in an establishment has design characteristics z that maximize profit

$$\pi = np(z) - C(n,z) \tag{5}$$

requiring

$$p(z) = C_n \tag{6}$$

$$np'(z) = C_z. \tag{7}$$

Condition (6) is the usual requirement that the extra revenue (equal to price under pure competition) from producing one more unit of a given product variety equal its marginal cost of production. Condition (7) requires the firm to produce that product variety at which the marginal revenue of any characteristic (or bundle of characteristics) equals its marginal cost.

An arithmetic example of the solution can be added to the example of consumer utility maximization given above. Suppose that a purely competitive firm is currently selling fifty units of a good embodying z^0 at a price of \$200 and that it is considering a design alteration to z^1 that would permit it to sell the good at \$225. The unit costs of producing fifty units of z^0 and z^1 are \$195 and \$215, respectively, so that

$$\pi^0 = np(z^0) - C(n,z^0) = \$10{,}000 - \$9{,}750 = \$250$$

$$\pi^1 = np(z^1) - C(n,z^1) = \$11{,}250 - \$10{,}750 = \$500.$$

Since $np'(z) = 50(25/6) > 50(215–195)/6 = C_z$, it pays the firm to make the change.

[9] A precursor to this part of the analysis is Lester Telser, "Advertising and Competition," *Journal of Political Economy*, vol. 72 (December 1964), pp. 537-562. An adequate representation of joint production and technical advantages of producing a product line with alternative characteristics is not available, but I doubt whether such a modification would affect the main outline of the analysis. Note also that the components of z are scaled to represent "goods" which require additional resources to produce greater amounts. That is the reason $p(z)$ increases in z. Local nonincreasing returns to scale in production is assumed in each production establishment at this point.

A diagrammatic representation of the solution can be obtained in a manner similar to that derived for buyers. Here we need to define a set of *profit* indifference surfaces, each one of which indicates the combinations of price and attributes that leave profit unaltered in the production establishment.[10] One member of this family is shown for two producers, A′ and B′, in Figure 1 (the curves labeled $\pi^{A'}$ and $\pi^{B'}$). Since profit is increasing in p and decreasing in z (the profit "direction" of the indifference surfaces is upward rather than downward as it was in the case of buyers), maximum attainable profit is achieved at the design where a profit indifference surface is tangent to the price surface $p(z)$. Establishments like A′ offer varieties with the amount z_a of characteristics, while those like B′ offer z_b. As illustrated, B′ has a comparative advantage in producing units with larger z content. If there were no comparative advantage, profit indifference surfaces for all producers would be identical, no firm would have a marked preference for producing any particular variety, and the profit indifference curve would be congruent with $p(z)$. Still, alternative varieties would appear on the market to satisfy the diverse preferences of different types of customers, verifying an assertion made above.

Competitive market equilibrium is in fact completely described by the buyer, seller, market price configuration shown in Figure 1. Buyers and sellers are matched to each other by common tangents along $p(z)$, the market price-product availabilities surface. Further, $p(z)$ contains all necessary information to sustain a competitive and efficient equilibrium in which buyers and sellers are optimally allocated to each other and sorted out along the differentiated product spectrum. Clearly there is a tendency for "assortive matching," since consumers of each variety purchase from sellers who have comparative advantages at producing them and who offer them at the lowest price. In Figure 1, A buys from A′ and B buys from B′. A could have bought z_a from B′, but only at a higher price than was paid to A′. Thus buyers and sellers are sorted out in the way that gives each customer the best bargain possible given his preferences. No resources are wasted in the process.

The Nature of Competition in Differentiated Product Markets

Strictly speaking, Figure 1 and the underlying discussion describe a static equilibrium that might persist forever, so long as supply prices have been bid down to their competitive no-entry level and tastes and technology

[10] These are nothing more than the level sets of indirect profit functions conditioned on z.

remain unchanged. However, it is useful and informative to go further and inquire into other aspects of competition.

The first point to notice is that there are strong incentives for firms to improve their products and offer better bargains than their competitors. This is immediately apparent in Figure 1. Suppose some firm finds a more efficient production method that allows it to offer variety z_c at a price lower than would cover costs before. In fact suppose costs are low enough to allow it to offer z_c at price p_c. Then it is no longer optimal for buyers A and B to remain with varieties z_a and z_b. z_c has become a better buy for both, and they should purchase it instead. In addition, customers who previously bought items offering attributes between and somewhat beyond z_a and z_b will find it advantageous to switch over to z_c rather than continue with their old brands. The seller who accomplishes such a maneuver gains the considerable advantage of drawing customers away from a broad band of neighboring brands and increases sales by a quantum leap. Supernormal (and monopolistic) profits are gained for a time, until the seller's competitors adopt the innovation and use it to improve their offerings of product varieties. Clearly the spectrum of varieties appearing on the market may be entirely changed by such operations. The feasible range of attributes may be extended or more desirable and entirely new attributes may be incorporated in the goods.[11] Examples of this kind of process are not difficult to enumerate. Think of stainless steel razor blades, synthetic fabrics in clothing, automatic transmissions, electronic hand calculators, new kinds of duplicating machines, frozen foods, and so on. Since the gains from getting a jump on the competition are so great, it is to be expected that sellers would devote considerable resources to change their offerings and attract customers. Well-known fiascoes such as the Edsel remind us that this process is subject to considerable risk and uncertainty. If the good turns out to have a price far in excess of the regression line, or if consumers perceive it as not lying in the interstices but duplicating an existing good at a higher price instead, or if there happen to be too few customer types in the middle it appeals to, it is not viable.

Filling gaps in the band spectrum of available goods is a most interesting phenomenon in the presence of scale economies; and, since information technology may exhibit certain scale economies, it is appropriate to explore the issue in more detail. This is the case of monopolistic competition rather than pure competition. When there are scale economies it is not necessarily socially optimal or even desirable to

[11] The role of entrepreneurship in this process is not unlike some of the discussion in Israel Kirzner, *Competition and Entrepreneurship* (Chicago and London: University of Chicago Press, 1973), and Joseph Schumpeter, *Capitalism, Socialism, and Democracy* (New York: Harper & Row, 1942).

produce goods that cater to each and every consumer taste group in the market. It may be more advantageous to achieve a compromise and have several different types of consumers all buy a good that does not precisely embody the combination of characteristics most desired by any particular consumer type. The cost savings from increasing the scale of production may make up for the utility losses from not getting precisely what each member most prefers. This problem is important in all cases where the number of varieties that appears on the market is much smaller than the number of distinct consumer types.

A modification of Figure 1 is useful for analysis. Assume that all potential and actual producers have cost functions of the form

$$c = k + nC(z) \tag{8}$$

where k is a fixed cost necessary to set up a production establishment and inform customers of the presence of the good in the market, while variable costs of production are subject to constant returns to scale in quantities produced, n, for given product design z. The minimum supply price necessary to break even on products of alternative designs is

$$p^s(z) = k/n + C(z) \tag{9}$$

$p^s(z)$ is decreasing in n for any given design, because a greater number of customers each share a smaller proportion of the fixed cost.

To put the problem in the simplest possible terms, assume that there are n_a type A customers and n_b type B customers with tastes like those pictured in Figure 1. Type B customers place a larger subjective valuation on the attribute and are willing to pay more for additional increments of z. Type A customers are assumed to be more numerous in the population, that is $n_a > n_b$. Two $p^s(z)$ functions are shown in Figure 2 in the one characteristic case, $p^s_a(z)$ relating to the type A customers and $p^s_b(z)$ relating to the type B customers.

Figure 2 shows what may be termed a separating equilibrium in the differentiated products market. Two varieties of product have appeared in the market, one with design characteristics z_a catering to type A buyers and the other with design z_b catering to type B buyers. The product offering z_a sells for $p_a = k/n_a + C(z_a)$ and the one offering z_b sells for $p_b = k/n_b + C(z_b)$. Type A customers have no incentive to buy z_b since their evaluation of the additional attribute it offers is less than its additional price, and type B people do not find it advantageous to switch over to z_a for exactly the opposite reasons. The sellers are covering costs and are content to offer both varieties on the market.

Figure 2

SEPARATING EQUILIBRIUM: TWO GOODS

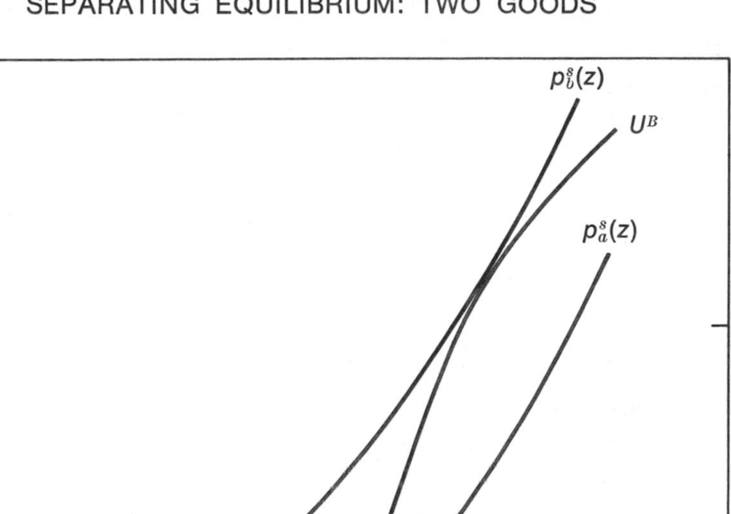

In fact the situation depicted in Figure 2 is not only an attainable market outcome, but also is Pareto optimal *given* the proviso that two or more goods appear on the market. No two varieties other than z_a and z_b can yield a higher level of utility for both types of customers, and more than two varieties obviously cannot yield more utility because of the presence of scale economies. However, the two-good separating equilibrium may not be stable or Pareto optimal if fewer than two varieties are permitted. It might be better for all customers together to buy only one variety. Look at the crosshatched area in Figure 2, where the price-attribute indifference curves overlap each other. If a seller offers an attribute-price package on a variety that falls anywhere within this area, both types of customers switch from z_a or z_b to the new good, and z_a and z_b are not viable in the presence of such a good. The entrepreneur offering it will have filled a genuine hole in the market and destroyed the competition.[12]

Whether or not a seller can come into the middle depends on the possibility of his covering costs in the crosshatched area. That is, there must exist a minimum supply price schedule $p^s(z) = k/(n_a + n_b) + C(z)$ that cuts through the set of p-z combinations where the indifference curves overlap. If such a $p^s(z)$ does exist, the result will be called a sharing equilibrium: only one variety appears on the market, the seller generates a sufficient volume of sales to justify the lower price and covers costs, and all customers are better off. If it does not, then two varieties are sustained and though there exists an apparent hole in the market, it is too shallow to fill. The separating equilibrium is stable in the latter case. The probability of one good or two depends on the magnitude of the fixed cost, the numbers of customers in each group and the extent of differences in tastes between them. For a given pattern of preferences, a sharing equilibrium is more likely the greater the fixed cost, because savings from joint consumption are larger when fixed costs are large. Given fixed cost, a separating equilibrium is more likely the more diverse are preferences between the two groups. Potential gains from a compromise somewhere in the center are a decreasing function of the distance that each group could obtain in the two-good equilibrium. Finally, if it pays to share, the attributes offered by the good actually appearing on the market are closer to the attributes most preferred by the more numerous group. This is easily seen in an extreme case where n_a is much larger than n_b. Then the minumum supply price function for the one good equilibrium is only slightly below $p^s_a(z)$, and the set of possible compromise equilibria must lie very close to z_a. Indeed, if group B is sufficiently small, the distance between $p^s_a(z)$ and $p^s_b(z)$ becomes so large that a separating equilibrium may not exist at all.

If customer preferences are sufficiently diffused and dense, an entrepreneur offering a new product anywhere below the hedonic price function $p(z)$ will attract customers from neighboring product types. When there are constant or decreasing returns to scale and complete information, this is always profitable. While sales increase also in the case of increasing returns, the increase may not be sufficient to make the product viable. Only if the increased market share is sufficiently large is the new product a profitable venture in the latter case, a fact

[12] Of course the seller's pricing policy is constrained by potential entry of others producing similar varieties and also by the original two-good equilibrium.

that explains in part why businessmen are continually concerned with their market share. The problem has not been studied very much, and what little evidence exists is mixed. K. Cowling and J. Cubbin[13] examined the British auto market and report that models priced below the estimated price-attributes plane increased their market shares over the period studied. But J. E. Triplet and Cowling report no correlation between change in market share and deviations from the hedonic price regression in the U.S. market.[14] The theory sketched above suggests the correlation should be greater among those models with extreme negative deviations and perhaps not for other observations.

In the increasing returns example above a separating equilibrium is Pareto optimal overall if a sharing equilibrium cannot be sustained, and a sharing equilibrium is better only if it is sustainable. Thus, with complete information the free market provides the correct number of goods in this case, and there are never too many varieties on the market.[15] However, if a sharing equilibrium is sustainable there is no guarantee from impersonal market forces alone that the seller offers the good with the socially optimal characteristic vector to the market.[16]

A more complete treatment of the introduction and adoption of new products would take account of the stochastic nature of information flows among buyers and how the rate at which they switch to new products is distributed over time. The formal analysis becomes an exercise in optimal capital accumulation, where the accumulated information content of past advertising messages on product attributes and

---

13 K. Cowling and J. Cubbin, "Price, Quality and Advertising Competition: An Econometric Investigation of the U.K. Car Market," *Economica*, vol. 38, no. 152 (November 1971), pp. 378-394.

14 J. E. Triplet and K. Cowling, "A Quality Adjustment Model for Determining Market Shares in Oligopoly," Working Paper no. 4, U.S. Bureau of Labor Statistics, Washington, D.C., 1971.

15 The analysis of this section with increasing returns bears some resemblance to Lester G. Telser, "On the Regulation of Industry: A Note," *Journal of Political Economy*, vol. 77, no. 6 (November/December 1969), pp. 937-952, and to Kelvin Lancaster, "Socially Optimal Product Differentiation," *American Economic Review*, vol. 65 (September 1975), pp. 567-585. However, it is a counterexample to their result that there are too many sellers in competitive equilibrium. More generally, results about the number of sellers and varieties with increasing returns are sensitive to underlying distributions of consumer preferences in the market. Also, two goods are always optimal if perfect price discrimination is allowed. However, price discrimination is presumed to be infeasible in my analysis since consumer types cannot be recognized when they are seen. In this sense the one-good equilibrium is a constrained optimum.

16 The problem becomes similar to the analysis of public goods. See Paul Samuelson, "Pure Theory of Public Expenditure," *Review of Economics and Statistics*, vol. 36 (November 1954), pp. 387-389, and "Diagrammatic Exposition of a Theory of Public Expenditure," *Review of Economics and Statistics*, vol. 37 (November 1955), pp. 350-356.

price is treated as a form of firm specific capital.[17] When the rate of adoption of the new good is not instantaneous, a situation arises that is analogous to the problem of infant industries. The innovating firm most likely incurs losses in the first part of the new product life cycle when few people have learned about it and its market share is small. If the product is viable, such losses are recouped in the later part of the product's life, after its market share has grown sufficiently large. The overall profit from the introduction of the good is properly considered to be a quasi-rent or return on the firm's information disseminating and advertising activities.

It is clear from this analysis that the effects of advertising on the number of differentiated products in the market is ambiguous. Indeed, the question is not well defined, depending as it does on the state of information in the market, the costs and ease of disseminating it, the nature of technical change, and how entrepreneurs perceive their opportunities for filling gaps in the market. However, as a broad generalization, *improvements* in the technology of advertising and information dissemination should increase the sustainable number of varieties appearing on the market in the steady state. The logic of this proposition is simple enough. The set-up costs k in the model sketched above may be identified in part with the gross costs of communicating information to buyers. Evidently the larger is k the fewer the sustainable product varieties and the more bunching of consumer types among existing goods. When an improvement in technology causes k to decrease, more goods appear on the market because entrepreneurs find it easier and more profitable to seek out additional markets and to accommodate consumer types with minority preferences. The increase in the number of varieties brought about by the decrease in k increases social welfare, since the distance between the most preferred varieties and those available to buyers is lessened. Buyers and sellers are more efficiently matched. People with "odd" tastes and preferences suffer when information about products is costly, since it is difficult and more costly for sellers and buyers to communicate and to find each other. We have here a result

---

[17] The most direct reference is J. P. Gould, "Diffusion Processes and Optimal Advertising Policy," in Edmund Phelps et al., *Microeconomic Foundations of Employment and Inflation Theory* (New York: W. W. Norton, 1970). Other relevant references are Kenneth Arrow and Marc Nerlove, "Optimal Advertising Policy under Dynamic Conditions," *Economica*, vol. 29, no. 114 (May 1962), pp. 129-142; Edmund Phelps and S. G. Winter, Jr., "Optimal Price Policy under Atomistic Competition," in Edmund Phelps et al., *Microeconomic Foundations of Employment and Inflation Theory* (New York: W. W. Norton, 1970); Sherwin Rosen, "Learning by Experience as Joint Production," *Quarterly Journal of Economics*, vol. 86, no. 3 (August 1972), pp. 366-382; Richard Schmalensee, *The Economics of Advertising* (Amsterdam: North-Holland, 1972).

of the kind where "division of product is limited by the extent of the market," since the extent of the market and product specialization is constrained by information channels. Finally, the fact that information diffusion depends on population density implies that the number of products available also depends on population density. Is it any wonder then that more product varieties are available in larger cities than smaller ones?[18] Similarly, more varieties should appear among product types that have national or international markets compared with smaller regional or area specific markets. Less product variety should appear in markets where there are outright bans and prohibitions on advertising.

Advertising and Perceptions of Product Attributes

If sellers can increase profit and sales by offering a genuinely superior design and price in comparison with the existing (p,z) configuration, there remains a possibility of accomplishing a similar result by changing buyers' perceptions of an existing good. What if sellers can convince buyers that existing products contain superior attributes through intensive advertising campaigns or by designing products in inessential ways? So far as individual firms are concerned, these activities have the same initial effects on sales and profit as were examined in the preceding section. But the nature of market equilibrium and the social consequences of such actions are markedly different.

Figure 3 illustrates the situation. The schedule $p(z)$ represents an initial equilibrium where products are packed into an attribute range from z_s to z_l, catering to a dense set of customers with continuously varying tastes. Now consider a firm selling a product with attributes z_d, which, through advertising or other means, convinces buyers that the product is better than z_d—for example, that it has attributes z_d+e embodied in it rather than z_d. Given product price $p(z_d)$ this action has the consequence of undercutting neighboring and closely competing products, moving a mass of customers away from rival sellers and producing a gap in the market some distance on either side of z_d+e. For the same reasons as were discussed above, such a maneuver looks very profitable. However, the gains are fleeting. If the seller of z_d can convince customers in this manner, the symmetry of the situation suggests that other sellers can do the same. The result is economic warfare with a vengeance.

The offensive action by the seller of z_d provokes defensive actions by close competitors. In order to maintain their market share, these

[18] The point is closely related to the well-known problem of constructing intercity cost of living indexes when some goods cannot be obtained in some of the cities.

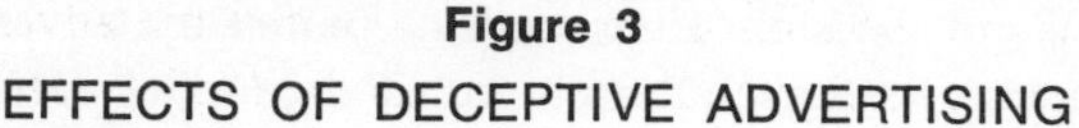

Figure 3
EFFECTS OF DECEPTIVE ADVERTISING

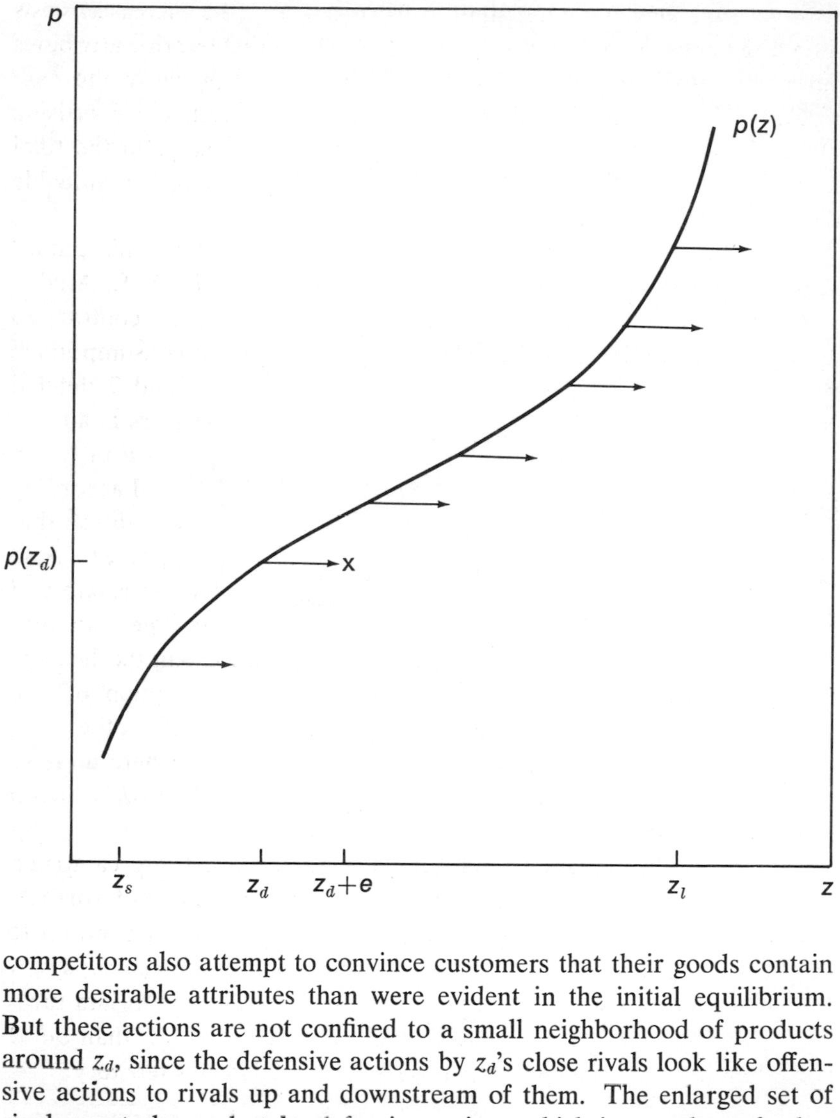

competitors also attempt to convince customers that their goods contain more desirable attributes than were evident in the initial equilibrium. But these actions are not confined to a small neighborhood of products around z_d, since the defensive actions by z_d's close rivals look like offensive actions to rivals up and downstream of them. The enlarged set of rivals must also undertake defensive actions which in turn have further upstream and downstream effects, and so it goes. Thus z_d's initial act has repercussions along the entire product spectrum, as illustrated by the arrows in Figure 3. The market result is that the perceived price-attributes schedule shifts to the right.

But this is not the end of the matter. Competing advertising campaigns have been cancelled out as it were, as each seller in turn attempts to maintain the proper "distance" from rivals. The only result is greater costs of sales with no redistribution of them, and the increased costs ultimately must be reflected in price. Thus the ultimate price-attributes curve must look much like the old one.[19] This is precisely the case discussed at the beginning of this paper. The total effects of advertising by all sellers together negate each other, leaving no change in the total market situation of either buyers or sellers and using up valuable resources in the process.

The above represents a rather blunt "sow's ear as silk purse" strategy. A more subtle analysis has been proposed by D. A. L. Auld,[20] using Kelvin Lancaster's approach to demand theory where, contrary to the above, the differentiated products are combinable in consumption.[21] For an illustration, suppose that there are two goods 1 and 2 defined according to the ratio in which they embody two characteristics z_1 and z_2. In Figure 4, let good 1 be defined according to the ratio *ol/al* in which z_1 and z_2 are embodied along line *oa* and let good 2 be defined according to the ratio *bj/oj* in which z_1 and z_2 are embodied along line *ob* (so that good 1 offers relatively more z_1 than z_2, and good 2 the opposite). Also let goods 1 and 2 be priced so that the consumer's budget set is *oab* and his consumption possibility schedule the line *ab*: the consumer can consume any combination (say *oi* and *ok*) of z_1 and z_2 along the line *ab*, but at any point on *ab*, he cannot increase his consumption of one characteristic without decreasing his consumption of the other. In Figure 4, the consumer's initial equilibrium is at point *c*, where he buys *cd* units of good 1 and *od* units of good 2 and where line *cd* is drawn parallel to line *oa*.

Now let the seller of good 1 undertake an advertising campaign aimed at convincing the consumer that good 1 contains more of attribute z_2 than it really does, moving its perceived attributes vector from *oa* to *oe*. The new perceived budget set becomes *oeb* and the consumer's new equilibrium lies somewhere along *eb*. As shown, if the equilibrium turns out to be anywhere between *e* and *f*, the consumer buys less than *od* of good 2 and the seller of good 1 has intruded on his rival's territory.

---

19 A possible exception would be at the boundaries (outer edges) of the market. The resemblance of this problem to recent discussions of competitive signaling should not pass unnoticed.

20 D. A. L. Auld, "Advertising and the Theory of Consumer Choice," *Quarterly Journal of Economics*, vol. 88 (August 1974), pp. 480-487.

21 Lancaster, "New Approach," pp. 132-157.

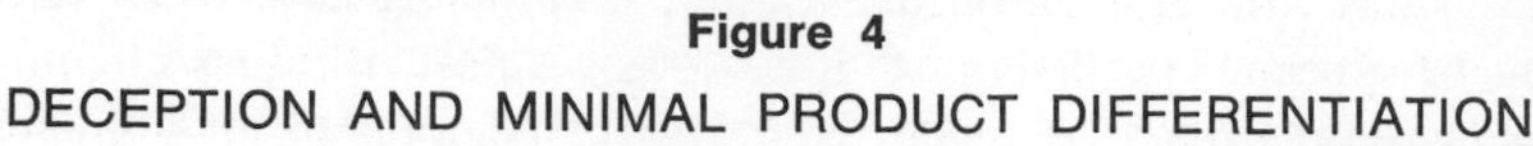

Figure 4

DECEPTION AND MINIMAL PRODUCT DIFFERENTIATION

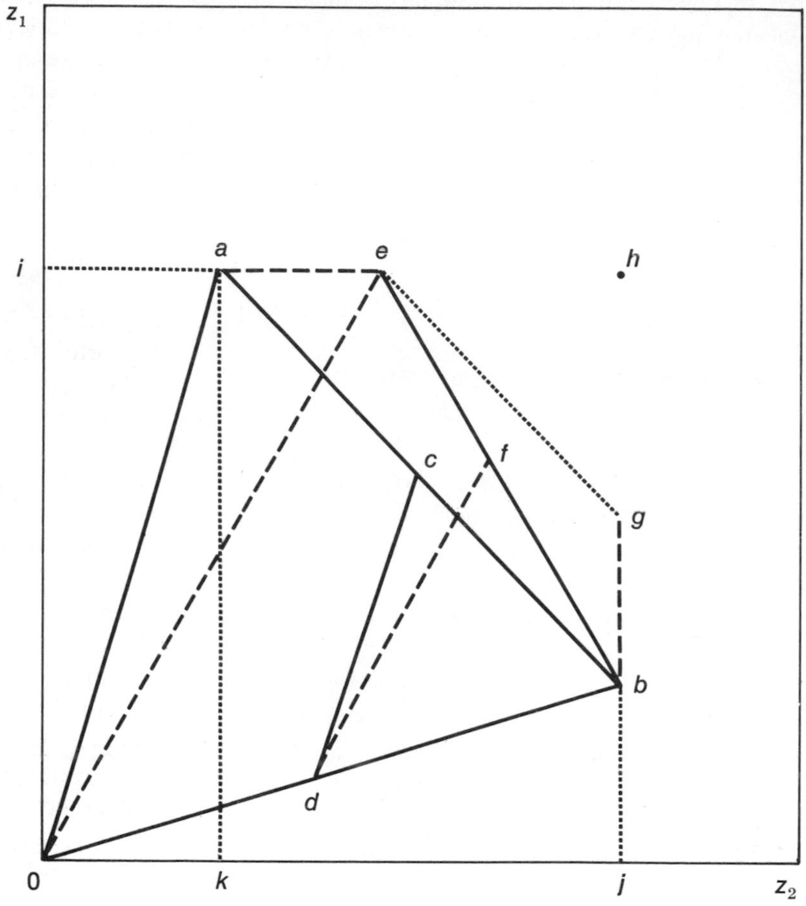

Again, however, we should not expect the rival to sit idly by and take this kind of punishment without retaliation. The seller of good 2 can redress the balance by convincing customers that his good actually contains the vector *og* rather than *ob*. The budget set becomes *oeg* and, by the same logic as before, seller 2 gets back sales lost to seller 1 in the first round so long as the new consumption vector lies in a certain range. Now the second round is ready to commence, then the third, and so forth. Indeed, it appears that the process converges to a point such as *h*, where both sellers have convinced the customer that their products are exactly the same! Instead of increased product differentiation we arrive at a kind of Hotelling's law of minimal product differentiation.[22]

Yet it is clear that *h* cannot be an equilibrium because selling costs have increased and total demand has not necessarily been redistributed. Thus the new equilibrium point may well lie closer to *c* than to *h*, though the minimum product differentiation feature would appear to remain intact. But why should there have been two firms offering two different goods, defined by the slopes of *oa* and *ob*, in the first place? If products embody characteristics in different proportions, it must be true that sellers can alter product designs to embody alternative proportions. Following a later approach to demand theory developed by Lancaster,[23] production possibilities of firms as discussed above suggest that the consumer's consumption possibility schedule should be concave (resembling, in smoothed-out form, the dashed line *a e g b*). Then any seller who would have produced a good with a characteristics ratio proportional to *oc*, that is, a seller who tailored his good to the desires of the customer depicted in the diagram, would have won all the business in the first place. In addition, if *oa* and *ob* actually do cater to certain types of customers who want exactly those proportions, the intrusion of each rival on the opponent's territory loses old customers as an expense of trying to attract new ones and new entrants find it profitable to cater to the neglected groups.

There are some very objectionable features to the scenarios discussed in this section. Surely not all silk purses are disguised sow's ears. At one time the label "made in Japan" was a negative attribute of a good, connoting shoddy and inferior merchandise. Has the quality of Japanese-made products genuinely changed, or have we only been led to believe that it has by clever packages and even more clever advertising campaigns? The real issue is how efficient consumers are at processing information. It seems unlikely that a general answer can be given to this question independent of the particular class of goods to be studied. The relevant factors probably include frequency of purchase and prior experience. For some kinds of goods it is easy and inexpensive for customers to ascertain "true" product attributes and false advertising claims. In this case there are long-run costs for firms pursuing deceptive

---

22 Harold Hotelling, "Stability in Competition," *Economic Journal* (1929), reprinted in American Economic Association, *Readings in Price Theory* (Chicago: Richard D. Irwin, Inc., 1952), pp. 467-484. Auld and Southey have extended Auld's analysis in "Advertising Strategy and the New Theory of Demand," *Southern Economic Journal*, vol. 42 (October 1975), pp. 225-230. They show that it is not always optimal to minimize apparent product differentiation, and this example should be modified to take that into account. Nevertheless, neither Auld nor Southey considers the actions of rival sellers in the market.

23 Lancaster, "Socially Optimal Product Differentiation," pp. 567-585.

strategies. There is value to a firm's reputation. Unfulfilled expectations and lack of credibility cut into repeat sales at a later date. For other kinds of goods it is difficult to ascertain a product's qualities, and false claims are more difficult to detect. But by the same token rational consumers should realize that claims are self-serving and that those claims that are least verifiable and potentially the most costly if false, should be regarded with the most skepticism.[24] Furthermore, it is in cases such as this that we expect private information services to arise that pool the experiences of many customers or undertake more systematic tests of various brands than any individual buyer is capable of accomplishing.

Nevertheless, some misleading information in advertising messages is to be expected, since information is too costly for consumers to be completely informed. In addition, it is well understood that production of attribute information services through private market agencies is likely to be insufficiently supplied, because information has many of the same features as common-property resources, and property rights in it are difficult to establish. Certainly one seldom encounters advertising messages that point out the negative features of a product, even though they may be a natural by-product of its admirable and desirable qualities. The most preferred and desirable attributes naturally are stressed instead.

The Value of Advertising Product Characteristics

A great deal of advertising is devoted to conveying information about the characteristics of goods. The value of knowing where individual sellers are located in the space of product attributes is comparable to knowing the seller's address on the geographical map. However, these values vary from buyer to buyer, depending on their own particular circumstances.[25]

The value of information about product characteristics varies directly with buyers' costs of search. When transactions and search costs are sufficiently small, buyers search more intensively and the additional advantage of intensive specialized search diminishes. The opposite is true for those with high search costs. Indeed, if search costs are sufficiently high it may not even pay to enter the differentiated products market at all. If advertising by firms economizes individual shopping effort, it may well induce some customers, who were pre-

---

[24] See Nelson, "Advertising as Information," pp. 729-754, and "Information and Consumer Behavior," pp. 311-329.

[25] A detailed analysis underlying this section is contained in the appendix, where advertising is treated as informing customers of the product attributes offered by particular firms.

viously out of the market because of high search costs, to enter the market. Thus advertising can actually expand the overall market. The value of a customer's time and search costs is similar from the seller's point of view to buyers' valuations of product attributes. Hence some sellers should cater to high search-cost customers by advertising and establishing reputations that effectively lower these costs. Sellers searching out customers by advertising and reputation are substitutes for buyers' search and shopping activities. Higher prices charged by sellers serving high search-cost customers represent equalizing differences on their "information attribute" qualities in much the same way that price differentials along $p(z)$ in the section above on the nature of competition represent equalizing differences for products with alternative characteristics and design.

The value of attribute information also depends on the difference between each consumer's preferences and market availabilities. If individual consumers exhibit little dispersion in their preferences and search costs, the gross value of advertising product characteristics is small and its net social value may be even negative, for the same reason it was in some of the examples in the section above on advertising and perceptions. Since advance knowledge of attributes allows customers to specialize search activities in the most preferred varieties, the value of catering to particular groups is correspondingly greater when there is greater dispersion in tastes among buyers.[26]

Advertising may allow better matching and more specialized search activities. If so, we expect that the market would not support as much pure price dispersion among product varieties, bringing consumers of each variety closer to the Pareto optimality condition of equal marginal rates of substitution in consumption. The effect on the number of varieties appearing on the market is more problematic. When attributes are not known in advance, but must be certified by personal inspection, firms gain less from offering the optimal characteristics in their products. Some varieties might be viable that would not be sustained in the presence of better information, and it is impossible to predict whether or not there would be a proliferation of varieties with advertising. It is clear, however, that those varieties appearing in the presence of superior attribute information are more likely to be closer to optimal, because the gains to firms from seeking out specialty submarkets are correspondingly greater, and customers purchase goods with more preferred characteristics.

Finally, there are systematic effects on market size and share due to scale economies in information diffusion, a point that calls into

26 See below, at the conclusion of the Appendix.

question Nelson's conjecture that more heavily advertised brands are likely to be better buys. It is a curious feature of attribute advertising that it informs some buyers not to shop among certain brands. Thus the incentives for advertising are clearly related to expected size of the market. On the one hand those varieties that would be less viable when information is less imperfect obviously have less incentives to advertise. In this sense the incentive to advertise depends on the seller's expectations of how well his brands cater to market preferences. Hence more heavily advertised brands are likely to be better buys. On the other hand, customers with minority preferences suffer in the presence of imperfect information because it is more costly for sellers to seek them out and tailor products to their needs and preferences. Specialized minority varieties may still appear in the market without much advertising if minority preferences are sufficiently intense relative to high volume alternative goods and their private costs of search are not too large. Clearly more heavily advertised brands are more likely to cater to "mass preferences" in the market and are unlikely best buys for those with more esoteric tastes.

Appendix

This is an analysis of the optimum search strategies of consumers in markets of the type described above, pp. 165-179, in the presence of imperfect information and costs of transacting. George Stigler and J. J. McCall examined search behavior in markets for identical and homogeneous goods that sustain price dispersion by transaction costs.[27] Here I attempt to generalize their results to markets where price dispersion is also sustained by transactions costs but where goods are heterogeneous. Again the heterogeneity is indexed by the attributes embodied by goods.

The model with full information in the second section of this paper showed that knowledge of the price-attributes function $p(z)$ contained all relevant data the consumer needed to make a correct decision. In the case of incomplete information, the immediate generalization of $p(z)$ is a joint probability distribution of product prices and characteristics. Denote the joint density defined over (p,z) by $\phi(p,z)\,dpdz$. The conditional distribution of price given z represents observed price dispersion among varieties in the market with identical attributes z. If all goods are homogeneous and equivalent in characteristics, the conditional density completely describes market observations, just as in Stigler and McCall. Thus one can view the present problem as a "distribution of

[27] See Stigler, "The Economics of Information," pp. 213-225, and J. J. McCall, "Economics of Information and Job Search," *Quarterly Journal of Economics*, vol. 84 (February 1970), pp. 113-126.

price distributions," the convolution of price distributions for each product variety and a distribution of varieties. The marginal distribution of z indicates the proportion of the differentiated products market accounted for by varieties embodying alternative attributes z.

The density $\phi(p,z)dpdz$ is meant to represent the circumstances underlying the construction of hedonic price indexes. For example, consider the regression model

$$ln(p) = \gamma z + \epsilon \tag{10}$$

where γ is a vector of regression coefficients and ϵ is a random variable with zero mean and variance σ^2. Many studies report fits of semi-log functions such as (10) to a wide variety of differentiated products. Equation (10) is the conditional regression of $ln(p)$ on z. Let ϵ be normally distributed. Then the conditional density of p given z is also normal and given by

$$N(p|z) = (1/p\sigma\sqrt{2\pi})exp - [ln(p) - \gamma z)/\sigma]^2/2.$$

Denote the density of product types z by $\lambda(z)dz$. Therefore, $\phi(p,z)$ is given by

$$\phi(p,z) = N(p|z)\lambda(z) = [\lambda(z)/p\sigma\sqrt{2\pi}]exp - [(ln(p) - \gamma z)/\sigma]^2/2.$$

in this case. Consumers' information about $\phi(p,z)$ is obtained by shopping around and comparing prices and attributes of alternative brands.

In the first problem to be considered the buyer has a generally correct notion of price and quality dispersion in the market and samples various sellers at random. Each sample (that is, shopping trip) costs $\$x$. The buyer does not know in advance the specific attributes and price offered by any randomly sampled seller, but gains this information after a sample has been taken and the good has been examined and inspected. The second problem considers a case where buyers have preknowledge of the attributes offered by each seller through prior information and advertising. The information revealed by sampling relates to price only. The difference in consumer welfare in these two situations is an important component of the demand price for attribute information. It is the value of knowing the product characteristics location of sellers in advance.

As before, the consumer has a utility function

$$u = U(c,z) \tag{11}$$

but is now subject to two constraints. One is the joint density of p and z, $\phi(p,z)$ described above. The other is a budget constraint

$$y = c + p(z) + xs \tag{12}$$

where y is income, c is other consumption goods normalized to have unit price, s is the number of samples taken, xs is the total shopping and search expenditure, z is the attributes of the product actually purchased, and $p(z)$ is the price paid for it. In contrast to the earlier problem, c, p, and z are random variables, depending on the accidents of search. Hence u is also a random variable and finding a maximum of u has no meaning. Instead, the objective function must take the form of maximizing the expected value of u, subject to $\phi(p,z)$ and the budget equation (12).[28]

Two types of solution have been proposed for this class of problems. One is an optimum sample size rule whereby the consumer decides in advance how many samples to take, retains all sample information, and returns to the seller offering the best deal. Another is a "stopping rule" strategy that has certain optimality properties. It so happens that describing a stopping rule for the problem at hand is much easier than finding a sample size rule.

Recall the stopping rule property in the case of sampling from a known price distribution over a homogeneous good. One computes a reservation price such that search ceases as soon as the buyer finds a seller offering the item at a price equal to or less than the reservation price. When a seller is encountered who quotes a price above the reservation price, the offer is rejected and another sample is taken. Things are not quite so simple as that in the present case, because goods are heterogeneous. Instead of a single reservation price there must be a whole set of reservation prices, one for each variety of the product encountered. The optimal search strategy turns out to be described by a reservation price-attributes *function* that divides the attainable price-attributes set into two regions, an acceptance set and a rejection set. If a sample yields an observation anywhere above the reservation price function the offer is rejected and another sample is taken. If the sample yields an observation below the reservation price function, it lies in the acceptance set, the item is purchased, and search ceases. The division of the sample space into acceptance and rejection sets depends on the buyer's tastes and on the costs of sampling. For example those for whom sampling costs are small obviously can afford to be more selective.

The problem is greatly simplified and the nature of solution is most clearly seen by a transformation of the data. Notice that any multivariate observation in (p,z) space is uniquely associated with a value of utility, from properties of the indirect utility function. Hence the multivariate problem can be converted to an elementary univariate problem: use (11) and (12) to transform the density $\phi(p,z)$ into a density defined on u.

I illustrate the procedure in the case where a consumer's utility function is linear

$$u = c + Bz. \tag{13}$$

Here B is a vector of marginal utilities of the z components expressed in terms of the consumption good (dollars). Each component of B

[28] And requiring the assumption, contrary to most of this paper, that $U(c,z)$ in (11) is concave.

directly gives the amount the consumer is willing to pay for additional increments of that component. Moreover, (13) conveniently represents differences in tastes among consumers according to differences in B. The indirect utility function corresponding to (13) gross of search costs is

$$\bar{w} = y - p + Bz \qquad (14)$$

w is a random variable because p and z are random variables. Define a set of dummy variables $R = z$, which along with (14) define a non-singular transformation from (p,z) to (w,R). The Jacobian of the transformation is unity and the density of (w,R) is simply

$$\psi(w,R)\,dwdR = \phi(y - w + BR,R)\,dwdR \qquad (15)$$

The marginal density of "gross utility" w is found by integrating over R in (15):

$$\theta(w)\,dw = \int_R \psi(w,R)\,dRdw = \int_R \phi(y - w + BR,R)\,dRdw \qquad (16)$$

We want to maximize expected utility net of search costs, subject to (16). The problem has now been cast in a form analogous to searching from a univăriate distribution and it is clear that a reservation *utility* policy is the optimal policy. Denote a reservation utility level by v such that offers yielding utility in excess of v are acceptable. The probability of stopping, that is, of finding an acceptable offer in any random sample must be

$$\pi = \int_v^\infty \theta(w)\,dw \qquad (17)$$

and if an acceptable offer is found, expected utility gross of search costs is

$$\bar{w} = \int_v^\infty w\theta(w)\,dw / \int_v^\infty \theta(w)\,dw \qquad (18)$$

where $\theta(w)/\int_v^\infty \theta(w)\,dw$ is the density of w conditional on an acceptable offer. Consequently the net expected utility from searching is

$$E(u) = \pi(\bar{w} - x) + (1-\pi)\pi(\bar{w} - 2x) + (1-\pi)^2\pi(\bar{w} - 3x) + \ldots \qquad (19)$$

where sx is search cost after s searches and $(1-\pi)^s\pi$ is the probability of taking exactly s samples given the optimal strategy. $\bar{w} - sx$ is expected net utility associated with exactly s samples. Factoring (19) into two components, one in $\pi\bar{w}$ and the other in πx, and solve the infinite series to arrive at

$$\bar{U} = E(u) = \bar{w} - x/\pi. \qquad (20)$$

$1/\pi$ is the average number of searches before an acceptable offer is found, and (20) shows that expected net utility is expected gross utility given an acceptable offer, $\bar{w}$, minus expected search costs, x/π. Finally, using (17) and (18), equation (20) can be rewritten in its functional equation equivalent form:[29]

$$\bar{U} = \int_v^\infty (w-x)\,\theta(w)\,dw + (\bar{U}-x)\int_0^v \theta(w)\,dw. \qquad (21)$$

Maximum expected utility is found by differentiating either (20) or (21) with respect to v and setting the result equal to zero. Denoting the optimal reservation value of w by v^* the result is

$$x = \int_{v^*}^\infty (w-v^*)\,\theta(w)\,dw \qquad (22)$$

which is readily verified to be a maximum because $\partial^2 U/\partial v^2 < 0$. Equation (21) shows that marginal search costs are set equal to expected marginal utility gains from search at the optimum.[30] Finally, since the right-hand side of (22) is decreasing in v^* at a decreasing rate, differentiation with respect to x proves that $dv^*/dx < 0$ and the acceptance utility level is decreasing in x. Since $1/\pi$ increases in v^*, an acceptable offer is more readily encountered when search costs are large.

The solution is illustrated in Figure 5. The ellipses display the probability contours of $\phi(p,z)$. The line labeled $p^* = y - v^* + Bz$ is the reservation price function and any observation below it is accepted. The reservation price function is a member of the family of price-attribute indifference curves discussed above, p. 168. If search costs had been larger v^* would have been smaller, and the reservation price function would shift upward, enlarging the acceptance region and decreasing the rejection region. The reservation price line depends directly on preferences. In the case shown, larger values of B increase the slope of p^*, and it is more likely that the customer purchases a variety with greater z content.

Now consider a problem where attributes of goods offered by individual sellers are known in advance. The solution consists of two parts: first fix an arbitrary value of z and find an optimal reservation price corresponding to it. Next choose z optimally. The difference between this problem and the other is that z is no longer a random variable. Here buyers can exploit conditional distributions rather than being constrained by unconditional distributions.

---

[29] A useful survey by S. A. Lippman and J. J. McCall, titled "The Economics of Job Search: A Survey," *Economic Inquiry*, vol. 14, no. 3 (September 1976), pp. 347-368, shows that the nature of the solution is similar when utility functions exhibiting risk aversion are considered. Since risk aversion is not essential to my problem there is little lost by ignoring it. It is interesting to note that the functional equation takes on a much more complex form than (21) when U is nonlinear, since the term analogous to $\bar{w}-sx$ in (19) are no longer linear and (19) cannot be factored into separate return and search-cost components. Also, I have analyzed the infinite horizon problem: the finite horizon problem has similar features, except that the reservation price-attributes functions shift upward and the acceptance set is enlarged as search continues.

[30] Compare with McCall, "Economics of Information and Job Search," pp. 113-126.

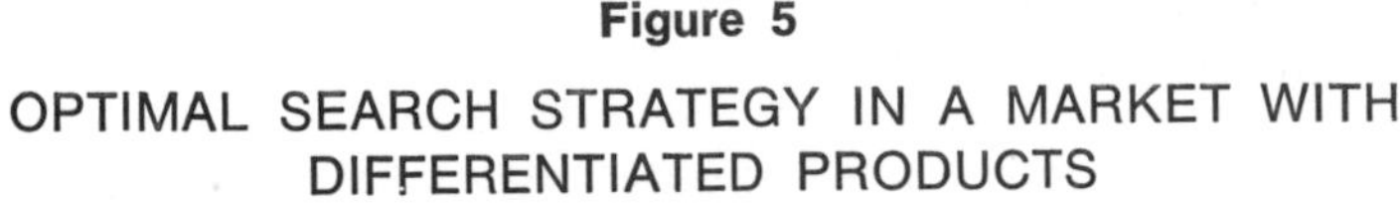

Figure 5

OPTIMAL SEARCH STRATEGY IN A MARKET WITH DIFFERENTIATED PRODUCTS

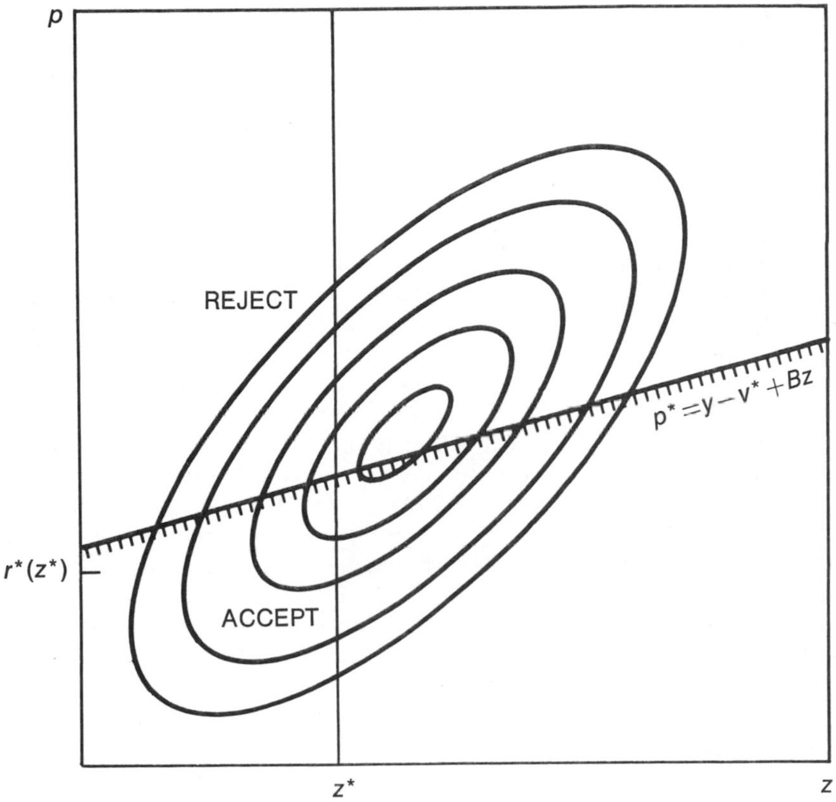

Let

$$\xi(p|z) = \phi(p,z)/\int_p \phi(p,z)\,dp$$

represent the conditional distribution of price for those varieties of goods embodying attributes z. Let $\overline{U}(z)$ represent expected utility conditional on this arbitrary value of z. By the same logic that was used to arrive at (21), here

$$\overline{U}(z) = \int_0^{r(z)} (y+Bz-p)\,\xi\,(p|z)\,dp - x + \overline{U}(z)\int_{r(z)}^{\infty} \xi(p|z)\,dp \qquad (23)$$

where $r(z)$ is the reservation price corresponding to goods with attributes z. Only products selling for prices below $r(z)$ are acceptable. Differentiate (23) with respect to r, set the result equal to zero and rearrange to obtain a conditional optimum analogous to (22);

$$x = \int_0^{r^*(z)} (r^* - p)\xi(p|z)\,dp, \tag{24}$$

a result identical to one found in McCall. However, (24) is only a conditional maximum. Substitute it into (23) and simplify to obtain

$$\overline{U}(z) = y + Bz - r^*(z) \tag{25}$$

Therefore, an unconditional maximum is found by differentiating (25) with respect to z and setting the result equal to zero, or

$$B = dr^*(z)/dz = -\int_0^{r^*} (r^* - p)\xi_z(p|z)\,dp \Big/ \int_0^{r^*} \xi(p|z)\,dp \tag{26}$$

where $\xi_z = \partial\xi/\partial z$. The first part of (26) has some features reminiscent of the optimality condition in the case of complete information in the second section of this paper.

The solution is also depicted in Figure 5. Optimality condition (26) is represented by the vertical line through the optimal variety, z^*, with $r^*(z^*)$ showing the maximum acceptable price for that class of goods. When attribute locations are known in advance, buyers completely specialize search and shopping activities among brands offering their optimal combinations of characteristics, and continue searching until acceptably priced items are found. Buyers with values of B other than that for the consumer shown in Figure 5 would have searched over a different class of goods. Buyers obviously do better on the average when locations of sellers are known in advance because search is concentrated on the most preferred varieties and shopping activities can be pursued more intensively.

A special case is worth noting. Consider the case in which the consumer has a linear utility function. He would then be willing to pay at most $\max_z \overline{U}(z) - \max \overline{U}$ for such information. This difference is a perfect index of the value of attribute information and must be nonnegative. (A similar compensating variation could be defined with nonlinear utility functions.) Consider also an empirically relevant case where the conditional density $\xi(p|z)$ corresponds to a linear hedonic price function of the form

$$\xi(p|z) = \Gamma z + \epsilon$$

where ϵ is homoskedastic, and Γ is a vector of fixed regression coefficients. In this case, where the probability contours in Figure 5 are all straight lines parallel to the points of means $p = \Gamma z$, it can be shown that the value of attribute information (the difference between $\max_z \overline{U}(z)$ and $\max \overline{U}$) is directly proportional to $|B - \Gamma|$. If B is very close to Γ it makes little difference to buyers which varieties are purchased, since average price differences on alternative goods more or less equalize subjective valuations of them all over the map. On the other hand when B is much different from Γ, a buyer's advantage from specialized search closer to the optimal variety is much greater.

The strong result of this second problem, that buyers completely specialize search to a unique class of goods offering the most preferred attributes, is due to the strong assumption that the underlying distributions $\phi(p,z)$ or $\xi(p|z)$ are known and that search yields no distributional information in and of itself. A Bayesian strategy must be followed when the distributions are not known precisely. Search modifies subsequent distributions as new sample information is combined with a priori distributions to produce new posterior distributions after each sample. However, it is known that the fundamental acceptance-rejection partition described above still applies to these more complex problems.[31] Thus while some details would be changed, the general nature of the solution and comparison between the two situations described above must still apply. For example, complete specialization does not occur when only limited prior information is known about individual sellers' product attributes, but certainly more specialization takes place than when no prior information is available at all.

[31] See Lippman and McCall, "Economics of Job Search."

COMMENTARIES

Yehuda Kotowitz

There are three very contentious questions in the economics of advertising. First, Is advertising a form of information or misinformation, or, more precisely, What are the conditions under which advertising will contain information or misinformation? Second, Is the correct amount of advertising supplied by the market? And, finally, Is advertising a barrier to entry that increases monopoly?

Because the papers in this part refer mainly to the first question, I shall concentrate my remarks on it. I shall also direct most of my remarks to Nelson's paper because I disagree with it. I find Rosen's paper to be excellent within the narrow confines that he sets for it. However, I think that these confines are much too narrow and beg some of the important questions.

Both Nelson and Rosen discuss advertising as information. They dismiss the possibility that advertising might transmit misinformation, by suggesting that consumers are able to verify such information fairly cheaply or that, if unable to do so, will disregard the information as coming from a suspect source. It is, consequently, not surprising that both papers conclude that social welfare is improved by the existence of advertising. This way of thinking seems to go against the grain of most people who are not economists. I find it puzzling that economists exposed to TV—perhaps some of them do not watch it—should claim that there is no such thing as misleading advertising.

My own casual viewing suggests to me that, at least on television and perhaps in other media, the amount of misleading advertising is tremendous, although, of course, there is a great deal of informative advertising as well. If survival of business practices over a long period of time is any indication of the profitability of these practices, we must accept the position that at least some misleading advertising pays. And this is true for firms that have long been established as well as for fly-by-night operations. Therefore it is important to have a theory that explains the circumstances giving rise to misleading advertising.

Nelson tackles the problem by recognizing that where prepurchase information or inspection cannot verify the advertising claims—that is, in the case of what he calls experience goods—consumers would simply disbelieve any direct information that is contained in the advertising message. In this case, he says, direct advertising will have no effect. This raises the question: Why do businesses bother to advertise such products?

According to Nelson, the relevant information is that the product is advertised, because advertised products are the best buys. This is, of course, a bootstrap argument. If consumers think that advertised products are the best buys, it will pay somebody to advertise an inferior product in order to create this impression. That is, the volume of advertising will constitute the misleading signal. It does not really matter whether the seller actually comes out and says that his product is better when in fact it is not. If he gives this impression by indirect means, it is misleading just the same. In this case, we will have Gresham's Law of advertising: false advertising will drive good advertising out of the market. All advertising will be misleading. And, consequently, consumers will disbelieve it whether it is direct information or indirect information.

The real question is whether the market will reward the transmission of correct information and discipline the transmission of misleading information, whichever way it is transmitted, directly or indirectly.

The key behavioral assumptions of both studies are that advertising leads consumers to try a product or to seek additional information about it and that, once the product is purchased, consumers can evaluate it. Therefore, misleading information yields only temporary gains and is suitable only for fly-by-night operations. If this is the case, direct information is clearly superior to indirect information from the point of view of both consumers and sellers, because blame and credit can easily be assigned. Consumers will value direct information over indirect information.

Nelson attempts to show that indirect information, in the form of heavy advertising, is likely to supply a signal which is correlated, albeit imperfectly, with low price per unit of quality and which therefore signifies a better buy. However, as argued before, under the assumption of easy verification consumers would be influenced by direct rather than by indirect information. Consequently, business will supply mostly direct information. Nelson's theoretical argument is therefore entirely unconvincing, even if we accept the technical arguments that advertising and price are likely to be negatively correlated and that consequently "the most heavily advertised goods are the best buys."

Moreover, the technical arguments are equally unconvincing and in some cases erroneous, so even the tentative negative correlation between advertising and price is not established. First, the analysis is conducted for the case of a very specific demand function—the translog. While this function has been extensively used in production analysis, its use as a demand function is questionable. In any case, any results obtained are valid only for this form of function and have no validity whatever for the general case. Moreover, even for this function the results are assumed rather than proven. For example, the results of Appendix A depend critically on the sign and magnitude of α_3 which is assumed to be negative *or* small. One might as well assume the desired relation.

Further, even if one accepts the result that a given change in price yields a change in advertising in the opposite direction (that is, $A' = dlnA/dlnP < 0$), it does not follow that "the more heavily a brand advertises, the more likely it is to be a better buy." This is because A' describes the relation between advertising and prices that a firm will follow at any output if the *ratio* of advertising to price is determined optimally. However, no firm will operate along this path (the *mutatis mutandis* demand curve in Demsetz's terminology), since only one point on it is relevant, that is, the point at which both instruments rather than just their ratio are set at optimum. Consequently, it is not clear why movement along this *mutatis mutandis* demand curve should occur at all. If one wishes to analyze differences among firms that are generally equal but different in one characteristic, such as MC^*, the correct procedure is to differentiate totally the first order condition with respect to this characteristic and observe the signs of $\frac{dP}{dMC^*}$ and $\frac{dA}{dMC^*}$. This Nelson has not done even for his narrow demand function. Consequently, most of the verbal arguments purporting to prove the effects of movement along the demand curve do not prove his contention.

I would like to return to the main point, which is that if consumers are unable to evaluate advertising claims perfectly, there are temporary gains from transmission of false advertising. These may be enough to offset the long-run cost of being found out, provided that consumers can be persuaded to believe the seller's claim to begin with. This caveat poses a serious problem because consumers know that advertising is suspect. Why, then, would they believe advertisers' claims when these are not easily verifiable?

To explain this, one must go back to fundamentals. I think the problem with most of the analyses of advertising is that we have not taken a good look at the psychology of how consumers actually make decisions and how they incorporate information of different kinds in the way in which they make purchasing decisions. In a series of unpublished papers, Professor F. Mathewson of the University of Toronto and I attempted to accomplish this task.

We show that before purchase, an individual, who is uncertain about the quality of a good, must form an opinion about the good by using whatever sources of information are available to him. Whether advertising affects this prior opinion depends, first of all, on the availability of reliable and consistent objective information. This depends, among other things, on taste diversity and, therefore, on the consumer's ability to find consensus among objective sources.

If there is a great deal of taste diversity, it is difficult for consumers to make up their minds clearly about any given product because they are given conflicting information by their friends and advisers. It is also difficult to obtain reliable advice when products are complex and verification of conflicting claims is difficult or expensive. In this case a diversity of opinion is likely even if tastes do not differ.

Where objective information is scarce, expensive, or conflicting, consumers must attempt to make up their own minds using whatever information is available. When information comes from a suspect source—advertising—consumers require such information to be more persuasive than that supplied by an objective source, but they do not ignore it. They may be willing to accept a *Consumer Reports* evaluation without much persuasion, but they generally require persuasion in accepting advertisers' claims. Thus, for example, the claim that enzymes improve washing ability by biological action is reasonably persuasive, even though it may be of limited validity. Consumers may be willing to accept it even if the source of the information is suspect.

The foregoing assumes that consumers operate rationally, knowing their limitations and the sources of the information. This, of course, is not always the case. Consumers may be subject to psychological manipulation, and the suspect source of the information may be disguised. Thus advertisers attempt to obtain "endorsements" from respected persons or media such as *Good Housekeeping*. (Apparently, many people believe that the *Good Housekeeping* seal implies that the magazine tested and approved the product in an objective fashion.) To the extent that such manipulation is effective (and there is a great deal of disagreement on whether it is) it will strengthen the foregoing argument on the persuasiveness of advertising.

Consumers' opinions about product quality are summarized in our analysis by a prior probability distribution that assigns a probability to each expected quality level. The variance of this probability distribution is a measure of the strength of the individual's belief in his preconceived notions. On the basis of this prior distribution the consumer decides whether to purchase the product. After purchase he must take the experience into account and modify whatever opinions he had before.

The previous speakers assumed that experience simply overrules consumers' previous opinions. In fact, however, most individuals change their minds only rather slowly, except, of course, in the face of overwhelming evidence.

We find that the optimal process in this kind of situation is a Bayesian procedure that determines an optimal rule for the revision of expectations about quality. The rule yields a set of equations that determine the learning process. The key elements of the analysis are the determinants of the speed of learning, that is, the speed at which experience modifies prior belief. It turns out that the more complex the product, the slower is the speed at which beliefs are modified. For instance, the consumer who takes a medicine and feels better does not really know whether this is because of the medicine or not—whether, in fact, the medicine hastened the cure or retarded it.

Claims about car repairs or appliance repairs are in the same category. It is often difficult to verify that repairs charged for were made and were necessary. So the improved performance is no guarantee of value received. Incidentally, there is a good deal of fraud in this area. For example, *Consumer Reports* loosened a tube in a radio and had it repaired in many different shops. They found that the bills ranged from nothing—which is what it should have been—to something over the value of the radio in the first place. Parts that were not needed were, in some instances, exchanged or not exchanged and charged for.

The second cause of slow learning is infrequent use. For example, seat belts may not be subjected to test until too late.

Another element, which has been stressed by Porter, is that if the valuation depends on the opinion of others, it is very difficult to know whether the product did its work or not.[1] Did the perfume really knock him out, or was he just drunk?

The less knowledgeable the consumer, on the average, the slower the speed of learning, although this is not always the case. In fact, less knowledgeable consumers sometimes learn too fast in the wrong direction.

It can be shown that the speed of learning will decline with time. That is, people who have accumulated experience tend to learn more slowly than people who are newly coming into the use of a product.

[1] Michael Porter, *Interbrand Choice, Strategy and Bilateral Market Power* (Cambridge: Harvard University Press, 1976).

But learning never ceases altogether because there is generally some attrition of information. The attrition of information can occur because of revision in product characteristics or simply because individuals forget. The rate of attrition of information is a lower bound to the speed of learning. Therefore, experienced consumers only learn enough from experience to offset the loss of information due to the passage of time, yielding a linear steady state model of learning.

When producers' decision models are analyzed using the consumer learning model, we find that the speed of consumer learning and the importance of the characteristics advertised are the main determinants of the producer's incentive to supply misinformation. To the extent that sellers can supply information that is not easily verifiable but is important to consumers, either in an objective or in a subjective way, it pays the seller to substitute a claim of quality for the actual quality. Consequently, under these conditions, advertising will tend to operate as a substitute for quality rather than as a complement. This tendency is stronger the slower the speed of learning. In this sense, advertising supplies misinformation and causes products of too low a quality to be sold at too high a price.

I would like to make one more point regarding the question of barriers to entry. There has been considerable argument whether there are economies of scale in advertising. This point is important because it bears on the use of advertising by established firms as a barrier to entry, which helps maintain their monopoly power over time. Our analysis, based on the signal detection literature, suggests an affirmative answer.[2] It appears that, in the presence of noise, listeners can perceive a signal only if the signal is at a considerably higher level than the noise. The shape of the signal detection curve is a cumulative normal distribution (S-shaped). Returns to increasing signal/noise ratio first increase and then decrease. This is precisely the form required to yield both barriers to entry *and* monopoly profits. By supplying a sufficient level of noise relative to the signal it is possible to keep the probability of detection quite low at relatively low noise/signal ratios. It is possible to think of advertising by established firms as noise that a newcomer must overcome in transmitting his signal to consumers. Because the relative amount of noise necessary to drown out any signal is low, the relative cost of established firms is low compared with that of newcomers, yielding an effective barrier to entry.

---

[2] See, for example, R. C. Atkinson, G. H. Bower, and E. J. Crothers, *An Introduction to Mathematical Learning Theory* (New York: John Wiley and Sons, 1965).

James M. Ferguson

One fundamental issue is the appropriate framework to be used in evaluating advertising. Let me propose that we evaluate institutions—and advertising is one of our social institutions—not in marginal but in total terms: Is the social product larger with or without the institutions? This is the theme of Professor Coase's work, "The Problem of Social Cost."[1] The issue is not whether advertising is perfect but whether the benefits of advertising outweigh the costs, so that the social welfare is greater with advertising.

This total approach is implicit in Nelson's earlier work, in which he basically argues that, in order to understand the role of advertising, we have to consider what the allocation of resources, the number of brands, and the quality of brands would be like in the absence of advertising. In this regard, let me quote from my book:

> Nevertheless, it is possible to conclude that the effects of advertising on elasticities of demand, barriers to entry, and concentration, are all irrelevant to establishing whether advertising benefits consumers. Contrary to the conclusion of the proponents of the view that advertising increases monopoly, consumers benefit from advertising, even if demands become less elastic, barriers to entry increase, and product differentiation increases. Consumers still benefit from the introduction of advertising, because advertising lowers the cost of information about brand qualities and leads to increases in brand quality, and because the average price per unit of quality, including sampling and alteration costs, are lower. Even if the critics of advertising were correct, therefore, that advertising decreases elasticities of demand, increases barriers to entry, and increases product differentiation, consumers are still better off. Advertising cannot increase the cost per unit of quality to consumers because, if it did, consumers would not continue to respond to advertising.[2]

Bear in mind that the consumer sovereignty principle advanced here does not mean that there is no deceptive advertising or that the most heavily advertised brand always offers the most quality per dollar of expenditure. The relevant comparison is between consumer welfare with and without advertising. The argument simply states that the cost to consumers of using alternative sources of information in the absence of

[1] Ronald Coase, "The Problem of Social Cost," *Journal of Law and Economics*, vol. 3 (October 1960), pp. 1-44.

[2] James Ferguson, *Advertising and Competition: Theory, Measurement, Fact* (Cambridge, Mass.: Ballinger, 1974), p. 36.

advertising exceeds the cost to consumers of using advertising, including the resource costs involved in advertising and including the costs of any deceptive advertising. We are comparing two alternative institutional arrangements, neither of which is perfect.

Economic theory predicts that when buyers lack perfect information—because information is not a free good and it is too costly to eliminate all ignorance—sellers will disseminate some false or misleading information. Sellers will act so that at the margin the returns from lying or misleading are equal to the returns from telling the truth. Thus, the existence of advertising that is not totally accurate and that fails to point out the limitations of advertised products is certainly not surprising. Nor is the existence of such advertising sufficient to condemn advertising as an institution. (It is, of course, true that the presence of imperfect information in the market does not justify government intervention, because intervention also has costs and these costs may exceed the benefits, as in fact they always appear to do.)

Thus, in my opinion, the critics of advertising who condemn advertising either because of its alleged adverse effects on competition or because of its alleged lack of truthfulness have paid insufficient attention to the benefits to consumers from the information provided by advertising.

Fortunately, the two excellent papers by Nelson and Rosen analyze the informative role of advertising. Two different pairs of assumptions underlie the analyses of the two authors. Nelson assumes identical consumer tastes and discusses the role of advertising in assisting consumers to ascertain the quality of brands with respect to product characteristics about which consumers agree. Rosen assumes that consumers' tastes differ and analyzes the role of advertising in assisting consumers to find the brands with the characteristics that best satisfy their specific tastes. Also, Nelson attempts to demonstrate the absence of increasing returns to advertising, while Rosen assumes increasing returns to informing consumers about product characteristics.

Perhaps the most fundamental point Rosen makes is his explanation of the benefit to buyers from advertising. Advertising informs consumers of the attributes of the goods offered by sellers. When consumers know in advance where the sellers' products are located on the product spectrum, which is what Rosen means by the location of the sellers, they can concentrate their search on the products that are most likely to offer the combination of characteristics they want. The information provided by advertising enables consumers to narrow their search and increases the likelihood that they will find the particular brand that best satisfies their tastes.

After an excellent discussion of competitive markets for differentiated products and the strong incentives for sellers to fill in gaps in the product characteristic spectrum by improving their products and thereby appealing to more consumers (a wider range of consumer tastes), Rosen introduces the problems that arise when there are scale economies and when, therefore, it is not necessarily socially optimal to produce goods that cater to every consumer taste. Under these circumstances the cost savings from production specialization to take advantage of the economies of scale can exceed the utility losses to consumers from not having every desired "product variety." For example, we see ready-made suits supplant tailor-made suits for most people, although people who have specialized tastes and want particular kinds of clothes that most people do not want, or are unwilling to pay for, can still go to a tailor. In most markets there is a wide range of products available.

In his discussion of the difficulties of introducing new products, Rosen seems to confuse the level of the reduction in the hedonic price with the presence or absence of increasing returns. Any given reduction in the hedonic price will have the same likelihood of success regardless whether there are increasing, constant, or decreasing returns to scale. What is different among these cases is that the reduction in the hedonic price in the case of increasing returns will be greater the greater the number of people attracted to the new product, whereas the reduction in the hedonic price is not a function of the number of customers attracted in the cases of constant or decreasing returns. It also appears that his statements about Pareto optimality do not apply if price discrimination can occur.

Rosen explains how advertising can expand market size by attracting new customers into the market. If search costs are sufficiently high, it may not be in the interests of some consumers with relatively unique tastes to enter the market at all, because it is simply too costly for them to find a brand that will reasonably, if not perfectly, satisfy their tastes. The introduction of attribute advertising, by reducing search costs, allows consumers to match their tastes more efficiently with the characteristic bundles offered by producers and thus to increase their welfare. As a result of advertising, some people enter the differentiated product market who would not otherwise be there. To me this point is especially important because of the not inconsiderable literature in this field that suggests that advertising shifts consumers among brands without any effect on industry sales. Also, lower gross costs of communicating information to buyers will tend to increase the number of brands, because sellers then find it less costly to cater to smaller groups of consumers with more specialized tastes.

Finally, Rosen is not sufficiently critical of the extreme argument that advertising has a zero social product. This argument states that advertising wastes resources because it only leads consumers to shift among brands without any change in the brands' market shares. A major implication of Rosen's model is that even if market shares were exactly the same after attribute advertising as before, there would be a major difference in that now consumers would be consuming brands with characteristic bundles that yield greater utility to them. Such a realignment of consumers and brands could happen without any change at all in market shares. Consumers are willing to pay the costs of advertising to achieve this better matching of brands and tastes, and the social product of advertising is definitely positive.

Now let me turn to Professor Nelson's work. In his previous papers, Nelson argued that all advertising is informative. The problem facing the consumer is to find the brands offering the most quality per dollar of expenditure according to his tastes. Consumers will respond to advertising only if it enables them to find higher-quality brands per dollar of expenditure, compared with using random sampling or using alternative information sources for purchase decisions. Nelson argues that there is a major difference between the content of search-good and experience-good advertising. Search-good advertising contains direct information about the characteristics and functions of the brand that allows consumers to rank brands. This direct information will be accurate, because consumers can observe whether the actual search characteristics are the same as the advertised characteristics before purchase.

Experience-good advertising provides only indirect information, namely, the fact that the brand is advertised and to what extent. According to Nelson, this information is valuable to consumers because heavily advertised brands are likely to be better buys. Consumer control over the accuracy of advertising is much weaker for experience-good advertising, because for experience goods it is cheaper to learn about brand quality by buying and trying the brand rather than by search before purchase. In this case, since the consumer cannot find out before buying whether the advertised characteristics are true or not, the opportunities for fraud are obviously greater, and I argue that some fraud will occur. However, consumers still exert substantial control over the accuracy of experience-good ads through their unwillingness to repurchase brands from a firm that has deceived them.

In this paper Nelson claims to provide much stronger arguments for the proposition that the indirect information provided by advertising of experience qualities is valuable to consumers because heavily advertised brands are generally better buys. He argues that advertising expenditures must be inversely related to price per unit of quality unless there are increasing returns to scale in advertising expenditures. He finds no direct or indirect evidence of such increasing returns. Therefore, more heavily advertised brands offer more quality per dollar of expenditure. This conclusion is especially important because in the final section of the paper, Nelson argues and demonstrates that there will be more advertising, the greater the relative importance of experience qualities compared with search qualities of goods. This means there will be more advertising, the more important the indirect information compared with the direct information provided by advertising.

One criticism of Nelson's analysis is that he uses the *mutatis mutandis* demand curve in estimating the firm's advertising elasticity without any discussion of the role of competitors' advertising, which is allowed to vary along this demand curve and with shifts in this curve. His estimates of the firm's advertising elasticities understate what they would be if competitors' advertising were held constant. A second criticism is that Nelson does not devote sufficient attention to cases where consumer tastes are not identical. Consumers who possess tastes different from the mass of consumers may not benefit by buying heavily advertised brands. However, I believe it is still correct to say that for any group of consumers with specialized tastes, among the brands with product characteristics that appeal to the group, the more heavily advertised brands would tend to be better buys.

In addition, I disagree with Nelson's argument that consumers with identical tastes will not believe the direct information that is contained in ads about experience qualities. If consumers will believe that heavily advertised brands are better buys, then I see no reason why they will not believe direct information about experience attributes. Firms spending large amounts on advertising to build up product reputations would not risk these reputations by supplying only false direct information in their advertising. Therefore, I cannot accept Nelson's argument that experience-good advertising provides only indirect information. Apparently, Nelson recognizes there will be believable direct information in experience-good ads for products that appeal to specialized tastes. Nelson needs to explain much more thoroughly the conditions under which direct information will and will not be believed.

A final criticism is that Nelson fails to examine adequately the returns to lying as distinct from the returns to telling the truth. This shortcoming may perhaps be due to his tendency to present his analysis from the point of view of the consumer rather than the seller. When buyers lack perfect information, sellers will engage in lying until at the margin the returns from lying are equal to the returns from telling the truth. Nelson has recognized the issue of the accuracy of information in his previous work. Consumers will especially rely on other sources of information about brand quality for durable experience goods. Consumers will be wary about buying expensive durable experience goods based solely on the information provided by advertising because they recognize the limited control they have over its accuracy and because of the high cost of being stuck with a lemon.

How does the market solve this problem? Sellers cannot be trusted to provide unbiased sources of highly accurate and complete experience-good information, especially for durable goods, but there is a demand for information on the part of consumers. Alternative sources of information about brand qualities become available, although, because of the public good aspect of information, they may provide less than the optimal amount of information. But information sources, such as Consumers' Union, arise to provide consumers with desired information. Why does Consumers' Union go to such great lengths to emphasize it does not accept advertising in its magazine and that it is not financed by any business firm? It does so in order to increase its reputation as an impartial source of information, or, at least, a source of information that is not subject to the biases of the business firms. Product warranties and "free" service contracts also assist consumers of durable experience goods. The market does provide alternative sources of information where needed.

Kelvin J. Lancaster

I will devote my remarks to expanding a little on the general analysis of product differentiation, information, and advertising, with the hope of adding some additional ideas to those in the main papers. What I have to say will complement Sherwin Rosen's paper in particular.

I want to draw two distinctions that are important here. The first is between the information *contained in* advertising and the information that the advertising occurs. Philip Nelson's analysis results in the rather McLuhanesque conclusion that the content of experience-good advertising does not matter; all that matters is that there is a certain amount of advertising. The second distinction is between what we can call "vertical" product differentiation (where the consumer faces a choice between a lower priced, lower quality product and a higher priced, higher quality product), and "horizontal" product differentiation (where the products are of comparable price and quality, but nevertheless different).

Since Sherwin Rosen's paper is primarily concerned with vertical product differentiation, I want to develop the theory of horizontal product differentiation somewhat, with particular reference to the extent to which sellers will wish to provide informational content to their advertising in this context.

Consider the case of pure horizontal differentiation where all the different product varieties can be considered to be of the same quality and sell at the same price, but have their characteristics in different proportions and appeal to consumers with different preferences. A simple example might be soft drinks, where the well-known brands conform reasonably well to this model.

Suppose, for simplicity, we could describe the various flavors of soft drinks in terms of their proportions of two characteristics only—sweetness and acidity, for example. If the preferences of the population were distributed uniformly over this spectrum of potential flavors we could, in principle, imagine drinks tailored to everybody's individual tastes. However, because of scale economics in production or distribution, both the socially optimal and the market solutions will lead to the production of only a finite number of different flavors.[1]

Let us reduce the example to its simplest possible form, by supposing that it turns out that the market solution results in only two flavors, one more sweet and the other more acid. We shall further suppose that these two flavors are so positioned on the spectrum of possible flavors that, if consumers were perfectly informed, exactly half would choose the more sweet and half the more acid, given that no other flavors are available. (This would indeed be the equilibrium market structure for a uniform distribution of preferences over the spectrum and for some specific degree of increasing returns to scale.) By perfect information here, we mean that every consumer knows exactly where his most preferred sweet-acid combination lies in the spectrum, and exactly where each of the available flavors lies, and he chooses the flavor closest to his most preferred combination; we implicitly assume that he cannot obtain intermediate flavors by mixing the available varieties.

Now consider the situation in which consumers are totally ignorant of where the two flavors lie on the spectrum, and possibly do not even know where their own most preferred combination lies. On the usual assumptions of random choice under total ignorance, we can suppose that each consumer has the same probability of choosing one flavor or the

[1] See Kelvin J. Lancaster, "Socially Optimal Product Differentiation," *American Economic Review*, vol. 45 (September 1975), pp. 567-585.

other, and thus that the market is divided evenly among the two—the same outcome, it would seem, as under perfect information.

The outcomes are identical only if the flavors chosen by the two firms are those that would divide the market evenly when consumers were perfectly informed, since the market would be split down the middle in the ignorance case whatever the two flavors but would divide at different points for different choices in the perfect information case. But we could argue that it will be in the interest of the firms to choose the flavors appropriate to the perfect information case unless they know for a fact that all consumers are perfectly ignorant, since that choice is the best if consumers should turn out to be informed and is as good as any other if consumers should be ignorant. (It should be pointed out that the underlying analysis here is really that of the n-good monopolistic competition structure. We use two goods merely to make a point as simply as possible, but we are not concerned with a duopoly structure.)

Now we come to the major question. Given an existing market equilibrium with the market divided in half (or in n equal parts in the more general case), would either of the two producers be interested in providing information as to exactly where its product lies on the flavor spectrum? The answer to this, in the simple case given above, would seem to be no. From the producer's point of view either each consumer is informed already—in which case the information is superfluous—or he is ignorant. If he is ignorant and already buys the producer's product, he is as likely to be buying it for the wrong reason (because he thinks it the more sweet, although it is the more acid) as for the right reason. The potential new customers are those who are buying the competitor's product for the wrong reason, but information which attracts these will lose those who are buying the *advertiser's* product for the wrong reason. Information as to the exact place of the product on the spectrum will be as likely to lose customers as to gain them, and there will be no incentive to provide it.

Thus we have a broad presumption that, in the case of pure horizontal product differentiation, there is no particular incentive for producers to inform potential customers as to the exact mix of characteristics in their product. This differs from the vertical differentiation case where, as Rosen has shown, there is an incentive to provide this information.

If we start introducing additional elements into our very simple model, we start modifying some of our conclusions. An obvious modification is to suppose that, in the total ignorance case, the probability that a consumer will choose a given product increases with his degree of familiarity with the brand name—a classic advertising hypothesis. In particular, we can suppose that informed consumers are not affected by advertising, but that the proportion of ignorant consumers choosing A rather than B increases if the amount of advertising of A is greater than that of B, instead of an equal division of the ignorant consumers. This will obviously provide an incentive to advertise with the classic oligopoly or monopolistic competition outcome that both (or all) firms will advertise equally and the market shares will again be equalized. This is advertising of the kind that involves shouting in order to be heard, but there is still no incentive to provide *information* in the advertising.

A more complex and more interesting case occurs when consumer preferences are not uniformly distributed. Suppose, for example, that the density of consumers along the spectrum is higher at the sweet end. It can be shown that, in such a case, the market equilibrium with full information will be such that flavors will be clustered more closely at the sweet end.[2] In the two-flavor (extreme) example, both flavors will be moved closer to the sweet end of the spectrum than in the uniform case.

If a "monopolistic competition" type of market solution exists for just two flavors, it will generally be such that the quantity is higher and the price lower for the flavor in the denser part of the spectrum, profits being equal and zero for both producers, if the market consists of perfectly informed consumers. If the consumers are ignorant, however, the market will be divided equally and both prices will be the same, since we assume consumers who choose at random will not pay more for one product than for the other. There will be an incentive for the producers to provide information that locates their products on the spectrum—the producer of the sweeter variety in order to catch its greater share of the market preference, the other producer to be able to raise its price by differentiating its product clearly.

However, it may not be to the advantage of the product with the smaller market to place itself *exactly* on the spectrum, merely to differentiate its product clearly—as in the "Uncola" advertising of Seven-Up. Thus we conclude that, although it may sometimes be to the advantage of some firms in a horizontal product differentiation situation to place their product correctly in the characteristics spectrum, there does not seem to be any presumption that it will pay to do so in general when we have horizontal differentiation.

Although it may not make any real difference to the firms whether the consumers have chosen their product on the basis of full information or as a result of random choice, it does make a difference in social

[2] Kelvin J. Lancaster, *Variety, Equity and Efficiency* (New York: Columbia University Press, forthcoming).

welfare.[3] In the simple (ignorance) case in which half the consumers who choose product A on a random basis would prefer B if they were fully informed, and half those who choose B would really prefer A, merely rearranging the consumers so that each purchased the appropriate product would increase social welfare unambiguously without affecting the firms in any way. Thus there is a potential social gain from information, but no incentive for the firms to provide it. The appropriate information might, of course, be provided at the cost of the consumers (who are the potential gainers) by consumer information services—but this assumes the consumers already know they may be choosing incorrectly, and does not really conform to the total ignorance case. There would seem to be a good case for, say, compulsory labeling or other forms of information provision that minimize the total cost of providing that information. It would seem that there is a potential social loss from lack of information that the market alone will not provide.

D. A. L. Auld

The task of commenting on both the Nelson and Rosen papers is a challenging one. Although there are obvious links between what the authors are doing, I have chosen to examine the papers separately.

Nelson's "framework" is designed to demonstrate a negative relationship between advertising expenditure and quality-adjusted price, P^*. This is important since it follows that the more advertised brands will be the better buy, according to Nelson. I do not think it *does* follow because (a) the question of what is a "better buy" has not been resolved; and (b) the logic is incomplete or ambiguous in that we are not told what the cause and effect relationship is.

Let us examine the relationship between P^* and advertising. The utility-corrected price P^* can be thought of as the market price divided by utility. If the utility derived from a product or service increases (or is at least perceived to increase) and market price is constant, P^* declines.

The decline of P^* is, if I interpret Nelson correctly, an index of a better buy. If advertising, very broadly defined, increases, and this results in increased utility derived from a good, P^* will decline, *ceteris paribus*. However, the paper appears to suggest that it is advertising that is responding to P^*. I do not believe this makes much sense since the market price, P, is not taken as a fixed parameter. It is not clear from

[3] We assume always that there are either some informed consumers or that the firms expect some consumers to become informed. If all consumers are always ignorant, there is no monopolistic competition equilibrium possible.

Nelson's analysis at this point just what is or is not allowed to happen to market price; given the definition of P^*, this is an important consideration.

Advertising A, utility-corrected price P^*, and quantity demanded Q_d must all be related in a particular way to ensure that as advertising increases, P^* declines. These relationships can be depicted visually, as in Figure 1. If the relationships in the upper left and lower right quadrants hold true, then A and P^* will be related as shown in the upper right quadrant. Nelson states that A cannot be negatively related to Q_d (in other words, it *must* be as shown) and hence the burden of proof rests with the P^* and Q_d relationship to obtain the A and P^* relationship. Given that P^* is equivalent to a price/utility ratio, it seems that for normal goods, quantity demanded will rise as P^* falls over a range of P^* as Nelson suggests. What worries me is the rather quick dismissal of the possibility that A and Q_d could be negatively related. Further-

Figure 1

ADVERTISING, UTILITY-CORRECTED PRICE, AND QUANTITY DEMAND

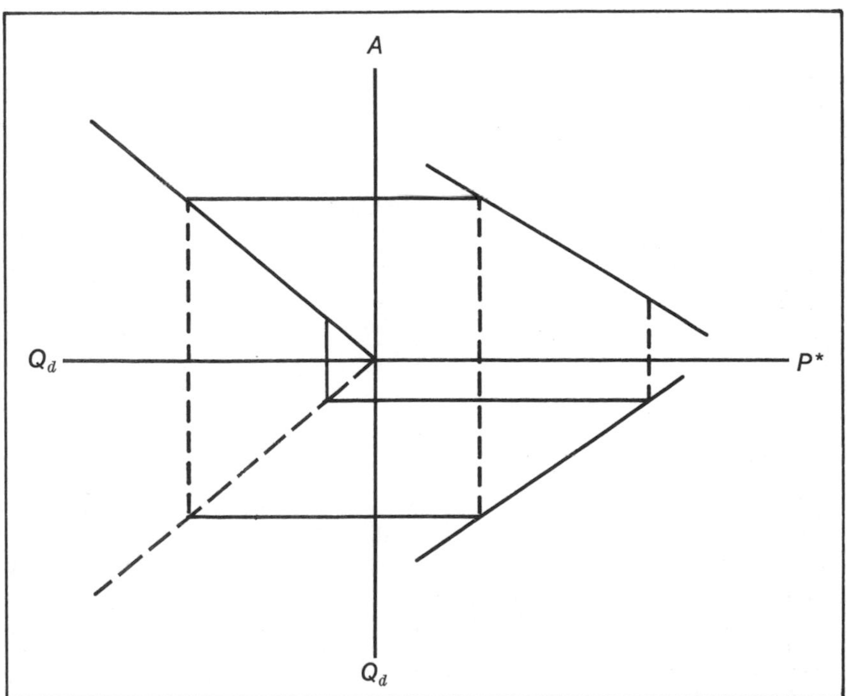

more, it is again not clear how everything is related. For example, the scenario could go something like this: advertising increases and P^* declines so that Q_d increases. It then follows that Q_d and A are positively related. Or the process could be explained in the following way: advertising introduces people to the brand; the rise in Q_d lowers the P^* (because people believe that a product "everyone is buying" is a good one) and that leads to further demands for the product.

Nelson's paper deals with the *mutatis mutandis* demand schedule. He feels that a test of this demand schedule is possible if a short time period is used such that "the brand's utility relative to other brands of the good probably has only a modest variation." I would argue that this depends in part on the range of competing brands. If there are many, then the probability increases that a dramatic change in an existing brand will occur or that a new brand will be introduced, and some adjustment for this will be necessary.

We next come to a discussion of shifts in demand curves as opposed to movements along the demand curve, the latter resulting from changes in P^* and A. Some clarification is needed at this point because of the earlier definition of P^* given by the author. Early in the paper it was suggested that P^* was equivalent to price per unit of utility. A rise in the market price increases P^*, and an increase in the utility received from a unit of a good lowers P^*. This implies that P^* responds to market price and perceived utility (or a combination thereof). But later on reference is made to movements along the demand schedule due to variations in P^* and A. Is this the P and Q_d demand schedule or the P^* and Q_d schedule? If the former, then a change in advertising results in a shift in the schedule and if it is the latter, advertising causes P^* to change so that *independent* changes in P^* and A do not seem possible. Nelson states that a movement along a demand schedule clearly "produces" a negative association between advertising and P^*. If we return to the simple diagram I have constructed, it is true that *if* the conditions established by Nelson hold, then a negative relationship between P^* and Q_d is *associated* with a negative relationship between P^* and A. But a reduction in market price (which is equivalent to a fall in P^*) does not *produce* a rise in A. To say that one can predict, though not with probability equal to 1, that advertising and quantity will have a negative relationship with price* again begs the question of the direction of causation and the existence of the prediction model itself.

Professor Rosen's paper is easier to follow than Nelson's, partly because Rosen has chosen a basically simple model of consumer utility maximization and producer profit maximization to develop his ideas.

Information derives its value from being able to match consumer-desired attributes and producer-supplied attributes as closely as possible, subject to the considerations of transaction costs, uncertainty, and scale economies.

Using the basic theory of Lancaster, Rosen correctly points out that it is a straightforward matter to transform observed prices of various items to implicit prices of observed characteristics. He goes on to say that the available values of z and the corresponding prices of z both are identified with the product varieties that are offered by the market. The Rosen model is then based on these two building blocks. It is, however, precisely the question of the "available values of z and prices $p(z)$" that is crucial to the role of advertising in the market. Although it is discussed somewhat indirectly in a later section of the paper, the role of information in transforming *potential* attributes and prices into *available* ones should be raised at this juncture.[1]

Some questions arise concerning Rosen's basic model. Is the function $p(z)$ supposed to represent a continuum of production possibilities by firms? If so, why does it follow this particular nonlinear path? Once we get to the profit indifference surfaces, we can perhaps see *how* the $p(z)$ function is generated; the locus of all southeast extremities of the profit-indifference schedules. But this still begs the question why profit indifference curves take on the configuration in p-z space that they do. Even in pure competition, these producers can, of course, have different prices for characteristics, provided the price of the product is equal for all producers. This can occur if the characteristic "mix" for each producer is different. But then, one might ask, does not the *heterogeneous* nature of the goods preclude the assumption (earlier) of pure competition? I raise this because the paper seems to drift quietly away from this assumption to that of two sellers only.

I think Rosen has emphasized a very important issue, certainly from the policy viewpoint, about the nature of the costs associated with filling in all the missing points on the *potential* spectrum of attributes. An excellent example is housing. Each family has a set of attributes it would desire, within its budget constraint. Many new subdivisions, however, do not possess homes with all possible combinations of attributes, for to do so would cancel the advantages of scale economies and similar sized lots. What makes the issue complex is the impossibility of actually measuring the welfare losses due to the selection of a good (house) that is not optimal (to the private individual).

---

[1] D. A. L. Auld, "Advertising and the Theory of Consumer Choice," *Quarterly Journal of Economics*, vol. 352 (August 1974), pp. 480-488.

Rosen explores the producer's incentive to enter the market to fill what is perceived to be a substantial mismatching of output characteristic mix and the consumer-desired mix. I do not think that there is anything particularly incorrect with the analysis as it stands except that it seems slightly restrictive. Several years ago, I published a note which dealt with this problem using the basic Lancaster model.[2] In that paper I tried to show what the "limiting price" had to be for a producer to enter a market and how it was quite possible to have consumers choose not only the new product but a combination of products to achieve maximum utility, given the budget constraint. We have to allow somehow for the explicit recognition of the market price of the product—perhaps a combination of my approach and Rosen's approach is possible. To get into a market, the product has to be made known. The extent to which it is necessary to advertise to enter the market will have a bearing on pricing policy and, naturally, on the product's degree of success in achieving a foothold.

In the section on advertising and buyers' perceptions of characteristics, Rosen indicates that no producer will sit by for long while his competitors undertake a massive advertising campaign to lure away his customers. He will respond in kind, and since one campaign supposedly negates the other, the consumer is left with a dead loss.

This scenario is possible but not likely. There are two additional features that must be considered. First, producers will in all probability have different abilities to "persuade" customers in terms of the cost of advertising. In other words, the competing ad campaigns will not cancel out, at least not exactly. In fact there are good chances one competitor will gain a decisive advantage in the short run.

Second, customers may quickly find out that what was advertised was not true and switch back to their original supplier. If this occurs with respect to search characteristics and the firm is prosecuted for false advertising, the impact could be severe. The difficult situation to resolve theoretically is the actual practice of advertising one or two characteristics for a limited time, then switching to another characteristic (or mix). My own feeling is that one could devise a model incorporating a "loss function" for each characteristic that was "extended" by advertising, allowing the possibility that constant switching of the characteristics to be advertised might well be an optimal strategy.

Let me conclude by drawing some inferences about the public policy issues with which this volume is concerned. It seems to me that advertising is a very personal thing and that one's use of it in maximizing

[2] D. A. L. Auld, "Consumer Welfare and Product Differentiation," *The Quarterly Review of Economics and Business* (Winter 1971), pp. 81-84.

utility depends upon the opportunity cost of search time, on people's aversion to trying new products, and on tastes. To limit or control advertising, at least with reference to experience qualities, would be futile.

As for the physical or measurable characteristics of goods and services, one's first reaction would be to recommend public policies to ensure heavy penalties for those who distort their product. Upon reflection, however, this approach may be extremely wasteful owing to the costs of controlling for minor and inconsequential deviations from the "truth." Obviously, the difficult policy question is to establish the range of public tolerance to these deviations.

PART FOUR

ADVERTISING, CONCENTRATION, AND PROFITS

ADVERTISING INTENSITY AND INDUSTRIAL CONCENTRATION–AN EMPIRICAL INQUIRY, 1947-1967

Stanley I. Ornstein and Steven Lustgarten

A basic tenet of traditional industrial organization textbooks holds that large scale advertising expenditures lead to monopoly power.[1] Advertising is believed to reduce price elasticity of demand and allow price to be raised above the competitive level. Resulting excess profits are said to persist because of advertising created barriers to entry due to (1) product differentiation or brand loyalty created by advertising and (2) economies of scale in advertising. In addition, supporters of this theory generally conclude that much advertising is misleading and wasteful and that consumers would benefit from restrictions on advertising.[2]

In contrast to this traditional view, recent literature argues that advertising increases competition[3] by providing information to consumers on product quality and characteristics and by allowing new entrants to overcome existing brand loyalties. Advertising helps the more efficient firms expand their market share, thereby resulting in an improved allocation of resources. According to this view, restrictions on advertising are harmful to consumers.

The behavior of the Federal Trade Commission in recent years illustrates these contradictory views on advertising. The FTC has examined restrictions on advertising by physicians, pharmacists, and optometrists

---

We are indebted to Edwin W. Eckard, Jr. for computer assistance.

1 See Joe S. Bain, *Industrial Organization*, 2nd ed. (New York: John Wiley and Sons, 1968), chapter 7, and Frederick M. Scherer, *Industrial Market Structure and Economic Performance* (Chicago: Rand McNally, 1970), chapter 14.

2 Scherer, *Industrial Market Structure*, p. 344.

3 Yale Brozen, "Advertising, Concentration and Profitability" in Goldschmid and Weston, eds., *Industrial Concentration: the New Learning* (Boston: Little, Brown and Company, 1974), pp. 115-137; Phillip Nelson, "Advertising as Information," *Journal of Political Economy*, vol. 81 (July/August 1974), pp. 729-754; Phillip Nelson, "Economic Consequences of Advertising," *Journal of Business*, vol. 48 (April 1975), pp. 213-241.

for possible anticompetitive effects.[4] At the same time it has issued a complaint that heavy advertising for ready-to-eat cereals enables sellers to enjoy a monopoly position.[5]

A popular test of the theory that advertising is anticompetitive has been to correlate advertising expenditures with industry concentration. Since the latter is widely used as an indication of monopoly power, previous investigators believed that the existence (or absence) of correlation between it and advertising would support (or refute) the textbook model.[6]

This paper will consider two basic questions. (1) Are advertising and concentration positively correlated? (2) Does a significant or insignificant correlation have any important implications for public policy?

Traditional tests of the hypothesis that advertising is a source of monopoly power have related advertising to industry rates of return as well as to concentration. Most of the hypotheses suggest that all three variables are related; however, no one has been able to derive the various interrelationships and directions of causality between the three variables. Part of the reason for this incomplete analysis is the difficult econometric and data problems involved. More importantly, there is no rigorous theory relating advertising intensity, concentration ratios, and profit rates. As a result, hypotheses, assertions, conjectures, and speculations abound. This investigation is confined to the empirical relation between advertising and concentration and only limited inferences are expected. The following section considers alternative explanations for a relation between advertising and concentration. A framework for testing certain hypotheses is then presented, followed by a discussion of the data used in previous studies and the sample used in this study. Finally, the empirical results are presented.

Alternative Hypotheses

Advertising Causes Concentration. The belief that advertising is positively related to concentration stems from the work of Kaldor and Bain.[7]

---

[4] "In the Matter of the A.M.A.," Federal Trade Commission, Docket No. 9064; "Disclosure Regulations Concerning Retail Drug Prices for Prescription Drugs," vol. 40, *Federal Register*, June 4, 1975; "Advertising of Ophthalmic Goods and Services," vol. 41, *Federal Register*, January 16, 1976.

[5] Federal Trade Commission, Docket No. 8883, April 26, 1972.

[6] Whether concentration is in fact a proxy for monopoly power is seriously questioned in Harold Demsetz, *The Concentration Doctrine* (Washington, D.C.: American Enterprise Institute, 1973).

[7] Nicholas Kaldor, "The Economic Aspects of Advertising," *Review of Economic Studies*, vol. 18 (1949-50), pp. 1-27; Joe S. Bain, *Barriers to New Competition* (Cambridge, Mass.: Harvard University Press, 1956).

Kaldor hypothesized that increasing advertising expenditures leads to higher concentration owing to: (1) increasing returns to advertising, which favor large firms over small firms as a result of the more severe capital market constraints on small firms, and (2) the greater degree of success of some firms' advertising programs, leading to greater sales and profits that may be reinvested in advertising to promote further growth in market share at the expense of rivals. According to Kaldor the end result is an oligopoly market structure rather than monopoly, since firms eventually reach the stage of diminishing marginal returns to advertising. Kaldor also hypothesized that a decrease in advertising would lead to a decrease in concentration.

Kaldor provided no empirical tests of his hypotheses. Two alternative tests of Kaldor's proposition seem reasonable. First, one can test whether high initial levels of advertising intensity are related to subsequent changes in concentration. Second, one can test for a relationship between concurrent levels or changes in advertising and concentration over time.

Bain stressed advertising's role in creating strong buyer-seller attachments or brand loyalty through its ability to differentiate products. His basic behavioral postulate was that buyers generally prefer established brands to new brands. Bain concluded that product differentiation—brought about by advertising and other factors such as product characteristics, distribution systems, and buyer motives—is the strongest of the various causes of barriers to entry in the twenty industries he examined. According to Bain, barriers arise to some extent from economies of scale in advertising, but primarily from the capital requirements imposed on new entrants who must overcome existing brand loyalty. He concluded that advertising expenditures play a leading role in determining the level of concentration. However, the mechanism of determination was not identified; that is, Bain did not explain how advertising economies of scale or capital requirements change concentration.

Thus, it is not clear how Bain's model is to be tested since changes in advertising economies of scale and capital requirements do not necessarily change concentration.[8] For example, economies of scale in advertising arise if successive advertising messages are either less costly to send (pecuniary economies) or more effective for the same cost (technological economies). Firms with larger advertising expenditures would then have lower costs per unit of advertising. Concentration might increase over what it would be in the absence of advertising if market

[8] Concentration is used in the generic sense of the number and size distribution of firms in an industry throughout this study. Thus any entry or exit changes concentration.

demand were not large enough to accommodate the same number of firms, each producing at a higher optimal level of output. However, since increased advertising will probably increase industry demand, the number and size distribution of firms may be unchanged after advertising is introduced, assuming all firms advertise with equal efficiency. If there are differential advertising efficiencies across firms, increased advertising would be likely to change the size distribution of firms and thus concentration. Alternatively, if advertising economies are purely pecuniary, concentration will not necessarily increase. For example, highly diversified firms could attain the same media volume discounts with small amounts of advertising for many different products.[9]

This ambiguity of advertising's effects on concentration extends to capital requirements as well. Higher capital requirements might benefit existing firms by reducing the number of potential entrants, but they would not necessarily change the existing size distribution of firms and thus concentration. Alternatively, if the cost of capital were lower for large firms, it might affect the size distribution of firms. In short, simple correlations between concentration and advertising intensity are not, as previous studies have asserted, properly specified tests of Bain's hypotheses. Nevertheless, for convenience we will continue the notion started in previous studies of a singular Kaldor-Bain hypothesis postulating a positive correlation.

In contrast to these traditional hypotheses, recent studies offer alternative hypotheses for a positive relationship that are unrelated to monopoly power. Nelson, for example, argues that, given quality variation among products and before the introduction of advertising, the more efficient firms are the largest firms and have the lowest price per unit of utility.[10] These large, efficient firms have the greatest incentive to advertise since their gains from advertising are greatest. They gain more because they have a greater probability of repeat purchase and a higher price-cost margin. Thus, advertising tends to drive out the less efficient firms and to raise concentration. Conversely, Nelson argues that advertising facilitates entry by reducing consumer search costs, thus leading to lower levels of concentration. He concludes that the effects of advertising are self-cancelling and that no systematic relationship across industries can be predicted.

Arguing in a similar fashion, another author notes that since the marketplace rewards product quality and since information flow is a

[9] This argument was made by James M. Ferguson, *Advertising and Competition: Theory, Measurement, Fact* (Cambridge: Ballinger, 1974), p. 17. This volume contains a clear and comprehensive analysis of most of the important theoretical and empirical issues surrounding the controversy on advertising and competition.
[10] Nelson, "Economic Consequences of Advertising," p. 232.

function of firm size or market share, firms with high quality and large market share will grow relative to small firms as a consequence of consumers' search for information on product quality.[11] Advertising is one means to dispense information and is itself a measure of firm size and thus of product quality. Hence, concentration and advertising may in part be positively related, simply by the nature of the market for information.

A recent study argues that advertising and concentration are indirectly related owing to the dynamic growth paths of firms and industries.[12] To illustrate, assume a firm producing consumer goods is operating in a relatively unconcentrated industry and is producing for a local or regional market at less than long-run optimum scale (that is, costs are above minimum long-run average cost). The firm makes the decision to expand its geographic market boundaries. A large scale advertising program is developed and introduced to attract new customers. This program is successful in encouraging new buyers to sample the firm's product, and these buyers become steady customers owing to the product's superior qualities. The resulting increase in production and market size leads to economies of scale in production and distribution, raising firm size and leading to lower price per unit of product quality. Rivals respond with advertising campaigns and attempts at market expansion, with only the most efficient firms ultimately raising their market share.

This process leads to an increase in concentration over time owing to changes in firm size and departures of unsuccessful firms. Firms will maintain high advertising intensity once a new equilibrium is reached in order to serve larger markets with greater buyer turnover. Further, as pointed out above, the most successful firms have the greatest incentive to advertise. Thus under this hypothesis, both levels and changes in the levels of advertising intensity and concentration are related, but there is no direct causal relationship.

There is nothing unique to advertising inputs in this scenario. Any factor leading to differential growth between firms, such as entrepreneurial skill, luck, or successful research and development may lead indirectly to increases in concentration over time.[13]

---

[11] Robert H. Nelson, "The Economics of Honest Trade Practices," *Journal of Industrial Economics*, vol. 24 (June 1976), pp. 281-293.

[12] Stanley I. Ornstein, "The Advertising-Concentration Controversy," *Southern Economic Journal*, vol. 43 (July 1976), pp. 892-902.

[13] Merely random chance will lead to increases in concentration over time and a positive relationship between concentration, profits, and sales, and possibly advertising. See Richard B. Mancke, "Causes of Interfirm Profitability Differences: A New Interpretation of the Evidence," *Quarterly Journal of Economics*, vol. 88 (May 1974), pp. 181-193.

Advertising is Spuriously Correlated with Concentration. Advertising intensity and concentration may also be related in cross-section analysis for purely statistical reasons. First, if large firms advertise more intensively than small firms, then industry average advertising intensity is most strongly affected by large firms. The higher the concentration, the more large firms dominate industry averages. Concentration is then a proxy for the weight of large firms, so concentration and advertising intensity are necessarily related. One means of distinguishing this statistical explanation from alternative hypotheses is to test for a relationship in both consumer and producer goods samples. Since this phenomenon is a function of large firm effects, it applies with equal force to both consumer and producer goods industries. In contrast, proponents of traditional monopoly power explanations concede that their models apply to only a subsample of highly advertising-intensive consumer good industries. Second, omitted variables that are related to both advertising intensity and concentration may account for a positive relationship in regression equations. Third, there appears to be, in theory, two-way causality, as explained below, so any single equation ordinary least squares estimate may suffer from simultaneous equation bias.[14]

Concentration Causes Advertising. Most early cross-section studies assumed that advertising leads to higher concentration,[15] while more recent studies reversed the function and assumed that it is concentration that leads to high advertising expenditures.[16] Some argue that nonprice competition, such as advertising, may be more profitable in highly concentrated industries.[17] Several authors have shown that the profit maxi-

[14] Richard Schmalensee, *The Economics of Advertising* (Amsterdam: North-Holland Publishing, 1972), pp. 222-226, has shown this bias to be positive in the case of advertising intensity and concentration. Estimates of simultaneous equation models by two-stage least squares (2SLS) have been made by Douglas Greer, "Advertising and Market Concentration," *Southern Economic Journal*, vol. 38 (July 1971), pp. 19-32, and Allyn D. Strickland and Leonard W. Weiss, "Advertising, Concentration, and Price-Cost Margins," *Journal of Political Economy*, vol. 84 (October 1976), pp. 1109-1121. Neither study found strong evidence of simultaneous equation bias.

[15] See, for example, Lester G. Telser, "Advertising and Competition," *Journal of Political Economy*, vol. 72 (December 1964), pp. 537-562, and H. M. Mann, J. A. Henning, and J. W. Meehan, Jr., "Advertising and Concentration: An Empirical Investigation," *Journal of Industrial Economics*, vol. 16 (November 1967), pp. 34-45.

[16] See, for example, Peter Doyle, "Advertising Expenditure and Consumer Demand," *Oxford Economic Papers*, vol. 20 (November 1968), pp. 394-416, and Brian C. Brush, "The Influence of Market Structure on Industry Advertising Intensity," *Journal of Industrial Economics*, vol. 25 (September 1976), pp. 55-67.

[17] See, for example, George J. Stigler, "Price and Nonprice Competition," *The Organization of Industry* (Homewood, Ill.: Richard D. Irwin, 1968), pp. 23-38.

mizing ratio of advertising to sales is equal to the ratio of advertising elasticity to the absolute value of price elasticity of demand.[18] If, as the conventional argument holds, the price elasticity of demand for the firm is inversely related to the concentration ratio, higher concentration will increase the optimum advertising-to-sales ratio, assuming no change in advertising elasticity.

It has also been argued that high concentration promotes collusion on advertising as well as on price.[19] Such behavior will yield an inverted-U or quadratic relationship in which both advertising intensity and concentration rise to intermediate levels of concentration, and then advertising intensity declines as concentration increases. Finally, as we have seen, it is sometimes argued that advertising reduces concentration by facilitating entry by new firms.

Summary. The net effect of the above hypotheses and statistical problems is not clear. It is clear that many economists expect *some* relationship, be it positive or negative, linear or nonlinear. It is also clear there is no practical means of distinguishing between all of the various hypotheses or of determining causality by regression analysis. Progress can be made, however, by distinguishing between some of the hypotheses and by removing potential sample bias, aggregation errors, and industry classification errors in the test data.

Framework for Analysis

Cross Section Analysis. While some studies have tested for a linear (straight-line) relationship between advertising and concentration, others have tested for a nonlinear relationship. In particular, economists have been interested in determining whether there is an inverted-U or "quadratic" relationship, whereby investment in advertising is heavier for oligopolists than for atomistic industries or for industries behaving as pure monopolists.[20] Since there is as yet no accepted theory of adver-

[18] See, for example, Robert Dorfman and Peter O. Steiner, "Optimal Advertising and Optimal Quality," *American Economic Review*, vol. 44 (December 1954), pp. 820-836, and Marc Nerlove and Kenneth Arrow, "Optimal Advertising Policy under Dynamic Conditions," *Economica*, vol. 29 (May 1962), pp. 129-142.

[19] Greer, "Advertising and Market Concentration"; John Cable, "Market Structure, Advertising Policy, and Intermarket Differences in Advertising Intensity," in *Market Structure and Corporate Behavior*, Keith Cowling, ed. (London: Gray-Mills, 1972), pp. 105-124; C. J. Sutton, "Advertising, Concentration and Competition," *Economic Journal*, vol. 84 (March 1974), pp. 56-69.

[20] See, for example, Greer, "Advertising and Market Concentration"; Cable, "Market Structure, Advertising Policy, and Intermarket Differences in Advertising Intensity"; Sutton, "Advertising, Concentration and Competition"; and Strickland and Weiss, "Advertising, Concentration, and Price-Cost Margins."

tising, there is no reason to choose one functional form over another. We therefore test linear, quadratic, and log-linear equations under the assumption (consistent with recent thinking) that advertising intensity is a function of concentration. The equations tested are:

$$ASR = a_1 + b_1 \, CR + e_1 \quad (1)$$

$$ASR = a_2 + b_2 \, CR + c_2 \, (CR)^2 + e_2 \quad (2)$$

$$ASR = a_3 + c_3 \, (CR)^2 + e_3 \quad (3)$$

$$LogASR = a_4 + b_4 LogCR + e_4 \quad (4)$$

where:

ASR = industry advertising-sales ratio
CR = four-firm value of shipments concentration ratio
e = error term

Under the traditional hypotheses the expected signs are:

$b_1 > 0 \qquad b_2 > 0 \qquad c_2 < 0 \qquad c_3 > 0 \qquad b_4 > 0$

Changes in Concentration. A framework for analysis can be developed using static equilibrium conditions for an industry.[21] For atomistic markets in long-run equilibrium, the number of firms and concentration are determined by the unique optimum firm size relative to total market size. Concentration is inversely related to total market size and directly related to optimum firm size, while the number of firms is directly related to total market size and inversely related to optimum firm size. Thus, concentration and number of firms are inversely related and are interchangeable measures of market structure in atomistic industries. As optimum firm size changes relative to market size, through shifts in demand and costs, the level of concentration will change. For example, changes in market size through upward shifts in demand will reduce concentration through new firm entry, assuming no offsetting changes in optimum firm size. A change in market size and a change in optimum firm size will cause concentration to rise, fall, or remain the same, depending on which change is greater.

These relationships hold, in general, in nonatomistic markets, although concentration and number of firms are not uniquely determined. In nonatomistic markets concentration is a function of economies of scale in the largest firms relative to total market size. The number of firms is influenced by the shape of the long-run average cost curve and

[21] These relationships are expressed more completely in Peter Pashigian, "The Effect of Market Size on Concentration," *International Economic Review*, vol. 10 (October 1969), pp. 291-314.

is a function of the minimum efficient firm size relative to total market size. Concentration and number of firms are inversely related, but not perfectly, owing to the unequal size distribution of firms. Nevertheless, as in atomistic industries, shifts in concentration are in general a function of relative changes in total market size and economies of scale.

Previous studies of changes in concentration ratios have focused on how changes in sales or market growth influence concentration ratios.[22] Clearly, this is incomplete. Changes in concentration are a function of changes in both cost and demand conditions and these are not unambiguously determined by industry growth rates. Industrial growth reflects the net change in cost and demand. It is an empirical question whether demand changes in any given period outstrip changes in costs (because of such factors as economies of scale), or are just offset by such changes, or are less than changes in economies of scale. Separating the two effects by properly specifying and estimating supply and demand functions for a large number of industries is impossible given existing data. However, since changes in concentration are a function of both changes in market size and changes in optimum size, both can be used to approximate shifts in demand and supply. Market growth in sales can be used as a crude proxy for changes in demand over long periods and changes in average firm size can be used as a proxy for changes in optimum firm size.[23]

In addition to the above determinants of concentration, the traditional industrial organization literature stresses the idea that concentration is a function of barriers to entry. These barriers can be defined as properly accounted cost differentials between entrants and existing firms. The most commonly mentioned sources of cost differentials are product

[22] These studies and others hypothesized an inverse relationship between concentration and growth for the following reasons: (1) the probability of entry varies directly with industry growth, (2) optimum size of plant and multi-plant economies do not increase as fast as industry growth, (3) growing firms choose to diversify to spread their risk and to avoid antitrust prosecution, and (4) dominant firms in highly concentrated industries get high prices and gradually give up part of the market to new entrants in order to maximize long-run profits. William G. Shepherd, "Trends of Concentration in American Manufacturing Industries, 1947-58," *Review of Economics and Statistics*, vol. 46 (May 1964), pp. 200-212; David R. Kamerschen, "Market Growth and Industry Concentration," *Journal of the American Statistical Association*, vol. 68 (March 1968), pp. 228-241; Malcolm C. Sawyer, "Concentration in British Manufacturing Industry," *Oxford Economic Papers*, vol. 23 (November 1971), pp. 352-383.

[23] There is great controversy as to how and at what level to measure economies of scale; for example, at the firm or plant level, for only the largest firms or plants, or for the minimum efficient scale of firm or plant. Pashigian's study shows the simple average firm size measure explained concentration almost as well as the weighted average firm size and was superior to two alternative survivorship measures of economies of scale.

differentiation, economies of scale in production and advertising, and capital requirements for entry. Large capital requirements are believed to stem from advertising-induced product differentiation and economies of scale in advertising and production. While these barriers are thought to explain concentration ratios across industries, increases in these barriers, as seen above, will not necessarily increase concentration.

Other potential entry barriers such as legal constraints, control of raw materials, and general technological know-how may also explain inter-industry concentration. However, this study is primarily concerned with advertising-induced barriers to entry. Hence, various measures of the levels and changes in advertising expenditures are used as proxies for these traditional hypothesized barriers to explain changes in concentration.

An alternative explanation of concentration changes is that, in the absence of barriers to entry, concentration is due to differential firm efficiency or luck.[24] Although size and large market share are not prerequisites of efficiency, they are the end result of a superior firm's growth. Thus, competition among firms in such areas as entrepreneurial skill, advertising, research and development, product quality, and customer service leads to greater market share for superior firms and higher industry concentration. Unfortunately, it is difficult to distinguish between efficiency and barriers to entry as determinants of concentration because the same variables, namely, profit rates, proxies for economies of scale, and advertising intensity, are generally used to measure both effects.

The final hypothesized determinant of changes in concentration is initial year concentration. Because concentration ratios are bounded between 0 and 100 percent, the initial level of concentration should explain subsequent changes in concentration. Low initial concentration is more likely to rise than fall, and high initial concentration is more likely to fall than rise. Consequently, the initial distribution of concentration ratios may influence subsequent changes. A distribution of industries skewed toward low concentration is more likely to experience a rise in concentration than a symmetrical distribution around a mean of 50 percent concentration. Similarly, for a subclass of industries such as consumer goods or nondurable goods, if initial mean concentration ratios are low, subsequent changes on average are likely to be positive. Hence, initial concentration is expected to be inversely related to changes in concentration.

These relations are expressed in the following equation:

[24] See, for example, Harold Demsetz, "Industry Structure, Market Rivalry, and Public Policy," *Journal of Law and Economics*, vol. 16 (April 1973), pp. 1-9; John S. McGee, *In Defense of Industrial Concentration* (New York: Praeger, 1971).

$$\Delta CR = a_5 + b_5 ASR + c_5 \Delta ASR + d_5 CR + e_5 \Delta AFS + f_5 \Delta GR + g_5 \tag{5}$$

where:

ΔCR = absolute change in four-firm concentration ratio
ASR = initial year advertising-sales ratio
ΔASR = absolute change in ASR
CR = initial year four-firm concentration ratio
ΔAFS = percentage change in average firm size
ΔGR = percentage change in growth measured by value added
g = error term

Under conventional hypotheses the expected signs are:

$$b_5 > 0 \qquad c_5 > 0 \qquad d_5 < 0 \qquad e_5 > 0 \qquad f_5 < 0$$

This equation is used to explain changes in concentration for comparable four-digit SIC industries from 1947 to 1967. In some cases the percentage change in total industry advertising (ΔADV) or the percentage change in advertising per firm (ΔAPF) were substituted for ΔASR. The logic of this substitution is that the absolute amount of advertising expenditures will be a better indicator of economies of scale or capital barriers due to advertising. Economies of scale would be realized in proportion to the total number of advertising messages, and this number would be more closely related to the total amount spent for advertising than to the advertising-to-sales ratio. Similarly, capital requirements relate to the total funds which must be raised to carry out a successful advertising campaign. In the estimated regression equations, ΔAPF and ΔADV gave very similar results. Therefore, in most cases, only the results using the latter variable were reported in the tables below.

As with cross-section regressions, the postulated direction of causality from growth and advertising to concentration is in question. Certainly the structure of an industry influences its growth and advertising. For example, advertising decisions are in part affected by rival advertising decisions which in turn are a function of interdependence among firms. As noted above, some economists claim advertising expenditures are strongly affected by high concentration. Similarly, growth is conditioned in part by endogenous decisions on such factors as production technology, managerial efficiency, and research and development expenditures. Such decisions, in turn, are frequently thought to be a function of industry structure. We simply wish to note this potential bias from two-way causality to caution the reader when interpreting the regression coefficients.

Data Problems in Previous Studies. All previous studies, especially cross-section analyses, have been strongly criticized for deficiencies in their data and samples selected.[25] Many studies of U.S. advertising have relied on a sample of IRS consumer good industries. There are at least three problems with IRS data. First, IRS samples suffer from measurement error owing to the mixing of consolidated financial data of diversified firms with more disaggregated four-digit Census concentration ratios based on establishment or plant data. Second, consumer goods industries appear to be selected subjectively in most studies without reliable data on the distribution of sales to various sectors. Finally, IRS industries are at the more aggregated three-digit level in contrast to four-digit Census industries and thus are less likely to conform to economic markets. Cross-section studies using IRS data generally find no significant linear relationship, but this may be due to these measurement errors.[26]

One attempt to avoid these problems by using four-digit Census data was made by Mann et al.[27] Using advertising data from media trade journals for large firms in fourteen SIC industries, they found a highly significant positive relation between advertising and concentration. This study was subsequently critized for: (1) introducing aggregation error by assigning firms to four-digit industries, (2) using a biased sample of a few highly concentrated advertising-intensive industries, and (3) using advertising data from trade journals, which are generally in error because of the exclusion of some advertising expenditures.[28]

Studies examining changes in concentration and changes in advertising fall into two groups. One group was primarily interested in cross-section regressions of advertising intensity and concentration and used first difference regressions to confirm cross-section results.[29] These studies used IRS data and found no significant relationship between changes in concentration and changes in advertising intensity from 1947 to 1963 and subperiods within those years.

[25] See, for example, "Symposium on Advertising and Concentration," *Journal of Industrial Economics*, vol. 18 (November 1969), pp. 76-101; W. Reekie, R. Rees, and C. Sutton, "Advertising, Concentration and Competition: An Interchange," *Economic Journal*, vol. 85 (March 1975), pp. 156-176.

[26] A sample of IRS consumer good industries was originally developed by Telser and used in subsequent investigations of both advertising and concentration and advertising and profit rates. Lester G. Telser, "Advertising and Competition," *Journal of Political Economy*, vol. 72 (December 1964), pp. 537-562.

[27] Mann, Henning, and Meehan, "Advertising and Concentration: An Empirical Investigation," pp. 34-39.

[28] Lester G. Telser, "Another Look at Advertising and Concentration," *Journal of Industrial Economics*, vol. 18 (November 1969), pp. 85-94; Richard A. Miller, "Advertising and Competition: Some Neglected Aspects," *Antitrust Bulletin*, vol. 17 (Summer 1972), pp. 467-478.

[29] Telser, "Advertising and Competition," p. 546; Robert B. Ekelund, Jr. and William P. Gramm, "Advertising and Concentration: Some New Evidence," *Antitrust Bulletin*, vol. 5 (Summer 1970), pp. 243-249.

A second group of studies examined the effect of the level of advertising on changes in concentration.[30] Each used a data set developed at the Federal Trade Commission by Parker[31] to classify industries into consumer and producer goods and into high, moderate, and low degrees of product differentiation, using advertising intensity as a proxy for product differentiation. They concluded that high levels of product differentiation have led to increasing concentration in consumer goods industries from 1947 to 1970. They further concluded that advertising is the main cause of increasing concentration. However, these studies suffer from potentially serious measurement errors due to their method of classifying industries. In fact, it is surprising that Parker's data set and classification scheme were adopted without question, since their results are crucially dependent on it.

Parker adopted the Federal Reserve Board's classification of industries into consumer and producer goods, defined at a mixed level of aggregation ranging from two to four digits, including various combinations. Since many Census four-digit industries do not correspond to these industries, it is hard to see how this classification would be useful. The potential error resulting from this procedure in, for example, the Mueller and Hamm classification of consumer and producer goods industries is clear from their definition. As they say, "Consumer goods are distributed primarily for use by households whereas producer goods are used mainly by other manufacturers or service industries."[32] In their sample of sixty-nine consumer goods industries, at least twelve are clearly misclassified by this definition since these twelve shipped over 50 percent of their output to other producers or had the largest percentage of their output shipped to other producer industries on the basis of the 1963 Input-Output Tables. Such errors tend to invalidate the study's findings.[33]

---

30 Willard F. Mueller and Larry G. Hamm, "Trends in Industrial Market Concentration, 1947 to 1970," *Review of Economics and Statistics*, vol. 56 (November 1974), pp. 511-520; Matityahu Marcus, "Advertising and Changes in Concentration," *Southern Economic Journal*, vol. 36 (October 1969), pp. 117-121.

31 Russell C. Parker, *Comparable Concentration Ratios for 213 Manufacturing Industries Classified by Producer and Consumer and Degree of Product Differentiation, 1947, 1954, 1958, and 1963*, Federal Trade Commission, 1967.

32 Mueller and Hamm, "Trends in Concentration," p. 513.

33 The twelve industries are 2087, 2292, 2394, 2397, 2741, 3636, 3691, 3717, 3861, 3872, 3962, and 3981. Their average weighted change in concentration from 1947 to 1970 (excluding 2292 whose concentration is missing in 1970) is 15.8 points, or 8.9 points above the weighted mean change in consumer goods found by Mueller and Hamm. Had these industries been properly classified into producer goods, the disparity in changes in concentration ratios found between producer and consumer goods would clearly have been far less. See Stanley I. Ornstein, *Industrial Concentration and Advertising Intensity* (Washington, D.C.: American Enterprise Institute, 1977), pp. 20-23.

Parker's classification of industries by degree of product differentiation is apparently based on the advertising-sales ratios of a few top firms in each industry. Advertising expenditures were collected from various media trade journals and used to classify industries. The FTC's explanation of this classification was the following cryptic note:

> Generally speaking, industries classified as undifferentiated made advertising expenditures of less than one percent of sales and those classified as highly differentiated made substantial expenditures for advertising, often in excess of 10 percent of sales and usually were heavy users of television advertising media.[34]

This description suggests that subjective standards were used to classify industries. The guidelines are general, suggesting a somewhat arbitrary classification system. Different threshold levels as well as different advertising media could have been used for different industries. In addition it appears that only one aspect of product differentiation was considered. Since product differentiation encompasses many dimensions across products, the use of advertising intensity alone is a poor proxy.

The use of a few large firms as proxies for an entire industry introduced a further source of error. Since most large firms are diversified, their advertising-sales ratios may have little relationship to a particular four-digit industry. The use of large firms may overstate or understate industries' advertising-sales ratios if such ratios vary across firm sizes within industries. There is substantial evidence in support of this argument.[35]

The classification of industries by degree of product differentiation was based on advertising-sales ratios for 1963, although the results were used to classify industries from 1947 to 1970. Use of a single year to classify industries over a twenty-three year period is subject to large potential error, since such ratios change from year to year. Finally, this method does not constitute a meaningful test of the Kaldor-Bain hypothesis. Even if the level of advertising and concentration were positively related it is not clear why the change in concentration over a long period should be related to the level of advertising at the middle or end of a period.

The Sample Tested. In order to eliminate incompatibility in industry aggregation between advertising data and concentration ratios (a prob-

---

[34] Parker, *Comparable Concentration Ratios.*

[35] William S. Comanor and Thomas A. Wilson, *Advertising and Market Power* (Cambridge, Mass.: Harvard University Press, 1974), pp. 196-216.

lem in studies using IRS data), advertising figures for four-digit industries were drawn from the U.S. Input-Output Tables. This source does not match perfectly all Census industries; however, sufficiently large samples were available using the 1947, 1963, and 1967 tables.[36] For 1963 and 1967, the sample comprises approximately 80 percent of all manufacturing industries and for 1947, approximately 60 percent. Advertising in each industry includes all major advertising expenditures except within-firm expenditures. This tends to bias advertising downward for industries with large in-house advertising departments. However, these advertising figures are much more comprehensive than media trade sources. They include, for example, talent and production costs, signs and advertising displays, art work, postage and printing, and space and time by media including newspapers, periodicals, network and spot TV, network and spot radio, outdoor, and motion picture. Advertising intensity for each industry is calculated as the ratio of inputs purchased from the advertising sector to total industry output, corrected for secondary transfers and imports.

An important advantage of the input-output data is their internal consistency. The construction of the input-output study is such that the summation of advertising inputs purchased by all users of advertising must equal the total advertising output of all producers of advertising. This provides a check of the accuracy of the input-output data that is absent from other sources of advertising data.

Consumer and producer goods industries were defined by the percentage of total output going to consumption final demand, intermediate production, and investment final demand, in the Input-Output Tables. If the highest percentage of output for an industry went to consumers, it was classified as a consumer good; if the highest percentage went to intermediate or investment goods, it was classified as a producer good.

In addition to the consumer-producer subsamples, the samples were divided into nondurable and durable subsamples for the cross-section regressions. This was done to reduce the extent of error owing to unaccounted determinants of advertising that are largely unmeasurable. For example, the type of advertising, retail outlets, consumer knowledge, buying frequency, and rate of new product introduction tend to be more uniform in consumer nondurable goods industries than in all consumer goods industries. The situation is similar with respect to producer nondurable and durable goods industries.

---

[36] The 1958 Input-Output Table does not have a comprehensive disaggregation of advertising by four-digit industries and could not be used. We were fortunate to obtain a mimeograph copy of the 1947 advertising figures from Philip M. Ritz of the U.S. Department of Commerce. The complete 1963 and 1967 tables are available on tape from the Department of Commerce.

The distinction between nondurable and durable producer goods was made by classifying industries whose output was primarily intermediate goods as nondurable and those whose output was primarily investment goods as durable. Consumer goods were classified by judgment into nondurable and durable goods categories. In general, products consumed within a short time such as foods, beverages, toiletries, and cleansers were classified nondurable. Consumer durables were dominated by long-lived household goods including appliances, furniture, and carpets.

Empirical Results

Cross-Section Results. The regression estimates of equations (1) through (4) for 1947, 1963, and 1967 are presented in Tables 1, 2, and 3 respectively. Each equation was estimated for seven samples: all industries, consumer industries, producer industries, consumer nondurable industries, consumer durable industries, producer nondurable industries, and producer durable industries.

The results for 1947, with the exception of consumer durables, show no significant linear or nonlinear relationship. These results are at odds with the traditional Kaldor-Bain hypothesis, which predicts a positive relationship in industries with the highest advertising intensity, in this case the consumer nondurable goods sample. In all cases except consumer durables, the explained variation in advertising intensity is not significantly different from zero, indicating that concentration plays no role in explaining levels of advertising intensity or vice versa. Thus, based on 1947 evidence, one would conclude that there is in general no significant relationship between advertising intensity and concentration.

The results for 1963 and 1967 present different evidence. In general, there is both a linear and log-linear significant positive relationship for the total sample as well as for individual subsamples. The results tend to be strongest in consumer goods subsamples. As stated above, advocates of the position that there is a positive relationship concede that it is likely to hold only in consumer goods industries with high advertising intensity. This is particularly so among those who argue that advertising leads to monopoly power because of economies of scale in advertising and advertising-created product differentiation. In the 1963 and 1967 samples, the mean advertising intensity is 4.1 percent in consumer nondurables and 0.9 percent in producer nondurables. Thus the results tend to support the expectation of a stronger relationship in consumer goods industries.

Table 1

ADVERTISING INTENSITY AND CONCENTRATION BY PRODUCT CATEGORY, 1947

Sample	Intercept	Coefficient of Concentration	Coefficient of Squared Concentration	Log of Coefficient of Concentration	Coefficient of Determination[a]
Total N=261	1.3057	−.0045 (0.60)			.00
	1.3162	−.0050 (0.15)	.0000 (.00)		.00
	1.2144		−.0000 (0.58)		.00
	−1.2272			.0525 (0.33)	.00
Consumer N=75	2.1169	.0063 (0.27)			.00
	3.3376	−.0597 (0.53)	.0007 (0.59)		−.01
	2.1764		.0001 (0.39)		.00
	1.2616			.3677 (1.30)	.02
Producer N=186	.7854	−.0041 (0.86)			.00
	.6291	.0040 (0.19)	−.0001 (0.40)		.00
	.7117		−.0000 (0.93)		.00
	−1.6420			.0456 (0.28)	.00
Consumer Nondurable N=41	3.2444	−.0073 (0.19)			.00
	4.4244	−.0721 (0.37)	.0007 (0.34)		−.02
	3.0442		−.0001 (0.13)		.00
	−1.1241			.3348 (0.85)	.02
Consumer Durable N=34	.7306	.0250[b] (1.82)			.09
	1.4532	−.0142 (0.22)	.0004 (0.62)		.08
	1.1775		.0003[b] (1.93)		.10
	−1.4886			.4250 (1.04)	.03

Table 1 (continued)
ADVERTISING INTENSITY AND CONCENTRATION BY PRODUCT CATEGORY, 1947

Sample	Intercept	Coefficient of Concentration	Coefficient of Squared Concentration	Log of Coefficient of Concentration	Coefficient of Determination[a]
Producer Nondurable N=134	.3814	.0012 (0.41)			.00
	.3518	.0028 (0.22)	−.0000 (0.13)		−.01
	.4079		.0000 (0.37)		.00
	−2.1481			.1800 (1.16)	.01
Producer Durable N=52	2.1269	−.0232 (1.47)			.04
	2.5669	−.0433 (0.59)	.0002 (0.28)		.02
	1.5672		−.0002 (1.37)		.04
	.7851			.5871 (1.17)	.03

Note: *t*-ratio in parentheses.
[a] Coefficient of determination adjusted for degrees of freedom.
[b] Significant at .05 level.

Table 2
ADVERTISING INTENSITY AND CONCENTRATION BY PRODUCT CATEGORY, 1963

Sample	Intercept	Coefficient of Concentration	Coefficient of Squared Concentration	Log of Coefficient of Concentration	Coefficient of Determination[a]
Total N=320	.9050	.0191[c] (2.39)			.02
	.4985	.0424 (1.36)	−.0003 (0.78)		.02
	1.2980		.0002[b] (2.10)		.01
	−1.3318			.3052[c] (2.89)	.03

Table 2 (continued)

ADVERTISING INTENSITY AND CONCENTRATION BY PRODUCT CATEGORY, 1963

Sample	Intercept	Coefficient of Concentration	Coefficient of Squared Concentration	Log of Coefficient of Concentration	Coefficient of Determination[a]
Consumer N=85	1.7388	.0524[b] (2.04)			.05
	.8784	.1007 (0.88)	−.0005 (0.43)		.04
	2.7876		.0005[b] (1.88)		.04
	−1.5205			.6354[c] (2.99)	.10
Producer N=235	.7042	.0039 (1.38)			.01
	.4189	.0204[b] (1.93)	−.0002 (1.62)		.01
	.8031		.0000 (0.89)		.00
	−1.1611			.1541 (1.54)	.01
Consumer Nondurable N=51	1.5764	.0654[b] (1.80)			.06
	2.2686	.0259 (0.16)	.0004 (0.26)		.04
	2.7507		.0007[b] (1.82)		.06
	−1.4582			.6298[b] (2.21)	.09
Consumer Durable N=34	1.8518	.0376 (1.06)			.03
	−1.5387	.2224 (1.39)	−.0020 (1.18)		.05
	2.8010		.0003 (0.77)		.02
	−1.6901			.6646[b] (2.03)	.11
Producer Nondurable N=186	.6467	.0058[b] (1.91)			.02
	.4938	.0150 (1.30)	−.0001 (0.83)		.02
	.7646		.0001 (1.62)		.01
	−1.2799			.1965[b] (1.78)	.02

Table 2 (continued)

ADVERTISING INTENSITY AND CONCENTRATION BY PRODUCT CATEGORY, 1963

Sample	Intercept	Coefficient of Concentration	Coefficient of Squared Concentration	Log of Coefficient of Concentration	Coefficient of Determination[a]
Producer Durable N=49	.9447	−.0030 (0.40)			.00
	.2331	.0323 (1.13)	−.0004 (1.28)		.02
	.9319		−.0001 (0.72)		.01
	−.6538			−.0150 (0.06)	.00

Note: *t*-ratio in parentheses.

[a] Coefficient of determination adjusted for degrees of freedom.

[b] Significant at .05 level.

[c] Significant at .01 level.

Table 3

ADVERTISING INTENSITY AND CONCENTRATION BY PRODUCT CATEGORY, 1967

Sample	Intercept	Coefficient of Concentration	Coefficient of Squared Concentration	Log of Coefficient of Concentration	Coefficient of Determination[a]
Total N=324	.5946	.0282[c] (3.92)			.05
	.2651	.0472 (1.63)	−.0002 (0.68)		.05
	1.1444		.0003[c] (3.62)		.04
	−1.7252			.4373[c] (4.25)	.05
Consumer N=87	1.1313	.0646[c] (3.05)			.10
	−.1076	.1324 (1.41)	−.0007 (0.74)		.09
	2.4664		.0006[c] (2.78)		.08
	−2.1500			.8358[c] (4.62)	.20

Table 3 (continued)
ADVERTISING INTENSITY AND CONCENTRATION BY PRODUCT CATEGORY, 1967

Sample	Intercept	Coefficient of Concentration	Coefficient of Squared Concentration	Log of Coefficient of Concentration	Coefficient of Determination[a]
Producer N=237	.5788	.0089[c] (2.44)			.02
	.4793	.0147 (1.04)	−.0001 (0.43)		.02
	.7495		.0001[b] (2.24)		.02
	−1.3305			.2172[b] (2.20)	.02
Consumer Nondurable N=54	1.4926	.0644[b] (2.11)			.08
	.4096	.1242 (0.91)	−.0006 (0.45)		.06
	2.7997		.0006[b] (1.94)		.07
	−1.9604			.7811[c] (2.95)	.14
Consumer Durable N=33	.3728	.0687[c] (2.81)			.20
	−1.5268	.1709 (1.56)	−.0011 (0.96)		.20
	1.8585		.0007[c] (2.46)		.16
	−2.5175			.9388[c] (4.85)	.43
Producer Nondurable N=184	.6333	.0077[b] (1.95)			.02
	.4474	.0191 (1.21)	−.0001 (0.75)		.02
	.7841		.0001[b] (1.70)		.02
	−1.4016			.2446[b] (2.22)	.03
Producer Durable N=53	.3790	.0128 (1.45)			.04
	.4080	.0113 (0.32)	.0000 (0.14)		.02
	.6383		.0001 (1.41)		.04
	−1.0949			.1283 (0.57)	.01

Note: *t*-ratio in parentheses.
[a] Coefficient of determination adjusted for degrees of freedom.
[b] Significant at .05 level.
[c] Significant at .01 level.

The results are weakest for the producer nondurable and the durable goods subsamples, yet in both 1963 and 1967 there is a significant positive linear and log-linear relationship in producer nondurable goods industries. Given the low level of advertising intensity in these industries, this result is inconsistent with the traditional Kaldor-Bain hypothesis. The result is consistent, however, with the hypothesis that large firm effects produce a spurious correlation, for this purely statistical artifact should apply with equal force to both consumer and producer nondurable goods. Although the finding of significant results for both consumer and producer nondurable goods industries does not refute the existence of advertising barriers to entry in consumer nondurables, it makes highly suspect the interpretation of a positive correlation in consumer goods industries as supportive of barriers to entry.

The explained variation in advertising intensity is typically very low. The 1963 figures are generally less than 5 percent, with the highest R^2 results in consumer durable goods. The R^2 results in 1967 are generally much higher than in 1963 but still typically quite low. The exception, again, is consumer durable goods. In general, over 90 percent of the variation in advertising intensity is unaccounted for by concentration. Indeed, with the exception of consumer durable goods in 1967, the R^2 results are generally so low that the influence of concentration on advertising intensity can be considered inconsequential.

The quadratic relationship receives no support in any year. This result is due in large part to extremely high collinearity (close association) between CR and $(CR)^2$, indicating that the range in which they are measured is approximately linear. The collinearity is typically in excess of 90 percent, making the regression results meaningless. An indication of the extent of collinearity is seen when $(CR)^2$ appears alone. Its sign frequently changes from negative in the quadratic equation to positive, and it becomes significant. Two alternative approaches were adopted to test the quadratic relationship. One was to apply the technique of slope dummies, both linear and logarithmic, by dividing the sample at the 60 percent concentration level. The results showed no evidence of a quadratic relationship. Secondly, the advertising-sales ratios were arrayed by concentration deciles to see if moderately high concentration levels were associated with the highest advertising-sales ratios. The results for the three years are in appendix Tables 1A, 2A, and 3A, respectively. They are difficult to interpret because few industries fell into certain decile ranges, particularly the highest decile ranges. Nevertheless, there does not appear to be an inverted U relationship in the most likely subsamples, consumer nondurable and durable goods. In fact, in 1963 and 1967 there is a bimodal distribution for consumer nondurables. Thus, there is no support for the hypothesis that oligopolists overinvest in advertising or collude on advertising.

Previous support for a quadratic relationship seems suspect since it most likely suffered from the same severe collinearity. In addition, the use of highly selective, small, and possibly biased samples may have affected previous results. Whatever the possible hypothetical basis for a quadratic relationship, there is no empirical support in our results.[37]

In summary, the results show a significant linear and log-linear relationship in 1963 and 1967, but not in 1947. The log-linear relationship appears to give a better fit to the data. There is a significant positive relationship in 1963 and 1967 in producer nondurables as well as consumer nondurables, although the relationship is stronger in consumer nondurables. The finding of a positive relationship for producer nondurables is inconsistent with traditional hypotheses that expect a positive relationship only in consumer goods industries. There is also no evidence of a quadratic relationship or much higher advertising intensity for moderate as opposed to low or extremely high concentration ratios. In short, there appears to be a significant positive but weak relationship between advertising intensity and concentration in the 1960s and none in the late 1940s; however, we cannot conclude from this that advertising leads to barriers to entry, is anticompetitive, or worsens industrial performance.

Analysis of Changes in Concentration. Tests of equation (5) were made with several alternative measures of advertising: advertising intensity in the base year (*ASR*47), absolute change in advertising intensity (ΔASR), percentage change in total industry advertising expenditures (ΔADV), and percentage change in advertising per firm (ΔAPF). Since previous studies, such as the ones by Marcus and by Mueller and Hamm, attribute their conclusion of high advertising intensity leading to increases in concentration to the existence of increasing economies of scale in advertising, it is important to choose a measure that is most likely to reflect possible economies of scale. It is not clear that their choice of dummy variables of high, moderate, and low advertising intensity reflects economies of scale. A high ratio (or change in the ratio) does not necessarily reflect intensive advertising because of pecuniary or technological economies of scale. A high ratio may simply reflect a high rate of product introduction. On the other hand, total advertising expenditures

[37] Strickland and Weiss, "Advertising, Concentration, and Price-Cost Margins," find support for a quadratic relationship and, like this study, use a large sample based on data obtained from the U.S. Input-Output Tables. However, their sample may suffer from measurement error. For further discussion, see Ornstein, *Industrial Concentration and Advertising Intensity*, pp. 35-38.

and changes in it are more likely indicative of possible economies of scale, and thus this measure is used as the best proxy for advertising economies of scale. There is a significant positive correlation between advertising intensity and total advertising expenditures in each year, as expected. However, there is no significant correlation between changes in each variable, indicating that they are not good substitutes for measuring increases in advertising expenditures. (See appendix Table 4A.)

Regressions were run for all comparable industries from 1947 to 1963 and 1967. There were 120 such industries for which SIC four-digit definitions did not change and for which concentration and advertising data were available in each year. Regressions for the total sample and for producer and consumer goods industries are in Tables 4–6. None of the advertising variables was significant in the producer goods industries for these periods. However, all of the other variables for producer goods were highly significant.

The results for the total sample show that base year concentration ($CR47$), changes in average firm size (ΔAFS), and market growth (ΔGR) are all highly significant and of the expected sign. These results support our earlier hypotheses derived from static equilibrium conditions. Specifically, large average firm size reflects large economies of scale. Thus, where there are few firms there are large economies of scale and high concentration and vice versa. Industries with the fastest growing markets tend to experience a decline in concentration, indicating that the largest firms are not growing as fast as the market. Either new firms are entering, smaller firms are growing faster than large firms, or both, leading to a decline in concentration. The simple correlation between market growth and net change in number of firms is 0.6 between 1947 and 1967, indicating that new firms are entering the fastest growing industries. The coefficients of both size and growth for the average firm are very small, indicating neither has a large influence on changes in concentration. For consumer goods these results do not hold between periods: change in average firm size and market size is insignificant in many cases for 1947 to 1963.

Initial year concentration is inversely related to change in concentration in each sample. This variable was included to account for a possible bias due to the bounded nature of concentration ratios. There may be a regression fallacy at work that causes industry concentration ratios to tend toward the mean. The significant inverse relationship suggests that this is a distinct possibility.

These three variables account for almost all of the explained variation in changes in concentration. However, nowhere do they explain

Table 4

REGRESSIONS EXPLAINING CHANGES IN FOUR-FIRM CONCENTRATION, 1947–1967, FOR 120 COMPARABLE INDUSTRIES

Period	Intercept	*ASR47*	Δ*ASR*	Δ*ADV*	*CR47*	Δ*AFS*	Δ*GR*	*I** Δ*ASR*	*D** Δ*ASR*	R^2
1947–1967	7.7080	−.0123 (0.04)			−.1744[b] (4.13)	.0246[b] (3.80)	−.0196[b] (3.90)			.23
	7.8161		.9025[b] (2.40)		−.1848[b] (4.47)	.0205[b] (3.35)	−.0172[b] (3.44)			.27
	8.2077			−.0001 (1.14)	−.1795[b] (4.26)	.0241[b] (4.00)	−.0192[b] (3.84)			.24
	6.8655				−.1828[b] (4.49)	.0168[b] (2.68)	−.0161[b] (3.25)	1.7120[b] (3.27)	−.2446 (0.38)	.29
	10.0000		1.2370[b] (3.16)		−.1809[b] (4.19)		−.0105[a] (2.14)			.20
1947–1963	7.4004	−.0085 (0.03)			−.1600[b] (4.04)	.0278[b] (3.52)	−.0218[b] (3.13)			.18
	7.5015		.4985 (1.56)		−.1641[b] (4.20)	.0248[b] (3.23)	−.0209[b] (3.01)			.20
	7.7909			−.0001 (1.14)	−.1649[b] (4.18)	.0275[b] (3.67)	−.0213[b] (3.06)			.19
	7.4258				−.1640[b] (4.17)	.0245[b] (3.13)	−.0208[b] (2.98)	.5471 (1.33)	.3990 (0.64)	.19
	8.369		.7500[a] (2.33)		−.1438[b] (3.57)		−.0121[a] (1.83)			.13

Note: *t*-values in parentheses.

[a] Significant at .05 level.

[b] Significant at .01 level.

Table 5

REGRESSIONS EXPLAINING CHANGES IN FOUR-FIRM CONCENTRATION, 1947–1967, FOR 39 COMPARABLE CONSUMER GOODS INDUSTRIES

Period	Intercept	*ASR47*	Δ*ASR*	Δ*ADV*	*CR47*	Δ*AFS*	Δ*GR*	*I** Δ*ASR*	*D** Δ*ASR*	R^2
1947–1967	11.4731	.1360 (0.31)			−.1772[a] (1.99)	.0219[a] (1.98)	−.0334[a] (2.19)			.17
	10.3343		1.2528[a] (1.82)		−.2115[b] (2.43)	.0171[a] (1.61)	−.0238 (1.57)			.25
	11.2729			.0001 (0.10)	−.1752[a] (1.93)	.0230[a] (2.17)	−.0326[a] (2.16)			.17
	8.2433				−.2038[b] (2.45)	.0125 (1.20)	−.0278[a] (1.90)	2.2225[b] (2.76)	−2.5747 (1.32)	.31
	13.3000		1.6290[b] (2.41)		−.2511[b] (2.66)		−.0210 (0.91)			.20
1947–1963	10.8455	.2981 (0.75)			−.1413[a] (1.74)	.0181 (1.31)	−.0419[a] (1.98)			.09
	10.8796		.3762 (0.70)		−.1535[a] (1.86)	.0180 (1.29)	−.0359[a] (1.70)			.09
	11.1035			−.0000 (0.09)	−.1441[a] (1.73)	.0206 (1.51)	−.0386[a] (1.85)			.08
	10.1844				−.1596[a] (1.92)	.0177 (1.26)	−.0397[a] (1.84)	.6783 (1.08)	−1.4090 (0.72)	.09
	11.8030		.5863[a] (1.76)		−.1574[a] (1.76)		−.0216 (1.20)			.05

Note: *t*-values in parentheses.

[a] Significant at .05 level.

[b] Significant at .01 level.

Table 6

REGRESSIONS EXPLAINING CHANGES IN FOUR-FIRM CONCENTRATION, 1947–1967, FOR 81 COMPARABLE PRODUCER GOODS INDUSTRIES

Period	Intercept	*ASR47*	Δ*ASR*	Δ*ADV*	*CR47*	Δ*AFS*	Δ*GR*	*I** Δ*ASR*	*D** Δ*ASR*	R^2
1947–1967	6.0131	−.0571 (0.37)			−.1874[b] (4.06)	.0342[b] (3.33)	−.0178[b] (3.58)			.25
	6.0460		.3898 (0.75)		−.1885[b] (4.10)	.0336[b] (3.28)	−.0176[b] (3.55)			.25
	6.5752			−.002 (1.49)	−.1938[b] (4.24)	.0338[b] (3.34)	−.0174[b] (3.59)			.27
	5.2797				−.1871[b] (4.07)	.0328[b] (3.19)	−.0173[b] (3.48)	1.6856 (1.21)	.0533 (0.08)	.25
1947–1963	6.3867	−.4957 (1.03)			−.1958[b] (4.67)	.0485[b] (4.34)	−.0194[b] (3.01)			.29
	6.0791		.5869 (1.23)		−.1942[b] (4.65)	.0479[b] (4.30)	−.0198[b] (3.08)			.29
	6.4213			−.0001 (1.47)	−.2009[b] (4.80)	.0486[b] (4.39)	−.0187[b] (2.92)			.30
	6.2378				−.1952[b] (4.62)	.0481[b] (4.27)	−.0197[b] (3.03)	.3099 (0.23)	.6542 (1.15)	.28

Note: *t*-values in parentheses.
[a] Significant at .05 level.
[b] Significant at .01 level.

more than 30 percent of the variation. Most likely some important explanatory variables have been omitted.

The advertising variables yield mixed results that are in some ways consistent and in other ways inconsistent with the Kaldor-Bain hypothesis. The change in the advertising-to-sales ratio is positive and statistically significant for both samples in most equations, and the magnitude of the regression coefficient of ΔASR is higher for the consumer goods sample. It is also higher in those equations in which average firm size (ΔAFS) is omitted. Thus it is possible that the average firm size variable is capturing some of the effect of advertising intensity. These results are consistent with the theory that advertising leads to concentration as well as with the theory that concentration leads to advertising.

Another plausible explanation for this regression result is the superior firm hypothesis outlined earlier. That is, in the absence of barriers to entry, concentration is explained by differential firm efficiency. Less efficient firms will lose market share or exit the industry as a result of rivalry with more efficient firms, leading to higher concentration over time in certain industries. Since more efficient firms have a greater incentive to advertise, advertising intensity rises as concentration rises, and the two variables appear to be related.

The results for changes in advertising intensity, as with changes in average firm size and growth, are inconsistent between periods. This suggests that results are strongly influenced by the choice of initial base and final years for first difference analysis. Such sensitivity to structural shifts does not produce great confidence in the reliability of the results.[38] It also shows that the method adopted in previous studies of using a single year to identify advertising intensity over a twenty-three year span is subject to great error.

In contrast to changes in advertising intensity, our best proxies for economies of scale in advertising—total industry advertising and advertising per firm (results not shown)—were insignificant in each sample and period tested. These results provide no support for the hypothesis that economies of scale in advertising lead to higher concentration. This is consistent with the fact that there is almost no evidence supporting the existence of economies of scale in advertising.[39] In fact, most studies

[38] This is similar to the findings of Kamerschen and others who investigated the relationship between changes in concentration and growth. Both negative and positive relationships were found, depending on the period tested.

[39] Recent comprehensive reviews of studies of advertising economies of scale concluded that there is no evidence of such economies. Julian Simon, *Issues in the Economics of Advertising* (Urbana: University of Illinois Press, 1970); Schmalensee, *Economics of Advertising*; James M. Ferguson, *Advertising and Competition.*

have found decreasing returns to advertising, which is not surprising since it is consistent with profit maximization. Of course, it may be the case that increasing returns exist but have not been detected because the techniques of testing are too crude, the data are too poor, or the output range in which such economies occur is not observable. Whatever the case, to date there is little evidence of such economies and our results are consistent with that finding.

The coefficient for initial year advertising intensity is also insignificant in each case. High initial advertising intensity is not related to subsequent changes in concentration, in contrast to what Kaldor's hypothesis implies.

The Kaldor and the "advertising-as-a-barrier-to-entry" hypotheses may be tested also by determining whether increasing and decreasing advertising intensity have symmetrical effects on concentration. Kaldor hypothesized that decreases in advertising will lead to decreases in concentration just as increases in advertising will lead to increases in concentration. Decreasing advertising should exert the stronger effect if advertising is indeed a barrier to entry. As stated earlier, this asymmetry results from the fact that only one type of barrier attributable to advertising will raise concentration, namely, differential increases in optimal firm size due to advertising economies of scale. However, a reduction in any alleged barrier such as brand loyalty, capital barriers, or economies of scale will facilitate entry and tend to reduce concentration. To illustrate the asymmetry further, suppose a new law blocked all entry into an industry. Passage of the law would not by itself cause concentration to rise. But if the law were repealed and if entry took place, concentration would fall.

The last regressions in each sample include slope dummy variables to test this hypothesis. The variables $I^{*}\Delta ASR$ and $D^{*}\Delta ASR$ represent increases in advertising-sales ratios and decreases in advertising-sales ratios respectively. Although we argued earlier for using change in total advertising expenditures as a preferred proxy for economies of scale, only change in advertising intensity gave significant results and was selected in order to bias the results toward the Kaldor hypothesis.

The results are contrary to those predicted by Kaldor and by the barrier-to-entry hypothesis. Increases in advertising intensity are significantly positively related to change in concentration in both samples from 1947 to 1967 but not from 1947 to 1963. Decreases in advertising intensity are not significantly related in either period. In consumer goods industries, the decreasing slope dummy is negative. Industries with increases in advertising intensity tended to experience increases in concentration, but so did industries with decreases in advertising intensity, although the latter were not significant.

A Larger Sample. One of the weakest aspects of this or any analysis of changes in concentration ratios is the need to use comparable industries whose industry definitions do not change over long periods of time. Such industries tend to be the slowest growing and least dynamic in terms of technological change and innovation. The Census explains the basis for its need to revise industry definitions periodically in the following manner.

> The need for redefinition arises particularly from the introduction of new products, the declining importance of older products, the introduction of new techniques, the growth of small fields into important industries, and similar dynamic development. While necessary to keep the classification abreast of the changing nature of the economy, an inevitable cost of redefinition is the loss of comparability for many categories over time.[40]

Clearly, industries not in these newer categories are generally the slowest growing and the least likely to attract new entrants and are likely to experience an above average amount of exits and to see a rise in concentration. Thus, there is a real possibility that such a sample of industries will be biased toward concentration increases.

The only period for which a much larger sample of advertising data are available is the short four-year span, 1963 to 1967. Although approximately 30 percent of all four-digit industries experienced a change in concentration of 5 percentage points or more over this period, the mean change in concentration was quite small, an increase of 0.5 points. Thus, the period may be too short to pick up substantial shifts in concentration.

Regression results for 317 comparable industries from 1963 to 1967 are found in Table 7. In contrast to the longer periods, absolute change in advertising intensity, percentage change in industry advertising expenditures, and advertising per firm are all significant and positive for the total industry and consumer goods samples. These equations are therefore more consistent with the hypothesis of increasing returns to advertising than were the previous regression equations. However, the slope dummy variable test is again inconsistent with the barrier-to-entry hypothesis. While the results are consistent with increasing returns to advertising, they are also consistent with other hypotheses that

[40] U.S. Bureau of the Census, Census of Manufacturers, 1972, *Special Report Series: Concentration Ratios on Manufacturing*, MC72(SR)-2, p. v.

Table 7

REGRESSIONS EXPLAINING CHANGES IN FOUR-FIRM CONCENTRATION, 1963–1967, FOR 317 COMPARABLE INDUSTRIES

Period	Intercept	*ASR63*	Δ*ASR*	Δ*ADV*	*CR63*	Δ*AFS*	Δ*GR*	*I** Δ*ASR*	*D** Δ*ASR*	Δ*APF*	R^2
1963–1967	.7126	.0504 (0.60)			−.0269[a] (2.05)	.0545[b] (4.33)	−.0431[b] (3.12)	all industries			.08
	.6577		.4192[a] (2.13)		−.0263[a] (2.05)	.0545[b] (4.39)	−.0400[b] (2.87)				.09
	.6379			.0010[b] (3.52)	−.0259[a] (2.04)	.0517[b] (4.20)	−.0400[b] (2.95)				.11
	.6639				−.0289[a] (2.25)	.0519[b] (4.17)	−.0392[b] (2.85)	.7498[b] (2.81)	−.0211 (0.22)		.10
			.4561[a] (2.25)		−.0409[b] (3.21)		−.0168 (0.02)				.04
					−.039[b] (3.13)		−.039 (0.03)			.8210[b] (4.08)	.07
1963–1967	1.3806	.0407 (0.38)			−.0285 (1.02)	.0738[b] (2.96)	−.0756[b] (2.59)	consumer goods N=84			.11
	.9657		.4552[a] (1.80)		−.0260 (1.00)	.0728[b] (3.00)	−.0570[a] (1.89)				.15
	1.1394			.0010[b] (3.45)	−.0256 (1.03)	.0632[b] (2.71)	−.0603[a] (2.20)				.23

Table 7 (continued)

REGRESSIONS EXPLAINING CHANGES IN FOUR-FIRM CONCENTRATION, 1963–1967, FOR 317 COMPARABLE INDUSTRIES

Period	Intercept	*ASR63*	Δ*ASR*	Δ*ADV*	*CR63*	Δ*AFS*	Δ*GR*	*I** Δ*ASR*	*D** Δ*ASR*	Δ*APF*	R^2
	1.1728				−.0368 (1.44)	.0633[b] (2.65)	−.0581[a] (1.98)	1.1004[b] (3.01)	−.1658 (.046)		.19
					−.044[a] (1.84)		−.0190 (0.80)			.803[b] (3.85)	.16
			.4996[a] (1.89)		−.0488[a] (1.91)		−.0090 (0.33)				.06
1963–1967	.6518	−.1942 (0.58)			−.0276[a] (1.85)	.0419[b] (2.79)	−.0262 (1.59)	producer goods N=233			.06
	.5285		.3107 (0.82)		−.0290[a] (1.94)	.0417[b] (2.77)	−.0261 (1.59)				.06
	.5484			−.002 (0.19)	−.0285[a] (1.91)	.0420[b] (2.80)	−.0267 (1.62)				.05
	.5721				−.0285[a] (1.91)	.0406[b] (2.70)	−.0218 (1.31)	.0919 (0.22)	1.6869 (1.48)		.06

Note: *t*-values in parentheses.
[a]Significant at .05 level.
[b]Significant at .01 level.

link concentration to advertising independent of monopoly power explanations, such as the efficient firm hypothesis.

Summary. Can something be learned from these various regression estimates despite the econometric difficulties and inconsistencies across periods? A few things seem clear. First, initial year advertising intensity is unrelated to subsequent changes in concentration. There is no basis to predict that industries today with high advertising intensity will experience increases in concentration in future years.

Second, increases in advertising expenditures relative to sales are generally positively related to increases in concentration. However, this is probably not a consequence of advertising-induced barriers to entry since decreases in advertising-to-sales ratios are not related to decreases in concentration.

Third, the advertising variables explain very little of the variation in concentration changes. Most of the explained variation stems from the measures of market growth, changes in average firm size, and the tendency of concentration ratios to change toward the mean concentration of all industries over time. Even these variables explain no more than 30 percent of the variation.

While barriers-to-entry hypotheses in general were not supported, the question remains unresolved whether the association between increasing advertising and concentration is due to advertising-induced changes in optimal scale. The lack of association between increases in total advertising or advertising per firm and concentration appears as evidence against this possibility for 1947–1963 and 1947–1967. However, the existence of an association appears to favor this hypothesis for 1963–1967. Unfortunately, the results are consistent with a number of other hypotheses as well.

Conclusions

Much of the controversy over concentration and advertising intensity has focused on data deficiencies and measurement error. This paper attempted to reduce these problems by matching a comprehensive measure of advertising expenditures with concentration ratios at the four-digit SIC level. This permitted tests between advertising and concentration with data that are less subject to sample bias, aggregation bias, and measurement error than data used in earlier studies. The results of these tests show the following:

- There was a significant positive linear and log-linear relationship across consumer as well as producer good industries for 1963 and 1967 but none for 1947.
- There was no significant quadratic relationship in any of the years tested.
- Levels of advertising intensity were not related to subsequent changes in concentration.
- Changes in advertising intensity were generally positively related to changes in concentration.
- Increases in industry advertising expenditures and advertising per firm were not related to changes in concentration from 1947 to 1967 but were related from 1963 to 1967.
- Decreases in advertising intensity were not related to decreases in concentration, suggesting that advertising is not a significant barrier to entry.
- The magnitude of the influence of advertising on concentration is very small, suggesting that any policy change in advertising will have little effect on concentration levels, and vice versa.

Although this study found a positive relationship between advertising and concentration, the nature and significance of this finding is unclear. A number of alternative hypotheses are consistent with the results. In general, the results do not support the orthodox view of advertising as a barrier to entry. It appears that greater understanding of the theory of advertising and the evolution of market structures is required to gain further insight into the various causal forces leading to this relationship. Far more research is required before public policy implications can be drawn from the types of results found in this paper.

Appendix

Table 1A

MEAN ADVERTISING INTENSITY BY TOP CONCENTRATION DECILES, 1947

Sample	Concentration Decile 30–39	40–49	50–59	60–69	70–79	80–89	90–100	N
Total	0.6	1.2	0.9	1.0	1.5	0.6	1.1	261
Consumer	0.9	2.7	1.1	3.5	3.3	0.9[c]	6.0[a]	75
Producer	0.4	0.6	0.8	0.3	0.5	0.5	0.4	186
Consumer nondurable	0.9	3.8[c]	0.7[c]	3.1[c]	3.2	0.8[b]	6.0[a]	41
Consumer durable	0.9	2.0	1.4	4.2[b]	3.6[b]	1.2[a]	[d]	34
Producer nondurable	0.5	0.2	0.5	0.4	0.6	0.5	0.5	134
Producer durable	0.3	2.3	1.3	0.2	0.2	0.3[b]	0.3[c]	52

[a] Based on one industry.
[b] Based on two industries.
[c] Based on three industries.
[d] No industries in this category.

Table 2A

MEAN ADVERTISING INTENSITY BY TOP CONCENTRATION DECILES, 1963

Sample	Concentration Decile 30–39	40–49	50–59	60–69	70–79	80–89	90–100	N
Total	2.3	1.6	1.5	2.1	2.1	4.2	1.3	320
Consumer	5.9	3.4	3.3	5.7	4.0	8.4	3.8[a]	85
Producer	0.9	1.1	0.8	0.9	1.0	0.7	0.9	235
Consumer nondurable	6.5	2.6	3.5	2.6[c]	5.2[c]	13.9[b]	3.8[a]	51
Consumer durable	4.8	4.2	3.1	10.2[b]	2.8[c]	3.0[b]	[d]	34
Producer nondurable	0.8	1.0	0.9	1.0	1.0	0.7	1.5	186
Producer durable	1.2	1.2	0.6	0.5[c]	1.1[a]	[d]	0.3[c]	49

[a] Based on one industry.
[b] Based on two industries.
[c] Based on three industries.
[d] No industries in these categories.

Table 3A
MEAN ADVERTISING INTENSITY BY TOP CONCENTRATION DECILES, 1967

Sample	Concentration Decile 30–39	40–49	50–59	60–69	70–79	80–89	90–100	N
Total	2.1	1.7	2.7	1.6	2.6	3.6	1.0[c]	324
Consumer	5.5	3.3	4.8	4.7	5.3	6.7	[d]	87
Producer	1.1	1.0	0.9	0.9	1.3	1.9	1.0[c]	237
Consumer nondurable	6.2	3.8	4.9	2.8	7.3[b]	7.5	[d]	54
Consumer durable	3.9	2.8	4.6	8.5[b]	3.9[c]	3.7[a]	[d]	33
Producer nondurable	1.1	1.0	1.0	1.0	1.3	1.0	2.5[a]	184
Producer durable	0.9	0.8	0.6	0.6	[d]	3.7[c]	0.3[b]	53

[a] Based on one industry.
[b] Based on two industries.
[c] Based on three industries.
[d] No industries in these categories.

Table 4A
CORRELATION COEFFICIENTS FOR 120 COMPARABLE INDUSTRIES, 1947–1967

	ΔCR	CR47	ASR47	ΔASR	ΔADV	ΔAFS
*CR*1947	−.32					
*ASR*1947	.09	−.03				
Δ*ASR*	.25	.11	−.32			
Δ*ADV*	−.08	−.11	−.09	.04		
Δ*AFS*	.20	.07	.36	.21	−.03	
Δ*GR*	−.17	.01	.13	−.10	.04	.39

Note: r is significant at .01 if $|r| \geq .23$. r is significant at .05 if $|r| \geq .16$.

Table 5A
CORRELATION COEFFICIENTS FOR 317 COMPARABLE INDUSTRIES, 1963–1967

	ΔCR	CR63	ASR63	ΔASR	ΔADV	ΔAFS
*CR*1963	−.17					
*ASR*1963	.04	.15				
Δ*ASR*	.12	.03	−.46			
Δ*ADV*	.21	−.01	−.05	.55		
Δ*AFS*	.20	−.22	.08	−.08	.05	
Δ*GR*	−.00	−.05	.02	−.15	−.02	.67

Note: r is significant at .01 if $|r| \geq .135$. r is significant at .05 if $|r| \geq .096$.

ADVERTISING AND OLIGOPOLY: CORRELATIONS IN SEARCH OF UNDERSTANDING

John A. Henning and H. Michael Mann

Not all economists interested in the competitive process are persuaded that advertising diminishes the strength of competitive forces. However, we are among those who believe that this proposition is confirmed by certain empirical regularities observed by various investigators. What is not clear, however, is why this seems to be the case, and it is this ignorance to which our paper is addressed.

We begin with a brief reference to the findings that lay the basis for the claim that advertising impedes competition, including our argument that economic theory provides plausible alternative mechanisms to explain the observed empirical results. We then offer some findings that suggest how the world may be working. We emphasize "may," for our efforts to date are necessarily tentative, pending further research. The working hypothesis suggested by our analysis is that intense advertising apparently follows from high levels of new product introduction by the leading established firms in an industry. It is this behavior, then, that requires further analysis if understanding is to be enhanced.

Advertising and Oligopoly. The evidence to date permits the following conclusions:

- Advertising intensity—the ratio of advertising-to-sales revenue—is positively associated with market concentration. Most studies find the positive relationship statistically significant, unlikely to be a chance occurrence. We are aware of three studies, though, that maintain that the association is positive and significant only up to a particular level of concentration. After that level the relationship becomes negative.[1]

[1] The number of studies is quite large. Surveys of them are contained in H. M. Mann, "Advertising, Concentration, and Profitability: The State of Knowledge and Directions for Public Policy," in *Industrial Concentration: The New Learning*, H. J. Goldschmid, H. M. Mann, and J. F. Weston, eds. (Boston: Little, Brown & Co., 1974); and James M. Ferguson, *Advertising and Competition: Theory, Measurement, Fact* (Cambridge, Mass.: Ballinger, 1975). A recent, unpublished paper is: Stanley I. Ornstein, "The Advertising-Concentration Controversy," 1975.

- Advertising, absolutely and as a percentage of sales revenue, is positively related to industry profitability, and the relationship is statistically significant. This is true even when advertising is treated as an investment and capitalized rather than treated as a current expense, the conventional method of accounting. The interpretation is that advertising acts as a barrier to entry and allows the exercise of market power.[2]

These empirical results indicate a connection among advertising, concentration, and profitability.[3] Why might this be so? One formal model rests upon a sequence that runs from concentration to profitability to advertising. The logic depends upon a demonstration that the optimal amount of advertising relative to sales, given profit maximization, will equal the percentage mark-up of price over production costs times the net advertising elasticity of demand. (See Appendix A.) If production costs are constant, then advertising intensity rises as price rises. Since maximum profit requires operation where there are diminishing net returns to advertising, profit as a percentage of sales rises with price. Therefore, it follows that an increase in market concentration, because it will be expected to increase price and, hence, profit as a percentage of sales, increases advertising intensity.[4] This model of the chain re-

---

[2] William S. Comanor and Thomas A. Wilson, *Advertising and Market Power* (Cambridge, Mass.: Harvard University Press, 1974). Michael Porter, "Consumer Behavior, Retailer Power and Market Power in Consumer Goods Industries," *Review of Economics and Statistics*, vol. 56 (Nov. 1974), pp. 419-436. The effect of the capitalization of advertising upon the statistical significance of the advertising-profits relationship is disputed. Some investigators maintain that capitalization reduced the association from statistical significance to nonsignificance. If this analysis holds up, it does not necessarily demonstrate the absence of oligopolistic pricing. Rather, it suggests that oligopolists may "overinvest" in this form of nonprice competition.

[3] Both studies cited in footnote 2 reported that concentration is unimportant in their respective statistical analyses of variables influencing profitability. If advertising is positively correlated with concentration, as we believe, this is a surprise since neither of the variables (advertising and concentration) would, in the presence of the other as explanatory of profitability, be expected to show statistical significance. The Comanor-Wilson and Porter results, then, indicate that concentration is inappropriately measured for it contradicts basic economic theory to believe that a barrier to entry, advertising, can ensure high profitability without the necessary condition for the coordination of a joint pricing strategy: few sellers.

[4] The substance of the presentation in the text is that of Richard Schmalensee, *The Economics of Advertising* (Amsterdam: North-Holland Publishing Co., 1972), pp. 223-227. Schmalensee states that "any exogenous change that increases the effectiveness of an oligopoly's price policy and raises P increases advertising as well as profits" (p. 226). An increase in concentration, thereby increasing dominance by the few, could well be an exogenous change that leads to a more effective oligopolistic price policy.

lation of the three variables is not the only contender. There are at least two others.

One model, articulated more than two decades ago, argues that increased advertising will promote an increase in concentration. The model starts with the assumption of an equilibrium of *n* firms in some industry that has a stable firm-size distribution. The adoption of advertising by all firms will destabilize the existing size-distribution.

> The reason for this is that the shift of the demand curve resulting from advertising cannot be assumed to be strictly proportionate to the amount spent on advertising—the "pulling power" of the larger expenditure must overshadow that of smaller ones with the consequence (a) that the larger firms are bound to gain at the expense of the smaller ones; (b) if at the start, firms are more or less equal size, those that forge ahead are bound to increase their lead, as the additional sales enable them to increase their outlay still further. Hence, after advertising has been generally adopted, and the trade settles down again to some sort of equilibrium, the pattern of the industry will have changed; sales will have been concentrated among a smaller number of firms, and the size of a "representative firm" will have increased.[5]

This reasoning posits a linkage of advertising to concentration. Since we expect increasing concentration to enhance oligopolistic interdependence and a coordinated pricing strategy, it follows that the sequence would be from advertising to concentration to profitability.

There is no reason, of course, why a third model might not be at work—one that combines the two just presented. Advertising may permit one firm to gain at the expense of others. As concentration rises, advertising expenditures rise, both because of an increasing price-cost margin produced by heightened concentration and because advertising is an acceptable means of nonprice competition. If Prisoners Dilemma considerations apply, advertising may escalate as an industry's structure passes into an oligopolistic setting. The recognition that advertising may have entry-barrier effects will encourage greater expenditures, linking advertising, through barrier consequences, back upon concentration.[6]

[5] Nicholas Kaldor, "The Economic Aspects of Advertising," *The Review of Economic Studies*, vol. 18 (1949-50), p. 13. Joe Bain suggests a chain like Kaldor's: "the ability of a few firms in an industry to secure strong product-differentiation advantages over all others has frequently been a primary reason for the emergence of oligopolistic market structures, including these with high seller concentration." Joe Bain, *Industrial Organization* (New York: John Wiley & Sons, Inc., 1968), p. 231.

[6] Comanor and Wilson, *Advertising and Market Power*, p. 145.

This sequence indicates feedback flows that generate a mechanism of joint determination.

To summarize, there is no a priori basis for believing that the observed empirical regularities referred to earlier result uniquely from any one of the theoretical mechanisms outlined. They are all equally plausible and all consistent with the empirical observation made at the beginning of the paper. The upshot is that economic theory alone cannot tell us why certain relationships turn up in empirical investigations. It is not that we have no explanations, but rather that we have too many. What does one do in such a situation? We propose a method which, if we are fortunate, will permit an inference about the mechanism —an ability to discriminate among equally probable alternatives.

Methodology. The advertising-concentration-profitability relationship involves three variables that are causally related to one another: between each two there runs a line of causation in one direction or the other (or possibly in both directions at the same time). We will not attempt to prove the existence of causation, but merely assume that it runs in some direction among the relevant variables—in our view an entirely reasonable assumption.[7] We hope to rule out, on statistical grounds, as many of the causal possibilities as we can. Ideally, we will rule out all but one set of causal connections among the three variables. The remaining set must then describe the laws governing their behavior.

Abstracting from statistical technicalities (we employ the method of least-squares regression), our method is simple and straightforward in principle and in interpretation.[8] We illustrate the case of two variables, granted to be somehow related to one another. Call these Y_1 and Y_2. Suppose the true relation is expressed as follows:

$$Y_1 \rightarrow Y_2$$

[7] We rule out a priori the possibility that profitability, advertising intensity, and concentration are determined independently of one another—that is, that there are no causal connections at all among these variables. No serious student, to our knowledge, has ever advanced such a hypothesis. No empirical outcome, including our own, is inconsistent with the hypothesis of independence. If one nevertheless insists on retaining the possibility of independent determination among these variables, then independent determination is merely added to the three directions of causation as possible explanations of our results in Table 1.

[8] A complete technical discussion of the statistical analysis, involving the permissible inferences that can be made about structural parameters from reduced form parameters, is contained in J. A. Henning and H. M. Mann, "Advertising and Concentration: A Tentative Determination of Cause and Effect," in *Essays on Industrial Organization in Honor of Joe S. Bain*, Robert T. Masson and David Qualls, eds. (Cambridge, Mass.: Ballinger, 1976). The technicalities only elaborate upon the very straightforward procedure described in the text.

We will attempt to discover this fact by making what are in effect statistical experiments. Suppose that when we induce a change in Y_1 we also observe a change in Y_2, but when we induce a change in Y_2, Y_1 does not change. We would correctly infer that the causal connection between Y_1 and Y_2 runs from Y_1 to Y_2, not from Y_2 to Y_1, and not in both directions. These latter inferences are simply inconsistent with the empirical findings given in the example. That is all there is to it: we statistically push each of the three variables in our problem and observe which of the other two respond. Those that do respond must be causally downstream, or at least not upstream.[9]

Statistical Analysis. Table 1 reports the results of five regressions[10] relating, respectively, two measures of advertising-to-sales ratios, concentration, and two measures of profitability to three independent variables—new products per firm, minimum optimal plant size, and average asset size of the sampled firms in fourteen industries. The results tell us we can induce a change in advertising intensity (Y_1) and observe concentration (Y_2) to change. An induced change in concentration (Y_2) does not change advertising intensity (Y_1). This conclusion follows from the fact that one of the three independent variables is "missing" (that is, not statistically significant) in the advertising equations, but all three are "present" (statistically significant) in the concentration equation.[11] Thus we can induce changes in concentration through a change in average assets, but not in advertising intensity.

[9] Professor Demsetz comments critically on the possibility of a statistical proof of the existence of causation between two variables. The reader will enjoy the skill and vigor he displays in demolishing this straw man. We have explicitly ruled out the possibility that Demsetz has in mind as the first paragraph of this section clearly states: the existence of causation must be given. What our analysis does, if we are fortunate, is to tell us in which direction the causation runs. We are grateful to Professor Demsetz for provoking us to add Appendix C where an algebraic version of our argument is presented for the interested reader.

[10] In order to maximize the number of degrees of freedom, we present pooled results in Table 1. These results combine the observations for three time periods: 1952-1956, 1957-1961, and 1962-1965. (See Appendix B.) A Chow test was employed to test the hypothesis that there is no significant difference between the goodness of fit when the regression coefficients are constrained to be equal for all periods and when they are not as constrained, that is, separate regressions of AS_1, AS_2, CR, PR_1 and PR_2 on NPF, $OPPL$, and $AVAS$ in each of the three time periods listed above. The F-ratio was not statistically significant at the 10 percent level for the regression with AS_1, CR, PR_1, and PR_2 as dependent variables. It was significant at the 5 percent level with AS_2 as the dependent variable. Thus, the constancy of regression for this variable must be regarded as forced and its quality lower than the other regressions.

[11] Some readers may question that the variable "new products per firm" (NPF) is exogenous. Although we do not share this view, the dropping of this variable from the statistical analysis does not change our conclusions at all. Clearly, our results and our interpretation are subject to revision if and when additional exogenous variables are incorporated into the analysis.

Table 1

POOLED REGRESSIONS RELATING AS_1, AS_2, CR, PR_1, PR_2 TO *NPF*, *OPPL*, AND *AVAS*

Independent Variables	*NPF*	*OPPL*	*AVAS*	Constant Term	*N*	R^2
Dependent Variables						
AS_1	0.796[b] (0.137)[a]	.109[b] (.028)	−.023 (.078)	.382	36	0.59
AS_2	1.074[b] (0.355)	0.223[b] (0.074)	−.018 (.020)	2.633	36	0.33
CR	4.062[c] (1.784)	2.597[b] (0.370)	0.036[b] (0.010)	30.906	36	0.36
PR_1	0.836[c] (0.373)	0.235[b] (0.773)	−0.002 (0.002)	9.689	36	0.28
PR_2	0.828[b] (0.331)	0.277[b] (0.069)	−0.002 (0.002)	8.268	36	0.40

[a] Standard errors in parentheses.

[b] Denotes significance at 1 percent.

[c] Denotes significance at 5 percent.

Note: AS_1: An average of the average advertising-to-sales ratios for the leading firms in fourteen industries, where the advertising data came from *National Advertising Investments*, for three time periods: 1952-1956, 1957-1961, and 1962-1965.

AS_2: An average of the average advertising-to-sales ratios for the leading firms in fourteen industries, where the advertising data came from *Printers' Ink* and *Advertising Age*, for three time periods: 1952-1956, 1957-1961, and 1962-1965.

CR: The four-firm concentration ratios as reported by the Bureau of Census for the fourteen industries for the years 1954, 1958, and 1963.

PR_1: The average of the average rates of return on equity of the leading firms in fourteen industries as reported by *Moody's Industrials* and Value Line Investment Survey, for the time periods 1952-1956, 1957-1961, and 1962-1965.

PR_2: The average of the average rates of return on total capital of the leading firms in fourteen industries, as reported by *Moody's Industrials* and Value Line Investment Survey, for three time periods: 1952-1956, 1957-1961, and 1962-1965.

NPF: The average of the average new product offerings of the leading firms in fourteen industries for the periods 1952-1956, 1957-1961, and 1962-1965, as determined by firm annual reports and by *National Advertising Investments.*

OPPL: A measure of the average establishment size of that group of establishments accounting for 70 percent of each industry's value of shipments for the years 1954, 1958, and 1963 as reported by the Bureau of Census.

AVAS: The average of the average asset size of the leading firms in fourteen industries for the time periods 1952-1956, 1957-1961, and 1962-1965, as computed from *Moody's Industrials.*

The inference is that advertising intensity is causally prior to concentration. If concentration determined advertising intensity or if these two variables were mutually determined, then a variable that influenced concentration would have to affect advertising intensity as well. Similarly, profitability is causally prior to concentration, since the average assets variable is "absent" from the profitability equations.

The only clear result of the experiment reported in Table 1, therefore, is that both advertising intensity and profitability are causally prior to concentration. To date we have been unable to establish prior causality between advertising intensity and profitability on statistical grounds. The following models are, therefore, possible:

(1) $AS \longrightarrow PR \longrightarrow CR$
(2) $PR \longrightarrow AS \longrightarrow CR$
(3) $\begin{matrix} AS \\ \updownarrow \\ PR \end{matrix} \longrightarrow CR$

Unfortunately, none of these models is completely consistent with those presented earlier in the paper. We have found that our powers of discrimination are limited to selecting the explanation that argues for advertising preceding concentration; we are left in ignorance with respect to the placement of profitability in the sequence.

Despite only partial success, we believe that our results do provide a start for a richer analysis of the causal mechanism that may be at work. We think we can improve upon the vague notion that the "pulling power" of larger advertising expenditures is at the heart of the process.

A Theory About the Results. Our previous work shows that the variable, new products per firm, surfaces as the key determinant of advertising intensity.[12] It is, therefore, to the behavior of this variable that we must

[12] Our paper, "Advertising and Concentration: A Tentative Determination of Cause and Effect," reports the following regression (standard errors in parentheses):

$$CR = 30.354 + \underset{(2.430)}{5.727}\, AS_1 - \underset{(.941)}{.689}\, AS_2 + \underset{(2.422)}{.240}\, NPF$$

$$+ \underset{(.433)}{2.125}\, OPPL + \underset{(.010)}{.036}\, AVAS \quad R^2 = .691$$

AS_1 is significant at 5 percent; *OPPL* and *AVAS* are significant at 1 percent. The regression indicates that *NPF* and AS_2 have no independent effect on *CR*. *NPF* apparently exerts its influence through AS_1. *OPPL* and *AVAS* apparently have a powerful independent influence on *CR*. It is the influence of *NPF* on AS_1 that lays the basis for the last section of the paper.

look for an explanation of the observed positive associations between advertising effort and market concentration. A beginning to the search for understanding may come from the following model, which plausibly links new products per firm to advertising intensity.

Assume an equilibrium of n firms of identical and efficient size, producing under conditions of L-shaped long-run average cost curves, but where the corner of the L occurs at an output level that is a modest fraction of the industry's output.[13] Each firm operates at the minimum efficient size, at the corner of the L, and each sells a brand of some particular product. Assume further that consumers switch periodically among the alternative brands such that each firm's (brand's) share remains unchanged and equal to $1/n$. Assume finally that the "product" belongs to a class of products that are

> purchased for their basic or functional utility, that the consumer can easily evaluate and appraise, and that, being nondurable, are purchased frequently and in small amounts, thus allowing the consumer a maximum opportunity for experimentation with and comparison of alternatives.[14]

This environment, one characterized by modest scale economies and negligible search costs, provides an opportunity for an expansion of brand offerings by one or more of the firms that will destabilize market shares, increase the importance of advertising as a source of information, and promote concentration.

Consider the case where each firm offers an additional brand. If consumers continue to distribute themselves as before, a new equilibrium will occur with twice as many brands, with the same number of firms, and with the same firm-size distribution as the previous equilibrium. However, each brand's market share will be $1/2n$. This means that the sales of any individual brand will not be sufficient to exhaust the scale economies that require $1/n$ sales.

Clearly then, if one of the firms began proliferating brands, all would be expected to imitate. Survival would depend upon "keeping up" and on a firm's capturing a large enough market share for the sum of the individual shares captured by its brands to equal the share required for efficiency.

It may be, though, that the firm which started first would gain a step not easily matched by its competitors. If one firm, in the initial

[13] "Modest" may be translated as a requirement that a 5 percent market share is needed to operate efficiently. The basic ideas for the model are in Richard Lipsey and Peter Steiner, *Economics* (New York: Harper & Row, 1966), p. 320.

[14] Bain, *Industrial Organization*, p. 459. This setting describes our sample with the exception of tires and tubes.

equilibrium, offers an additional brand, its market share will rise to $2/(n+1)$, the remaining firms' brands each having a $1/(n+1)$ share. Since this is not an efficient share, the others will offer a second brand, but, if our "first-starter" offers a third brand while the others are still expanding their line by one, the others will again find themselves below the efficient share. It is quite conceivable that some firms may begin to exit if they lag sufficiently far behind the first-starter.

This process is especially likely to generate a change in the firm-size distribution if switching consumers begin to distribute themselves according to intense advertising campaigns attending new product introduction rather than, as originally posited, indifferently and proportionately over the number of brands offered.[15] The reason that heavy advertising may influence consumer choice is that new product introduction will raise search costs.[16] Consumers find, in the face of increases in the number of brands, that previously accumulated knowledge gained from purchase experience is worth little because untried alternatives are continually being presented.[17] Advertising, then, becomes an important source of information, telling the consumer about new brands that will satisfy his desires more fully than the existing alternatives. Such advertising may well influence the decision to shift brands, thereby reducing the switching that comes from periodic experimentation. Thus, sales become increasingly dependent upon advertising.

The result of the process of moving from *n* brands to *n* plus *m* brands is the escalation of the costs of competition. A firm must offer a number of brands to be sure of obtaining an efficient market share. Each brand, once ready to market, will impose certain fixed costs—those of production, marketing, research and development, and introductory advertising. The firm will need a certain level of sales, at a given price, to amortize these investment expenditures.[18] Successful

---

[15] New product introductions substantially inflate advertising budgets. R. D. Buzzell and R. E. M. Nourse, "Product Innovation in Food Processing, 1954-1964" (Graduate School of Business, Harvard, 1967).

[16] Comanor and Wilson, *Advertising and Market Power*, p. 11.

[17] The importance of advertising will heighten in cases where new brands bump old brands, for example, those whose sales have dropped to what the firm considers a negligible level. The value of the prior purchase experience for a brand removed from the marketplace becomes zero. The cereal industry is a case in point. "Shelf space in the supermarkets is at such a premium that a new brand usually earns room for itself only at the expense of another—a situation that sharply increases the costs of initial and continuing promotion." Sheldon Zalanik, "The Fight for a Place at the Breakfast Table," *Fortune*, December 1967, p. 129. Also, Comanor and Wilson, *Advertising and Market Power*, fn. 7, p. 11.

[18] John A. Menge, "Style Change Costs as a Market Weapon," *Quarterly Journal of Economics*, vol. 76 (November 1962); Spencer Klaw, "The Soap Wars: A Strategic Analysis," *Fortune*, June 1963.

amortization becomes more difficult the smaller the expected market share of any individual brand and the higher the fixed costs of brand introduction. Brand proliferation reduces the former and heavy advertising raises the latter. That some firms will drop out and that other firms will not replace them is not surprising, nor are our statistical results.

In fact, the model is a plausible explanation for Joe Bain's lament:[19]

> We are at loss to explain, for example, in terms of the preceding argument [i.e. the expectation of substantial selling outlays for prestige, complex, or durable goods], the very high level of selling costs that persists in the soap industry.

Our data show that the soap firms, for each of the time periods examined, had the largest or second largest value for the "new products per firm" variable. It is clear that any public policy concerned with intense oligopolistic advertisers should start with those factors that promote advertising. Brand proliferation looks like a good place to start.

Appendix A

Schmalensee's model starts with the profit function:

$$\pi = P\,Q(A, \bar{A}, P) - C[Q(A, \bar{A}, P)] - AT$$

where P = price, C = cost, Q = quantity, A = "number of advertising messages . . . purchased by the firm at a constant cost of T per message," and $\bar{A}$ = "number of advertising messages purchased by competitors."

The first order condition is:

$$(P - C_Q)\;(\partial Q/\partial A + \partial Q/\partial \bar{A}\,\frac{d\bar{A}}{dA}) = T.$$

The term $(d\bar{A}/dA)$ indicates the reaction expected from one's competitors if advertising is increased. Multiplying this expression by $\bar{A}/PQ$, the second expression in the second parentheses by $\bar{A}/A$ and setting $T = 1$, we obtain:

$$\frac{(P - C_Q)}{P}\,(E_A + E_{\bar{A}}\,E_{conj\ A}) = A/PQ$$

E meaning elasticity, and the expression $(E_A + E_{\bar{A}}\,E_{conj\ A})$ measuring net advertising elasticity of demand.

Therefore, A/PQ depends upon the price-cost margin and the elasticities of Q with respect to A and $\bar{A}$, and the reaction of competitors. Assuming C_Q, long-run marginal cost, is constant, it follows that when P rises, so does A/PQ. Interpreting $P - C_Q/P$ as the Lerner index of monopoly, it follows that profitability rises with P and therefore A/PQ rises with profitability.

[19] Bain, *Industrial Organization*, p. 460.

Further manipulation permits the same conclusion if profitability is defined as profit as a percentage of sales. Since other measures of profitability, return on equity or on assets, are closely correlated with the return on sales, "it thus seems that profitability, no matter how measured, rises with *P*."[20]

Appendix B

There are forty-two observations potentially contained in the data in Table 2, a set of AS_1, AS_2, CR, PR_1, PR_2, NPF, $OPPL$, and $AVAS$ for three time periods, 1952–1956, 1957–1961, and 1962–1965 for fourteen industries. The results of the regressions in Table 1, based upon the data pooled over the three time periods, rely upon thirty-six observations because measurement of all of these variables was not possible for every industry in each of the time periods. (See notes a, b, and c following Table 2).

Appendix C

To show the essential simplicity of what we mean by "determining the direction of causality," we offer the following exercise. Set up two linear equations in the two endogenous variables Y_1 and Y_2 with any number (say K) of exogenous variables. Call the latter Z's. Assign arbitrary numerical values, including zero, to the parameters of this system (as from a telephone book, random number table, or the like). As a simple example, the model at this point might look like the following:

$$Y_1 = 6.0 + 2.0Z_1 - 4.0Z_2 + 3.5Z_3 + 1.6Y_2$$
$$Y_2 = 0.8 - 4.4Z_1 - 3.0Z_2 + 7.1Z_3 - 2.8Y_1$$

None of these specifics is known to us, except the general form. Now, either delete Y_2 from the first equation or delete Y_1 from the second equation. The former makes the model one in which Y_1 is causally prior to Y_2; the latter makes Y_2 causally prior to Y_1. Next, make sure that at least one of the Z's does not appear in the equation from which the Y variable has been deleted, but does appear in the other equation. These requirements result in a system of two equations: one of them contains both Y's and as many as K Z's; and the other contains only one of the Y's and no more than $K-1$ of the Z's. If Y_1 and Z_1 were deleted from the second equation, for example, the system would be:

$$Y_1 = 6.0 + 2.0Z_1 - 4.0Z_2 + 3.5Z_3 + 1.6Y_2$$
$$Y_2 = 0.8 - 4.4Z_1 + 7.1Z_3$$

[20] Schmalensee, *The Economics of Advertising*, pp. 223-225.

Table 2

INDUSTRY DATA

Industry	AS_1	AS_2	*CR*	PR_1	PR_2	*NPF*	*AVAS* (000)	*OPPL* (%)
				1952–1956				
Chewing gum	2.49	6.3	86	15.09	14.60	0.00	58.828	25.4
Soap	5.35	7.0	85	12.00	10.58	3.00	326.027	3.3
Cigarettes	3.39	4.8	82	10.36	7.98	2.25	536.351	7.6
Biscuits	0.68	1.7	71	12.13	12.05	0.50	136.559	2.4
Tires and tubes	0.42	0.6	79	14.29	10.67	1.75	580.512	3.3
Cereals	3.22	4.4	80	16.72	15.30	3.00	103.667	9.8
Brewing	1.24	5.1	27	10.55	8.76	1.00	93.960	1.9
Soft drinks	2.17	4.4	53	14.49	13.00	1.33	131.183	1.4
Flour	2.76	3.3	73	8.47	7.60	1.50	140.196	6.0
Baking	0.32	1.5	20	15.25	11.04	0.50	54.381	0.1
Meat packing	0.18	0.4	39	4.82	4.32	0.75	298.740	0.4
Liquor	2.36	6.7	64	7.51	6.68	—[a]	368.851	3.0
Pens	4.08	5.2	57	13.18	11.56	2.50	18.510	7.0
Canned fruits and vegetables	0.81	1.2	28	8.06	6.58	0.50	127.486	—[c]
				1957–1961				
Chewing gum	3.37	9.1	88	16.24	15.93	0.66	75.092	22.9
Soap	4.70	7.7	90	13.05	11.44	3.00	601.927	2.6
Cigarettes	3.78	5.7	79	12.69	10.80	1.50	606.892	6.2
Biscuits	0.33	2.3	65	12.05	12.04	2.50	165.714	2.3
Tires and tubes	0.51	0.7	74	10.70	10.01	0.25	750.600	2.3
Cereals	3.87	6.2	83	16.60	15.68	4.00	144.252	15.2
Brewing	1.40	5.4	28	7.56	6.90	1.33	123.894	1.7

Soft drinks	1.85	5.1	55	15.45	13.51	1.66	168.875	1.6
Flour	3.40	5.0	75	8.53	7.58	1.00	184.080	10.6
Baking	0.15	2.7	22	12.40	10.24	0.00	79.450	0.1
Meat packing	0.20	0.4	34	5.78	4.97	0.75	298.002	0.2
Liquor	2.58	6.9	60	7.52	7.15	—[a]	451.500	3.1
Pens	3.16	7.0	51	7.53	6.19	1.66	24.503	3.1
Canned fruits and vegetables	0.86	1.4	29	6.83	6.17	1.00	180.731	0.2
1962–1965								
Chewing gum	2.00	12.7	90	14.31	14.10	0.00	107.858	17.2
Soap	4.29	10.8	72	12.70	11.66	6.50	822.932	2.6
Cigarettes	5.24	9.0	80	12.27	11.10	4.25	676.318	7.1
Biscuits	1.36	6.1	59	12.96	11.88	1.50	209.586	2.35
Tires and tubes	0.61	1.9	70	9.06	7.99	1.00	976.848	2.9
Cereals	4.20	8.8	86	15.74	15.25	3.00	190.800	12.0
Brewing	1.68	10.6	34	10.44	9.66	1.00	160.959	1.9
Soft drinks	2.27	8.7	62	15.58	14.09	2.33	252.766	1.6
Flour	3.20	7.4	70	9.13	8.08	1.00	226.329	3.4
Baking	0.09	2.7	23	9.39	7.70	0.00	106.785	0.1
Meat packing	0.27	0.8	31	6.39	5.53	1.00	343.386	0.25
Liquor	2.57	9.6	58	7.66	7.45	—[a]	539.172	3.3
Pens	2.85	—[b]	48	8.14	7.08	1.50	27.605	3.0
Canned fruits and vegetables	1.00	—[b]	24	6.47	5.89	0.00	225.456	0.25

[a] Application of the criteria contained in R. D. Buzzell and R. E. M. Nourse, *Product Innovation in Food Processing 1954-1964*, (Division of Research, Graduate School of Business, Harvard University, 1967) for distinctly new products indicated that the liquor firms offered only product improvements or line extensions throughout the periods covered.

[b] Advertising data were unavailable for the leading companies in this period from *Printers' Ink* and *Advertising Age.*

[c] No estimate was made for canned fruits and vegetables in 1954. The revision of the standard industrial classification in 1957 reassigned about 30 percent of the pre-1957 SIC value added to new SIC codes established in the 1957 revision. (*Concentration Ratios in Manufacturing Industries, 1958*, table 7, pt. 2, p. 419.)

Finally, construct an artificial "data" matrix of K values for each of the K exogenous variables, a $K \times K$ nonsingular matrix Z. Given this matrix Z and the two resulting vectors of K "observations" on each of the endogenous variables Y_1 and Y_2, we will be able to infer which Y has been deleted from which equation and therefore, which Y is causally prior. We will do this given only the "data" matrices $Z(K \times K)$; Y_1 and Y_2 (each $K \times 1$). We reach our conclusions by examining the $K \times 1$ vectors $Z\,Y_1$ and $Z\,Y_2$.

For the logic of this procedure, consider the case where Y_1 has been deleted from the second equation, as above. Then, the system in terms of the "data" matrices Z, Y_1, and Y_2 would be:

$$Y_1 = Z\,A + a_0\,Y_2$$
$$Y_2 = Z\,B$$

where a_0 is a nonzero scalar and A and B are coefficient vectors. (Recall that we required at least one of the Z's to be missing from the second equation, that is, one element of the B vector to be zero.) It follows now that we know Y_1 and Y_2 vectors must be related to the Z matrix and the unknown (to us) A and B vectors and the scalar a_0 in the following way:

$$Y_1 = Z\,(A + a_0\,B) \rightarrow (A + a_0\,B) = Z^{-1}Y_1$$
$$Y_2 = Z\,B \qquad \rightarrow B = Z^{-1}Y_2$$

The vectors we calculate, $Z^{-1}Y_1$ and $Z^{-1}Y_2$, will thus be $(A + a_0B)$ and B respectively. The first will have no zero elements, and the second at least one. In general, the Y variable dependent on only some of the Z variables (the Y_i for which $Z^{-1}Y_i$ contains at least one zero) must be causally prior.

COMMENTARIES

Harold Demsetz

Why is it that we do not yet have good positive theories of advertising expenditure, with apologies to excellent beginnings by Nelson and Telser? The answer, I believe, is that we have no theoretical precedents to guide us. Economists have never seriously tried to explain the intensity with which firms use fertilizer, copper, or any other specific productive input. They have not found this problem sufficiently interesting. This judgment is, I believe, generally correct, even in the case of advertising. Yet, the use of advertising inputs has received attention from economists, even if no good positive theories have been developed.

If we asked people to rank the importance of problems that face our society, I doubt very much that they would rank advertising very high, if at all. The source of our interest in advertising is in the concern shown by intellectuals, not the general public. That is why we are contributing to this volume. Intellectuals have forced us to discuss something that is not worth discussing.

The intellectual—and over persistent objections I include myself in that category—looks at this life and finds things not quite to his liking. People do not behave as he would like them to. They purchase swimming pools, Cadillacs, and tickets to football games. Since many of us are in the business of selling a different life style, it is quite natural for some of us to view commercial advertising, which, after all, is a mechanism by which consumers and producers get together to communicate about wants and life styles, as an obstacle to our effort to persuade others to adopt the good life as the reformist intellectual sees it.

Galbraith wrote a book that says that commercial advertising causes the private sector to be too large and that we need a compensating expansion of the public sector, a position that might be interpreted as a basis for concern about advertising.[1] We find intellectuals rising in

[1] John K. Galbraith, *The Affluent Society*, 3rd ed. (Boston: Houghton Mifflin, 1976), pp. 129-131.

defense of First Amendment protections for politicians and academics, but not for commercial communication. Great costs are imposed upon the perpetrators of fraud in the commercial world, but not in the political world, where congressional immunity reigns, or in the classroom, where fraud is protected by academic freedom, nor in the pulpit, where we are told that everlasting life can be ours if only we believe.

The attitude of intellectuals toward advertising is revealed by the ease with which normative judgments are made when, in fact, the path by which they are reached is not at all obvious. Do we want an economy in which competitors are penalized for calling attention to their products through commercial advertising, even when such advertising is used in conjunction with some degree of product or firm uniqueness (monopoly, if that term is preferred)? A system that makes it easy for competitors to imitate each other perfectly surely undermines the incentive to undertake risky and costly investments in new products and goodwill creation. We have a system of patents, trademarks, and copyrights specifically designed to maintain such incentives by raising the cost of imitation. Is it really desirable to penalize business success within this institutional setting because advertising is used as part of the investment process? Such successes may provide a part of the explanation for the correlations between profit rates, advertising, and concentration that have been discovered by economic researchers. These statistical findings are a puzzle in search of explanation; they do provide a scientific basis for interest in advertising.

The correlation between concentration and advertising intensity could be explained in a quite harmless way by a spillover theory, according to which firms do not use advertising very much when many of the benefits of advertising fall upon their competitors. The more concentrated an industry becomes, the more the benefits of advertising fall upon the firm doing it, and so advertising intensity may increase with concentration. But there are all sorts of ad hoc explanations for the phenomenon that could be trotted out in the absence of any serious theorizing about the problem.

The explanation provided by Henning and Mann is an example—one that does not seem to me to make sense in terms of the corpus of economic theory. Their rationalization presents a situation in which firms produce more and more brands and incur higher costs of advertising and communication; yet, their explanation is couched in the context of experience goods, which people can judge on the basis of use. In such a situation, economic theory would seem to call for a firm to produce an "unbranded" good at lower cost since people can judge on the basis of experience and, in this way, undercut "high cost" advertised brands. Instead, Henning and Mann have firms doing things that cause losses both to themselves and to the industry. Their rationalization does not seem consistent with profit maximizing behavior. Perhaps they can improve upon it, but as it stands, it is of the ad hoc variety. In fact, much of what is said in this volume must be of ad hoc variety.

So let me now turn to what I consider the non-ad hoc portions of the papers. I do not have much to say about the Ornstein-Lustgarten paper because I have no reason to dispute their statistical studies. They make no great claims for a theoretical explanation of the relationship, so they are fairly immune from attack, except for their failure to provide an explanation.

Not so with Henning and Mann. They claim to have devised a statistical technique for establishing causation. Their basic methodology can be illustrated as follows: If *A* causes *B*, then any set of exogenous factors that influences *A* must also influence *B* if those factors are relevant to the model. They influence *B* either directly or indirectly through their influence on *A*, which in turn will influence *B*. But exogenous factors that influence *B*, where *B* is caused by *A*, will influence *A* only directly since there is no causal link through *B* to *A*. Hence, if the relevant exogenous factors all influence *B*, but do not all influence *A*, we can infer that *A* causes *B*.

Confidence in this procedure requires that their model be complete and correct, and in the absence of any good theory of advertising, there is no way of knowing whether it is. Indeed, in the present instance, we have little or no theoretical basis for believing that minimum optimal plant size or average asset size of firms has any theoretical connection to advertising-sales ratios. Nor are we sure that a new products-per-firm variable is relevant to concentration, profitability, or even advertising-sales ratios. We seem to have regression equations containing *available* variables rather than *theoretically sensible* variables.

A few examples will suffice to reveal how the lack of theory undermines any finding obtained through this procedure. Suppose we observe that height and blueness of eyes are correlated, and we wish to know which way the causation runs. Take two variables, such as latitude of residence and quality of diet, call them exogenous, and alternately regress blueness of eyes and height on these exogenous variables. Height will be positively related to quality of diet and latitude of residence (it is well known that Mediterranean types are shorter than northern European types). But blueness of eyes will be positively related only to latitude of residence. If we were foolish enough to apply the Henning-

Mann methodology to this problem, we would conclude that blueness of eyes causes increased height.

Or, suppose we wish to know whether structural monopoly causes greater price-marginal cost margins or vice versa? If we regress structural monopoly on the existence of patents and on the newness of products, two positive regression coefficients are likely to result. If we regress profit margins on the same two variables, we are likely to find that the regression coefficient of only patents is significant; since some new products earn high profit margins but others must be introduced at a loss, the regression of profit margin on newness of product is not likely to be significant. Applying the Henning-Mann methodology, we conclude that high profit margins cause structural monopoly.

These examples fully reveal that statistics without theory is a weak technique for establishing causation. The statistical technique used by Henning and Mann is likely to give unreliable results unless we have confidence in the theoretical relevance of the exogenous variables and in the existence of a causal relationship between concentration, advertising intensity, and the profit rate. Henning and Mann are quite confident that some causal relationship involving advertising intensity does exist—so much so that they fail to give serious consideration to the possibility of a purely spurious relationship deriving from the manner in which accountants treat advertising expenditures as current expenses. The observed positive correlation between advertising intensity and profit rate may disappear when advertising is treated as an investment and capitalized.

There have been several studies of the advertising-profitability relationship, and to my knowledge, only one is consistent with the Henning-Mann position.[2] Studies by Bloch and Ayanian, on the other hand, find no relationship between profit rate and advertising intensity when adjustments are made for the investment quality of advertising.[3] A study that I have just completed, using a very different approach, verifies the importance of accounting techniques to the existence of this correlation.[4]

---

[2] See Leonard W. Weiss, "Advertising, Profits, and Corporate Taxes," *Review of Economics and Statistics*, vol. 51 (November 1969), pp. 421-430.

[3] See Harry Bloch, "Advertising and Profitability: A Reappraisal," *Journal of Political Economy*, vol. 82 (March/April 1974), pp. 267-286, and Robert Ayanian, "Advertising and Rate of Return," *Journal of Law and Economics*, vol. 18 (October 1975), pp. 479-506.

[4] Harold Demsetz, "Accounting for Advertising as a Barrier to Advertising" (unpublished manuscript).

Michael P. Lynch

The debate concerning advertising and concentration has been going on for more than a quarter of a century now. In fact, the first paper on the subject was published in the *Journal of the American Statistical Association* in 1900.[1] The modern controversy really began, however, with the publication of Kaldor and Silverman's book in 1948.[2] Two major questions have been raised: Are advertising and concentration positively correlated and if so, does the correlation have any causal significance? The paper by Ornstein and Lustgarten focuses on the first of these questions but does take a stab at the second. The paper by Henning and Mann assumes that the answer to the first question is yes and then addresses the second.

While the focus of the papers and the views of the authors differ considerably, they also share some very important common ground. Both papers assume that the "industry" is the smallest unit relevant for investigating possible relationships between advertising intensity and market power. Both assume that the industry advertising-to-sales or shipments ratio is the appropriate one, rather than similar ratios by brand or firm. Neither paper presents a microeconomic model that can be aggregated up to an industry level or discusses what conditions have to be met to make such an aggregation permissible. I fear that this common ground may be a shared swamp.

I will comment on the Ornstein-Lustgarten paper first. This paper seems to me to provide some more evidence that advertising intensity and concentration are positively correlated, though the correlation is rather low over the broad expanse of American industry. Everybody now seems agreed on that point. That is progress. The use of Input-Output Tables to generate the advertising intensity measures is an interesting and, I think, useful addition to the data base in this field. I note, parenthetically, that Professor Leonard Weiss has made a similar use of them in a study published in 1974, where he used the advertising-to-shipments ratio as a determinant of industry price-cost margins.[3] The

1 Sidney Sherman, "Advertising in the United States," *Journal of the American Statistical Association,* December 1900, pp. 119-162.

2 Nicholas Kaldor and Rodney Silverman, *A Statistical Analysis of Advertising Expenditure and of the Revenue of the Press* (Cambridge: Cambridge University Press, 1948); see also Nicholas Kaldor, "The Economic Aspects of Advertising," *Review of Economic Studies,* vol. 18 (1950), pp. 1-27.

3 Leonard Weiss, "The Concentration-Profits Relationship and Antitrust," in *Industrial Concentration: The New Learning,* Harvey J. Goldschmid et al., eds. (Boston: Little, Brown & Co., 1974), pp. 184-231; see also Allyn D. Strickland and Leonard W. Weiss, "Advertising, Concentration and Price-Cost Margins," *Journal of Political Economy,* vol. 84 (October 1976), pp. 1109-1121.

sample size the authors use is quite large, and this does free the authors from the charge of selection bias. But large samples have a price, like most other things, and the authors can be criticized for including four-digit industries that bear little relation to economically relevant markets and for using national concentration ratios when regional ratios would be more appropriate. Nevertheless, I, for one, am prepared to accept the conclusion that there is a small, but significant, positive correlation between advertising intensity and concentration.

On the more important issue of whether advertising is causally related to concentration, Professors Ornstein and Lustgarten make some modest claims based on their attempts to explain changes in concentration by changes in advertising expenditures. While the authors admit that it is not possible in a single equation model to determine the direction of causality, they, like most other people, go ahead and draw some conclusions anyway. They conclude that the evidence from their study indicates that advertising is not a barrier to entry. The basis for this statement is their finding that, although increases in advertising intensity are associated with increases in concentration, decreases in advertising intensity are not related to decreases in concentration.

Frankly, I do not know how to interpret these results. This is an example of how difficult it is to draw any conclusions from data when the theory being tested has not really been spelled out. The absolute level of the advertising-to-sales ratio is taken to be a direct measure of the height of the product differentiation barrier. In a cross-section study of industries, then, the higher the entry barrier, the more highly concentrated we expect the industry to be. Fine. But what happens now if, in one of these industries, there is a change in the function relating advertising to sales, such that advertising exhibits even greater economies of scale? Presumably, if nothing else happens (advertising input prices do not change, there is no growth in unit sales, which might reduce manufacturing costs, et cetera), there will be a shake-out, those firms with the largest initial market shares using their new advantage to increase them. In this case, in the new equilibrium we would expect higher concentration but a lower industry advertising-to-sales ratio. Thus, if the source of change is in the sales promotion function, I think the theory says that changes in concentration and changes in advertising intensity should be negatively correlated in the same industry over time. On this interpretation, the authors' first finding could be interpreted as being inconsistent with the barrier thesis and the second consistent, exactly the reverse of their interpretation. Of course, the prediction depends on the source of the underlying change and on the assumption that all other changes cancel out. As a professional economist, I have been well trained to believe four impossible things before breakfast, but I cannot believe that there have been no important systematic changes that might affect advertising-to-sales ratios over a broad class of U.S. industry in a twenty-year period.

In short, I think the Ornstein-Lustgarten results tell us very little, if anything, about the causal relationship between advertising intensity and concentration. The problem is not that their results are inexplicable, but that there are all too many theories consistent with them, a complaint also raised by Henning and Mann.

Let me make a few more brief points on the first paper, and then I will turn to the second. Ornstein and Lustgarten suggest that the Federal Trade Commission is schizophrenic on the subject of advertising, since it seems to view advertising as sometimes informative, procompetitive, and beneficial to consumers and sometimes as misleading, wasteful, anticompetitive, and harmful to consumers. I see no logical contradiction here, and I believe that both cases are found in the real world. Second, I would be interested to see the effects in their change equation of running a continuous variable for percentage of output going into final consumption, rather than the dummy variable approach the authors used. Lastly, I wonder if the failure to use changes in real rather than nominal advertising expenditures over this long period of time creates any serious bias in the results.

Let me now turn to the Henning and Mann paper. Their work focuses directly on the question of causality, and that is surely the right place to focus. They make use of some ideas developed by Herbert Simon to argue that there is a simple procedure whereby one can determine when one variable is causally prior to another.[4] I might mention that I do not think they will go down in history for it. On my reading of the subject, the method was invented by a biologist by the name of Sewall Wright, who, I believe, has received credit for it.[5] And the general techniques have been discussed in the econometrics literature by Herman Wold and Robert Strotz and others.[6] It seems to me that industrial organization economists (even Harold Demsetz) frequently make causal statements on the basis of regression results. Somebody must believe that it can be done with statistical models.

In their sample of fourteen industries, Henning and Mann reach the interesting conclusion that concentration is not causally prior to

4 Herbert Simon, "Spurious Correlation: A Causal Interpretation," reprinted in *Models of Man* (New York: John Wiley & Sons, 1957), pp. 37-49.

5 Sewall Wright, "The Method of Path Coefficients," *Annals of Mathematical Statistics*, September 1934, pp. 161-215.

6 Robert H. Strotz and H. O. A. Wold, "A Triptych on Causal Systems," *Econometrica*, vol. 28 (April 1960), pp. 417-463.

advertising intensity or profitability. This is a rather surprising conclusion, because, if I read it right, it says that if an industry concentration ratio increases, say, from 40 percent to 80 percent, industry profitability will not be affected. I would argue that much more work needs to be done before any such conclusion can be accepted. First, the authors' new product intensity variable appears to have a powerful effect on the regression results. Yet it is hard for me to believe that it is an exogenous variable. Perhaps the rate of new product introduction could be considered exogenous in the semiconductor industry, but I hardly find it plausible in the chewing gum, soap, liquor, cereal, and soft drink industries. Second, if I have a wide range of exogenous variables to choose from, it seems to me that it may be possible to choose a subset of them to give any causal ordering desired. In particular, choosing different subsets may give different and contradictory causal orderings. Third, the mathematics of the method have not been fully presented for this particular case, either in this paper or in the paper that Henning and Mann have contributed to the Bain volume.[7] Fourth, it is not clear to me just what hypothesis is being tested, and what hypotheses are being maintained. I would be more comfortable with a paper that compared predicted with actual correlations, or coefficients, from alternative causal models.

Henning and Mann assert, and I agree, that there are all too many explanations for their findings. That is not a rare problem in economics. At the end of their paper, they offer a theory about their results that I find very interesting. Essentially, they suggest (1) that the new product intensity variable reflects a strategic sort of brand proliferation that ends up by increasing concentration and profitability rates for the survivors; (2) that being first in a particular product field confers an advantage that is difficult to overcome; (3) that the process of brand proliferation will raise the cost of search for consumers, and lead to heavier reliance on advertising material; and (4) that there are economies of scale by brand, in part because of the necessity of advertising them heavily. Thus, the process of brand proliferation also increases the capital required to enter the industry.

This is all very plausible for some consumer product industries and is at least partially supported by some work that various staff people have been doing at the FTC.[8] I think this type of theorizing is

[7] J. A. Henning and H. Michael Mann, "Advertising and Concentration: A Tentative Determination of Cause and Effect," in *Essays on Industrial Organization in Honor of Joe S. Bain*, Robert T. Masson and P. David Qualls, eds. (Cambridge, Mass.: Ballinger Publishing Company, 1976), pp. 143-154.

[8] See the staff report entitled *Sales, Promotion, and Product Differentiation in Two Prescription Drug Markets*, Ronald Bond and David Lean, FTC Staff Report, February 1977.

a step in the right direction but, obviously, it is only a first step. It goes behind industry aggregates, to a microeconomic model at the firm or brand level. It does not assume that all firms will generate the same additional sales from the same advertising expenditures, face the same elasticities of demand, and so on. I have little doubt that being first in a market with a different and perhaps superior product is immensely important. Economists may have just discovered this, but marketing people have been talking about it for a long time. It is the marketing people who have given us the contemptuous expression "me too" brands, and who have said that imitators will not only be poor seconds in sales, but also in profits.[9]

The marketing and trade literature focuses on market shares at a much more refined level than four-digit SIC industries. It considers product characteristics and timing of introduction as being extremely important. I suggest that people who make their living advising firms how to change their sales through promotion have a good command of what the relevant markets are and which variables are important to a successful promotional strategy. Economists may be good at modeling their knowledge. Economists might gain much by paying more attention to what marketing experts do. In particular, I think the work of A. S. C. Ehrenberg and his colleagues should be of great interest to economists.[10] They have compiled very impressive evidence that consumers behave in a very simple and predictable way in the repeat purchase of consumer goods. They appear to have found the routine way in which people behave, and it should be highly useful in explaining just what it takes to shock people out of that routine.

I also believe that the following stylized facts have to be taken into account if we are ever to make much progress in this field. First, consumers do behave in a routine way unless they are shocked out of it. They are not little computers. Second, many consumer product fields are dominated by one brand. Relevant markets may well be much smaller than four- or five-digit levels, and even fairly homogeneous product classes may have identifiable market segments within them. Therefore, the relevant economic model may very well turn out to be something like the dominant firm model, and one would look at dynamic pricing strategies of the type explored by Darius Gaskins.[11]

9 See, for example, the very interesting work titled "The Wheel of Marketing," copyright 1975, by James Peckam, Sr. This work contains summaries of many Nielsen studies where Mr. Peckam was consultant on marketing operations.

10 A. S. C. Ehrenberg, *Repeat-Buying, Theory and Applications* (New York: American Elsevier Publishing Company, Inc., 1972).

11 Darius W. Gaskins, Jr., "Dynamic Limit Pricing: Optimal Pricing under Threat of Entry," *Journal of Economic Theory*, vol. 3 (1971), pp. 306-322.

Third, the dominant firm is likely to behave very differently from the others and is the key to understanding how the whole product field behaves. In particular, its advertising-to-sales ratio may well be much smaller than those of the other firms in the field. Fourth, there is a life cycle for a brand, and pricing and promotional strategies are geared to it. The age of the brand is an important consideration in making sense out of observed advertising-to-sales ratios. Fifth, I think we have to face up to the distinct possibility that the firms themselves have nothing like precise knowledge of the relationship between their advertising and promotional expenditures and their sales. Indeed, marketing reports that I have seen indicate that even careful experiments frequently lead to nonsense results. Even when experiments fail, what hope is there for statistical estimation? Sixth, serious consideration should be given to the possibility that advertising does not affect industry demand. If so, any model must be formulated in terms of market shares rather than absolute sales and is subject to the very stringent adding up constraints that have been laid out for the linear case by Richard Schmalensee in his well-known book.[12] I do not know of any results for a nonlinear case.

Where does all this leave us? I believe we will never be able to answer the basic causal question posed here by using aggregate industry data. It is natural and proper for economists to seek general and simple results that will hold across broad classes of industries. It was useful to see if analysis of industry aggregates could yield general laws. If we have not found them after twenty-five years of effort, then I do not believe it is likely that we shall. Causal, quantitative, industry case studies using good data are our best hope. Perhaps they will form a basis for a general inter-industry theory that works. Some of us may have to learn far more about the chewing gum business than we ever wanted to know.

William S. Comanor

In reading the papers here and elsewhere in this volume, one is struck by the continuity of the debate. It seems that, through the years, the same issues are raised, the same arguments made, and, by and large, the same positions taken, without any resolution of the issues. We should be able to agree on this point, if on no other.

Although consumers may learn about products from past purchases, it seems that for consumers, like professors, learning is not quick, easy, or perhaps even possible. Positions once formed seem difficult to change

[12] Richard Schmalensee, *The Economics of Advertising* (Amsterdam: North-Holland Publishing Co., 1972).

—a fact that probably has more to do with the psychology of the individual and the sociology of the discipline than with economics. In principle, we carry out empirical studies and look for statistical evidence regarding the theories advanced and the models constructed. We test our positions to enable us to decide between conflicting views. But, as the foregoing papers attest, the evidence is never as clear or precise as we wish. Inevitably, there are differences of interpretation.

The primary question at stake here concerns the nature of the relationship between advertising and monopoly. Does advertising lead to monopoly, or does monopoly lead to advertising, or both, or neither? The evidence examined in these papers is the empirical relationship between advertising-sales ratios and concentration ratios. Whatever their differences, both sets of authors accept the concentration ratio as a valid index of monopoly.

This similarity to what other authors have done seems particularly pronounced in the case of Ornstein and Lustgarten, who examine the simple correlation and regression coefficients between advertising-sales ratios and concentration ratios. The principal difference between the Ornstein-Lustgarten studies and other studies lies in the choice of data. Where others have used IRS statistics or data on large firms allocated to SIC four-digit industries, Ornstein and Lustgarten use data from the U.S. input-output tables. Although their data may be better, it is possible to find problems with any data, including theirs.

In reading an empirical paper, I try to look at the statistical results before I read the text that accompanies them. Generally, the text explains and interprets the tables to the reader, and generally, the two fit together. But I notice that there are many instances in the economics literature when the tables and the text do not seem to go togeher. And if I must choose between a man's text and his tables, I will take his tables every time. Interpretations are more likely to be based on other factors, while empirical results are less subject to bias.

Tables 1–3 in the Ornstein-Lustgarten paper suggest that there is generally no significant relationship between advertising and concentration in 1947 for most of the economic sectors they consider, although there does appear to be a significant association between these variables in both 1963 and 1967. As might be expected, this relationship is stronger in the consumer goods industries, although it is found also in producer nondurables.

From these results, we might expect the authors to conclude that there is a significant relationship between advertising and concentration, which they associate with barriers to entry, at least after the immediate postwar years. But, no, that would be too straightforward—too simple an interpretation. They argue that, since advertising intensity is lower in producer goods industries, this finding cannot be due to an entry barrier effect, which therefore casts doubt on whether this effect exists in consumer goods industries as well. They expect to find a significant relationship in the consumer goods industries but not in the producer goods industries. However, because they find a significant relationship for producer nondurable goods as well, they conclude that their finding invalidates the hypothesized result for consumer nondurable goods. This is a strange interpretation indeed.

They write that although the finding of similar results for both consumer and producer nondurable goods industries does not refute the existence of advertising barriers to entry in consumer nondurables, it makes this interpretation "highly suspect." I wonder what evidence would have convinced them.

Even if we were to accept the authors' comment that the positive association in producer nondurables is a statistical artifact, this hardly invalidates the results for consumer nondurables. And this is especially true when one looks at the size of the relevant coefficients. For 1963, the reported elasticity of advertising with respect to concentration is 0.63 for consumer nondurables and 0.20 for producer nondurables. Clearly, there is a significant economic relationship here even if the producer nondurable effect were a statistical artifact. For 1967, the advertising elasticity is 0.78 for consumer nondurables, and 0.24 for producer nondurables, and the difference between these coefficients is statistically significant. It is difficult to conclude from this evidence that there is not a significant relationship between advertising and concentration in the consumer goods sector. It remains even if we concede the existence of a statistical artifact and take the estimated coefficient for producer nondurables as a measure of the size and extent of that artifact.

The paper by Henning and Mann is also concerned with the empirical relationship between advertising and concentration. Unlike Ornstein and Lustgarten, Henning and Mann assume the existence of a positive relationship between these two variables. They try to determine which variable causes the other or, as they put it, which variable is causally prior to the other, since there are explanations for both.

Any attempt to infer causation from correlation statistics is a tricky business. Professor Demsetz has pointed out some of the defects in this procedure, and I find myself happily in full agreement with his admonitions concerning the pitfalls involved.

Henning and Mann estimate reduced-form equations in which advertising and concentration are regressed on a set of exogenous variables. However, the reduced-form coefficients that they estimate are not the same as the structural coefficients they seek. A reduced-form coefficient of zero does not necessarily imply a zero structural coefficient, and furthermore, it is quite consistent with the joint determination of both variables.

The main problem with this procedure is that the authors have not included all possible exogenous variables that could influence the dependent variables. I can imagine other factors affecting advertising or concentration that should be included in the reduced-form equations, which might produce quite different results. Unless one has included all possible exogenous variables in the reduced-form equations, it is terribly difficult to conclude anything from the results obtained.

There are questions of how to interpret the statistical results for both papers. However, this is true of most empirical research. By far the most important issues are the conceptual ones. Just what are these two variables designed to indicate? In particular, what does the concentration ratio measure?

The primary justification for using the concentration ratio in either paper is the Ornstein-Lustgarten comment that the concentration ratio is "widely used as an indication of monopoly power." This seems to be a rather weak basis for an empirical investigation. Elsewhere, Ornstein and Lustgarten view the concentration ratio as measuring barriers to entry. In fact, the concentration ratio is not a very good measure of either barriers to entry or the degree of monopoly power in an industry. What the concentration ratio does measure is one dimension of the size distribution of firms, namely, the relative importance of large firms in an industry. While concentration may influence firm behavior, it is certainly not the only factor affecting monopoly power.

If we are concerned with the possible effects of concentration ratios on monopoly or on advertising, we need to deal explicitly with what is likely to be the impact of concentration. We need to consider the impact of concentration on advertising, which depends on the role of inter-firm communication. For example, when products are differentiated, we would expect the advertising of one firm to reduce the sales of its rivals. When products are homogeneous, we would expect the advertising of one firm to increase the sales of its rivals. In our book, Thomas Wilson and I examine these matters in some detail.[1] Our analysis suggests that the relationship between advertising and concentration is a more complex issue than either of these papers suggests. While it is sadly true that concentration ratios are a widely used index of monopoly, this fact should prod us on to further work, rather than serve as a stone on which to rest.

[1] William S. Comanor and Thomas A. Wilson, *Advertising and Market Power* (Cambridge, Mass.: Harvard University, 1974).

Richard Schmalensee

The two papers in this session provide interesting contrasts in method, data, and conclusions. While both are innovative, in very different ways, I am afraid that neither manages to resolve any central issues.

I will begin with the Henning-Mann paper, which I found the more interesting of the two. Their method of testing for causal direction appears correct in principle, but its application requires a great deal of care. Consider the following simple structural system:

$$C = c_1 + c_2X + u_c \qquad (1)$$

$$A = a_1 + a_2Z + a_3C + u_a \qquad (2)$$

Here C and A are endogenous variables relating to concentration and advertising, respectively; X and Z are exogenous variables; the a's and c's are constants; and the u's are disturbance terms. Given this structure, any reasonable definition of causality (there are apparently many) would indicate that C causes A while A does not cause C.

The reduced form corresponding to this structure is the following:

$$C = c_1 + c_2X + u_c \qquad (3)$$

$$A = (a_1 + a_3c_1) + a_2Z + (a_3c_2)X + (u_a + a_3u_u) \qquad (4)$$

With a large enough sample, one will be able to establish (through least squares) that X appears in both equations and Z appears only in the second. The presence of X in equation (4) establishes that a_3 is non-zero, so that C causes A, while the absence of Z from (3) establishes that A is not present on the right of equation (1). Note that if Z were present in the first structural equation, no test would be possible, since Z would appear in both reduced-form equations regardless of the causal relation between C and A. In order to detect C causing A, there must be exogenous variables, like Z, that enter the structural relation for A but *not* that for C. On the other hand, in order to detect causation from A to C, one needs exogenous variables appearing in the first structural equation but *not* the second.

While one can make inferences about causation from reduced-form coefficients in this fashion, the hypotheses under test are actually about structural coefficients, like a_3, that can be estimated directly. Such direct estimation would require explicit presentation of the maintained *structural* hypotheses. (In the example, one such hypothesis is that a_2 is not zero.) Maintained hypotheses are usually considered important in sta-

This comment was prepared while the author was associate professor of economics, University of California, San Diego.

tistical work, since only if they are plausible can the validity of tests based on them be defended. Henning and Mann unfortunately fail to present a set of maintained structural hypotheses from which their reduced-form equations can be derived. Still, certain hypotheses are implicit in what they have done.

One structural hypothesis that clearly is made is that new products per firm (*NPF*) is exogenous, uncorrelated with the structural disturbances. Surely this element of conduct is, absent any definite theory, on the same level of endogeneity as the advertising-sales ratio. Further, the tentative theory Henning and Mann present implies that both variables will be increased by whatever chance factors lead to outbreaks of nonprice rivalry. This in turn implies a correlation between *NPF* and the disturbance term in the structural equation for advertising intensity. If such a correlation exists (or, in other words, if *NPF* is really endogenous), all reported coefficient estimates are biased and inconsistent.

Another maintained structural hypothesis must be that no additional exogenous variables are important determinants of the three endogenous quantities considered. Because I think the world is a complicated place and that industries differ in many ways, I find it hard to believe that no other exogenous variables are involved here. It is difficult for me to imagine a defensible model in which concentration, profitability, and advertising intensity ultimately depend on only two exogenous variables: average establishment size (*OPPL*) and average asset size (*AVAS*). If any relevant exogenous variables have been omitted, the reduced-form coefficient estimates are biased. Particularly noticeable by their absence, as I see it, are exogenous variables that can be expected to appear in the structural equation for advertising, but not those for concentration or profitability. Without such variables, like *Z* in the example, one cannot detect causation from concentration or profitability to advertising.

On a more speculative level, since *OPPL* and *AVAS* relate to economies of scale, they clearly belong in the structural equation for concentration. If they are also thought to affect the height of entry barriers, they probably belong in the structural equation for profitability as well. But it is difficult to reconcile this latter hypothesis with the insignificance of *AVAS* in the reduced form equation for profitability.

Henning and Mann are unable to find clear indications of the causal relation between advertising and profitability, but they find both causally prior to concentration. This seems consistent with the "disequilibrium hypothesis" of Yale Brozen and others, in which advertising, new product introductions, and high profits on the part of leading firms are symptomatic of the sort of differential skill and/or luck that will enable them to grow at the expense of their rivals and thus increase concentration.

Henning and Mann suggest that the evidence is also consistent with a model in which advertising and new product introduction are both symptomatic of outbreaks of nonprice rivalry, which, by destabilizing an existing order protected by entry barriers, leads to divergences in firm size and thus to increases in concentration. The difficulty with the latter explanation, at least in its present form, is that it does not address the observed positive correlation with profitability. If advertising and new product introduction are symptomatic of more intense rivalrous behavior, one might expect them to undermine profitability.

The main innovation in the Ornstein-Lustgarten paper would appear to be the large data set employed. Their sample of industries is much larger than that of Henning and Mann, which is a good thing if and only if one believes that Census industries are in general defined approximately correctly. Their data cover all firms in each industry, while Henning and Mann use information on leading firms only. I would argue that the preferable approach depends on precisely what hypotheses are being considered, along with one's feelings about the importance of small specialized or misclassified firms in Census aggregates. I am not familiar with the compilation of the advertising data in the Input-Output Tables, though I somehow find it easy to doubt that the published numbers are quite as "quirk-free" as the authors' presentation suggests. Still, the sheer size of the sample of four-digit industries covered makes the input-output data well worth exploitation.

Ornstein and Lustgarten present over a hundred cross-section regressions, relating advertising intensity to concentration for various years, various groupings of industries, and various assumed functional forms. Their finding of a typically positive, significant, but weak association between the two variables is of interest in light of earlier studies, and it may serve to cast doubt on some structural hypotheses. On grounds of elementary logic, however, I do not see how the presence of a correlation in producer goods samples can cast any real doubt on the Kaldor-Bain analysis, which explicitly does not apply to such samples. Obviously other mechanisms are at work in the producer goods samples, but until they are identified, it cannot be seriously argued that they serve to explain *all* significant correlations. I must endorse the authors' apparent acknowledgement that bivariate regressions of this sort simply cannot discriminate among a large number of structural specifications with very different policy implications.

The regressions "explaining" changes in concentration are more interesting. It is not clear, however, whether we are to interpret the estimates as reduced-form coefficients (in which case advertising intensity is being assumed exogenous) or as structural coefficients (in which case least squares is inappropriate). The lack of explicit structural specification again invites multiple interpretations of the estimates obtained. These regressions do not have much power to discriminate among alternative structures either. Still, some of the findings are suggestive and do deserve comment.

The failure of lagged advertising intensity to contribute to the explanation of changes in concentration, after controlling for other influences, suggests that advertising does not cause concentration. But, in order to reconcile this with the cross-section results, one would need to look for causation in the other direction in the same fashion, by seeing whether lagged concentration helped to explain changes in advertising intensity after controlling for other influences. Given the weakness of the contemporaneous correlations (and the difficulty of "holding other things constant"), I doubt that causation from concentration to advertising would be detected by such procedures either.

Ornstein and Lustgarten find that changes in advertising intensity were more closely related to changes in concentration than were changes in total advertising or advertising per firm. They interpret this finding as evidence against economies of scale in advertising. It is of course true that the average cost of advertising should depend on the total amount purchased. But advertising intensity determines the impact of any economies in persuasion on average total cost. To illustrate, let Q be output and A advertising messages, so that the average total cost function of a typical firm may be written as

$$ATC(Q,A) = [TPC(Q) + TAC(A)]/Q = APC(C) + [A/Q]AAC(A), \quad (5)$$

where TPC and TAC are total production and advertising cost, respectively, and APC and AAC are the corresponding average costs. The ratio (A/Q) is the natural measure of advertising intensity, and it determines the impact of average advertising costs on average total costs.

Ornstein and Lustgarten argue that their results imply that if advertising intensity increases, the larger the increase the larger the associated increase in concentration, while if advertising intensity decreases, no such relation is present. I do not think this argument is well supported by their regressions. The relevant comparison is between the coefficients of two variables that are orthogonal by construction. Orthogonality means that the t-statistics relevant to the hypothesis that the coefficients are in fact equal can be easily computed, though the authors do not present them. Four time intervals are examined. For producer goods, the coefficients differ in the alleged way only for 1947–1967. The t-statistic for that period is 1.06, so the difference is not significant. For consumer goods, the coefficient difference is as alleged for all periods. While the difference is significant for 1947–1967 ($t = 2.27$) and for the sub-period 1963–1967 ($t = 2.47$), it is quite insignificant for 1947–1963 ($t = 1.01$) and 1963–1970 ($t = 0.63$).

Even if the pattern claimed were clearly present in these data, its interpretation does not seem obvious. Simply lowering an entry barrier need not induce entry unless prices are far enough above costs. Even if entry occurs, concentration as measured here will not fall unless entrants' sales come mainly at the expense of the top four firms, and no model I know of suggests that this is especially likely.